DISCOVERY TIME

for COOPERATION and CONFLICT RESOLUTION

SARAH PIRTLE

CHILDREN'S
CREATIVE RESPONSE *to* CONFLICT
Nyack, New York

Published by the Children's Creative Response to Conflict Program
521 N. Broadway
P.O. Box 271, Nyack, NY 10960
(914) 353-1796
Fax: (914) 358-4924
e-mail: ccrcnyack@aol.com

ON THE COVER: Tawnne Gonzalez, Charles McRae, Victoria Melendez, and Jeremiah Murphy of Brightwood Magnet School, Springfield, Massachusetts.

EDITING, DESIGN, AND PRODUCTION:
   Potter Publishing Studio, 3 Bridge Street Rear, P.O. Box 126, Shelburne Falls, MA 01370
   Cover design, text design, and copy editing by Jeff Potter
   Text production by Linsey Kelch and Abe Loomis

COVER PHOTOGRAPH: Will Elwell, Shooting Star Photography, Greenfield, MA 01301

ISBN 1-891955-09-8

CONTENTS

PREFACE by Priscilla Prutzman vi

C H A P T E R   1 :   **BUILDING BLOCKS** 3
How to Use this Book • A Broader Perspective: Our Common Flame •
Acknowledgements • An Overview on Working with Groups: The Magic of Groups •
Insights from CCRC • Perspectives on Conflict •
For School Counselors • Music for All of Us

C H A P T E R   2 :   **COMMUNITY** 15
SCHOOL-WIDE ACTIVITIES: Social Responsibility Assembly •
School Contract • Know Your Neighbor • "Talk It Out" Family Night •
Song: "There's Always Something You Can Do."

CLASSROOM PRACTICES: Morning Greeting Circle • Class Meeting After Recess •
Good News Board • Affirmation Goodbye

C H A P T E R   3 :
CORE CURRICULUM
Integrating cooperation and the arts into language arts, science and social studies 29
LANGUAGE ARTS: Tribbles • Anger Poetry •
Communicating Memories: Sounds, Smells and Sights •
Cooperative Dialogue Writing • Conflict Resolution and Literature •

SCIENCE: Peace Flowers • Tell Me Why • Our Sense of Sight •
Cooperative Study of Animals • The Decisions of Cell Membranes •

SOCIAL STUDIES: Biographical Scrolls • Conflicts of Community Builders •
Mystery Bags • An Encounter of Cultures • Picturing the Future •
What the Spirals Say: Art and Archaeology • Cooperative History Fair •
Local Women in History

C H A P T E R   4 :
DISCOVERY UNITS
Exploring Cooperation With all the Senses 59
ESSAY: Discovery Units — How to Lead Daily Cooperation Groups
ACTIVITY UNITS: Cooperative Construction • Story Drawings •
Listening Pairs • Making Cooperation Board Games • Peer Teaching • The History in Our
Hands: Affirmation Drawings • Affirmation Activity: Send A Rainbow
CREATIVE MOVEMENT: Spider Web Hands • Magic Pebbles • Discovery Dance •
Movement and Writing • Storytelling Dances: The Return of Unity

ACTIVITY UNITS: Cooperative Songwriting ◆ *Songs:* "I Talk to My Food," "That Quiet Place" and "Outside My Window" ◆ The Songs We Carry Inside ◆ Songs for Cooperation ◆ Children's Peace Statue ◆ Cooperative Boat Building

CHAPTER 5:

AWAKENING THE PEACEMAKER

Conflict Resolution Activities 91

ESSAY: Helping Students with Conflicts

ACTIVITIES: Conflict Interviews ◆ Will the Castle Be Built? ◆ Feelings and Conflicts ◆ *Song:* "Talk It Out" ◆ Writing Conflict Resolution Songs

ESSAY: How to Make Your Conflict Resolution Plan

ACTIVITIES: Conflict Book ◆ Always Something You Can Do: Puppet Role Play ◆ Sharks, Turtles and Kangaroos: Role Plays ◆ Two Kinds of Power ◆ "You Made Me" ◆ Heart Statements: Role Plays ◆ Conflict Cartoons ◆ People Can Change ◆ Friendly Voices ◆ Our Whale Hearts ◆ Peacemaker Council ◆ Changebringers ◆ Yes and No Drawings ◆ Yes and No Dances ◆ Opposites Meet

PROBLEM-SOLVING METHODS: River Listening ◆ Fishbowl ◆ Spokes

CHAPTER 6: BIAS AWARENESS ACTIVITIES 131

ESSAY: Building Bridges

ESSAY: Bias Reduction and Mediation

ACTIVITIES: Please Touch Table ◆ Name Celebration ◆ Musical Walls and Bridges ◆ *Song:* "Walls and Bridges" ◆ Naming Differences ◆ Prejudice Exists ◆ I Remember ◆ Recognizing Stereotypes ◆ Make Assumptions ◆ Speaking Up ◆ Who Likes this Activity? ◆ Word Watch ◆ Open and Closed Circles

ESSAY: Interrupting Targeting

ACTIVITIES: Singing Spanish ◆ Gender Peacemaking ◆ The Web of Human Unity Heritage Quilt Squares ◆ This Beautiful River

APPENDIX 165

The Developmental Acquisition of Social Skills ◆ Features of a School-wide Conflict Resolution and Bias Awareness Program

INDEX: Language Arts and Expressive Arts

RESOURCE LIST

PREFACE

DISCOVERING NEW AND creative ways of building classroom communities and responding to conflict is what this wonderful new book of ideas and activities is about. It is particularly rewarding to see the influence of the major themes of Children's Creative Response to Conflict (CCRC) interwoven throughout *Discovery Time*: developing self esteem and communication skills — especially listening and cooperation — and teaching creative conflict resolution and bias awareness.

From the beginning, our goal at CCRC has been to help young people learn creative responses to conflict and violence before they reach an age where aggressive responses might become ingrained. We began in 1972 as a grassroots organization founded by the Quaker Project on Community Conflict to work in the New York City schools. The original founders were teachers who had also done nonviolence training. CCRC wanted to create an open and safe environment where people would choose cooperation, open communication, and positive ways of responding to problems.

We saw the need for adults to model the skills and approaches of creative conflict resolution. Today, CCRC is often referred to as CRC — Creative Response to Conflict — because we work with so many different ages. As we grew, the new themes of problem solving, mediation, and bias awareness also grew in importance.

One of the special new aspects of *Discovery Time* is the emphasis on using the expressive arts — music, creative writing, dramatics, movement, and drawing — for the development of all these themes. Readers will learn how the arts open new perspectives for students, engaging children's senses, opening up the full range of their intelligences, and helping children experience themselves as part of a caring community. By developing creativity, we help children know themselves better, and we help them learn how to handle problems that arise with confidence. Sarah Pirtle shows how to use the arts to further cooperation rather than competition by respecting each person's contributions. She applies this not

only to conflict resolution, but also to bias awareness. CCRC's approach to bias awareness is to help children appreciate their own and others' cultures, to help them examine the ways that bias is directed against themselves and others, and to help them explore ways of responding to biased comments using their communication and conflict resolution skills. This book presents teaching methods developed by many teachers and trainers over the past decade to meet these aims.

We are pleased to have had the support and inspiration of Dr. Elise Boulding during our nearly three decades of work in CCRC. She comments, "If I were an elementary school teacher today I would feel very keenly the burden of parental and community concerns; they hope that what happens in the classroom will somehow produce a new generation which can begin to repair the stresses and strains of our idealistic but conflicted society." In response to *Discovery Time*, Dr. Boulding says, "Good news! Here is a book about the transformation of social conflict into a creative classroom discovery process that will empower teachers and children alike to develop all their senses, inner and outer, and to deal positively with the strains that arise from the basic facts of human difference."

Dr. Boulding adds, "The only equipment needed is an open mind and a listening ear. The author draws upon her own years of teaching and on a remarkable network of teachers in a variety of school systems, to describe how classrooms can become mini-communities where children learn to arrive at cooperative solutions to a variety of perplexing situations. One of the best things about the book is that once started on any of the activities suggested, teachers will find new ideas sprouting in their own minds."

We echo Dr. Boulding's assessment of the important contribution this book makes toward empowering teachers. The author keeps a central focus on helping all people know their own creativity. Sarah Pirtle has been working in schools since 1972 as a teacher, artist-in-residence and a trainer on social skills. Since 1986, she has taught graduate education courses to pass her expertise onto other teachers. Over the years she has invented numerous activities for her students, and she shares them here. Her early conflict resolution song, "There Is Always Something You Can Do," written in 1984, has become the theme song for many conflict resolution and mediation programs worldwide. Sarah Pirtle so fully represents the tone and spirit of CCRC in both her words and her ways. We are pleased and honored, as publishers, and as colleagues, to support her in developing this important curriculum.

As the field of conflict resolution develops, we hope that many people will learn and grow from the depth of experience that the author and her many colleagues bring to us.

Enjoy these wonderful new ideas!

Priscilla Prutzman
Cofounder, Children's Creative Response to Conflict
Coauthor, The Friendly Classroom for a Small Planet
CCRC, Nyack, NY, February 1998

How the Activities are Presented

CATEGORY: At the beginning there is an indication whether it is a single activity or a collection of related activities (a unit). In Chapter 3, activities are further identified as pertaining to language arts, science, or social studies. In Chapter 5, information is provided as to whether it is a problem-solving method or art activity.

ORIENTATION: A teacher can use this brief statement to introduce the activity.

PROCEDURE: Every step of the activity is detailed. This book clearly distinguishes between the author's advice to "you" (the teacher) and the suggested words from the teacher to "you" (the students).

EXTENSIONS: Ideas for elaborations and follow-up activities are provided.

SOURCES: These activities include the creations, contributions, and collaborations of a variety of talented and dedicated educators, who are credited in this section to the best of the author's ability. Activities and units that list no sources are from Sarah Pirtle.

SYNOPSIS: This quick guide provides a suggested grade level span, the purpose and goals of the activity or unit, and a list of any materials. The grades listed are intended as a general reference; teachers should use their professional judgment.

✖ ACTIVITY ✖
Two Kinds of Power

SOURCE

This activity was created by Maggie Carlson from Bemidji, Minnesota, with additions by Candy Roberts, also from Bemidji, who offers another way to present it.

GRADES: 3rd–6th
FOCUS: Comprehend personal power that is different than aggressive force
MATERIALS: hammer hidden in a bag

ORIENTATION

Tell students: "Today we look at two different kinds of power."

PROCEDURE

1. *The Hammer:* "Here is one kind of power." Take out a hammer hidden in a bag and process the students' reactions. Ask, "What kinds of words or actions have the power of a hammer?" *Examples:* "Make me!", "Go away!", "I hate you!", hitting, kicking, pushing.

2. *The Light:* If we wanted to change ice, we could crack it with a hammer, but how could we change it without the use of this kind of force? Discuss the power of heat and light. What words or actions have the power of light? *Examples:* "Let's talk about this?", "That's not okay with me," "How can we change this?", talking, listening, asking, stating how you feel.

   Discuss: Who on television uses the power of a hammer? Who is a person you know that uses the power of light? Related activity: "The Web of Human Unity" (p. 159) distinguishes power-over from power-with.

   Variation: Candy Roberts starts this activity simply by setting up a lamp and shining it on ice. She leaves this without explanation. Then she brings out the hammer. Usually the students back away, and she helps them explore their negative reaction. All this is done before talking about power. Next, Candy hits the ice with a hammer. Now, students are directed to the melting ice, as she asks, "What happened to the ice under the lamp?" Finally, she poses the question, "If someone was trying to change you, which way would you want them to use — like the light or like the hammer?"

3. *Role Play:* Tell the group, "Let's have a chance to compare the two kinds of power. I'm going to pretend that I'm a person who uses my fists everytime I want something. I'm out

at recess, and I want to be team captain of the recess game, but I've already been captain for two weeks. How can you talk to me about being fair? I'm going to ask you to try to help me change."

"Try first using power like a hammer." Bring up volunteers to work with you or ask the whole class to work on the problem simultaneously. "What do you notice when you hammer at me?"

"Now help me change using the power of the light." Encourage the group to work with you from the direction of the second kind of power. "How did I react differently when you approached me with the power of light?"

EXTENSIONS

Read or tell the Norwegian folk tale, "The Sun and the Wind," which recounts a struggle between the sun and the wind to see which is the more powerful. They both try to get a traveler to take off his coat. The wind uses forceful blowing but it doesn't work. The sun succeeds by shining. Act out the story with your class.

Sing the song, "This Little Light of Mine," a traditional African American gospel song.

Chorus:

This little light of mine, I'm gonna let it shine. (3x)
Let it shine, let it shine, let it shine.
1. Everywhere I go, I'm gonna let it shine.
2. All around this world, I'm gonna let it shine.
3. All around this class, I'm gonna let it shine.

Awakening the Peacemaker   109

CHAPTER 1
Building Blocks

How to Use This Book

DISCOVERY TIME explores how to teach social skills through experiential learning. Teachers, school counselors, principals, and expressive artists from Massachusetts, Vermont, and Minnesota in the United States, and from Israel and Canada, have contributed to this collection.

LESSON PLANS

This book is designed for teachers with a variety of needs and interests. You will find many new activities by skimming the pages in search of interesting approaches. If you need curriculum ideas for an entire year, there are more than 45 week-long units from which to choose.

ACADEMIC CURRICULUM

Most of these lesson plans are designed to be part of your language arts or social studies curriculum. This book can help you incorporate affirmation, communication, cooperation, conflict resolution, and bias awareness into what your students are already studying.

EXPRESSIVE ARTS

The arts provide powerful tools for learning. They help us begin with our senses and involve the whole person, including our emotions. For this reason, you'll find drawing, movement, music, writing, storytelling, and creative dramatics integrated into all the chapters.

DISCOVERY-BASED LEARNING

The material in this book rests upon these core ideas:

◆ Students need our guidance to learn how to treat themselves and others respectfully, to learn how to include rather than exclude, and to learn how to be productive group members.

◆ Collaboration, cooperation and conflict resolution are essential life skills that students will carry as adults into every work situation and human relationship.

◆ We help them develop positive social skills not by telling them how to behave and not by punishing them when they have trouble, but through active learning over an extended period of time.

For students to develop important communication skills — how to collaborate with others, how to solve conflicts creatively, how to advocate for fairness over bias — they need time to learn by doing. In short, children need opportunities to make their own social discoveries. In this book you will experience a variety of fun, informative, and educational activities that provide time for students to participate in cooperative structures, experience their value as members of the class, and choose to use new skills consciously.

There is no "multiplication table" of facts about social skills to memorize, but students can develop an internalized bank of experiences that function as a map. Incremental skill development is exciting to watch. For example, kindergartners may begin the year knowing only hitting as a solution. However, as they develop inner speech and start to gain impulse control, they can become first or second graders who say forthrightly, "I don't like to be called names." As a younger student learns how to listen and restate what someone says, he or she can grow into a fifth or sixth grader who is able to hold several points of view and is ready to take on a neutral position as a peer mediator of disputes.

A BRIEF TOUR OF THE CHAPTERS

Each chapter in this book presents one of five different ways that schools can teach the social curriculum.

Chapter 2: *Community*
This chapter describes ongoing practices that create a positive framework and strengthen the classroom community.

◆ Morning Greeting Circles (p. 22) acknowledge each individual.

◆ A Class Meeting after Recess (p. 23) directly guides students in handling their most pressing issues.

◆ Making daily lists on the Good News Board (p. 25) encourages positive behavior.

Also in this chapter are strategies that link the entire school:

◆ Monthly school Social Responsibility Assemblies (p. 15) help classrooms focus on specific social skills.

◆ School Contracts (p. 17) with students highlight bias reduction as well as academic issues.

Chapter 3: *Core Curriculum*

The suggestions in this chapter, which integrate cooperation and the arts into language arts, science, and social studies, relate directly to academic curriculum:

◆ Teachers learn five ways poetry can be used to increase students' understanding of how to express anger constructively. ("Anger Poetry," p. 30.)

◆ Students explore the way that cell membranes make decisions about what to let in and what to keep out (p. 39).

◆ Educators can change the traditional science fair and create an event where students cooperate by portraying scientists. ("Cooperative History Fair," p. 54).

◆ Teachers can go back 7000 years in time to Old Europe through "What the Spirals Say" (p. 50) to share information about a time without weapons and warfare.

Chapter 4: *Discovery Units*

Delineated in this chapter are thirteen different collections of themed activities that assist students in cooperation skills.

◆ In "Cooperative Construction" (p. 62), students work in small groups each day to create a different kind of construction. This provides a chance to focus specifically upon collaboration skills.

◆ In "Peer Teaching" (p. 68), students identify hobbies and activities they can teach each other.

◆ In "Cooperative Songwriting" (p. 80), small groups create a verse of a song together.

Chapter 5: *Awakening the Peacemaker*

Familiar conflict resolution concepts, like "I Statements," and methods like puppet plays are approached from new directions. In addition, new activities show ways of incorporating art and language arts into conflict resolution training.

◆ Students observe four parents or older students not cooperating, allowing the class to reflect upon what is helpful behavior in a group. ("Will the Castle Be Built?", p. 96)

◆ In "Peacemaker Council" (p. 118), visualization and reflection helps students engage the wisdom they already have inside themselves.

◆ In "River Listening" (p. 124), students learn how to reach consensus.

Chapter 6: *Bias Awareness Activities*

Students become aware of bias, stereotypes, prejudice, and unfairness through a variety of methods. Several of the activities can be incorporated to create a month-long unit.

◆ Role models of people who have worked to create fairness are illuminated. ("This Beautiful River," p. 161)

◆ Students learn examples of organizations of men who work together to end sexism and gender-based violence. ("Gender Peacemaking," p. 154)

IMPLEMENTATION

As we bring these activities to students, it helps to keep our overall objectives in mind. Carol Corwin from Brattleboro, Vermont summarizes: "The most valuable decision for me was to make building social skills in my classroom an ongoing project and to schedule a definite slot for it in my weekly schedule. It has been beneficial in several ways." Carol describes the benefits:

◆ It has given a clear-cut vehicle for problem solving.

◆ It has brought the group closer together emotionally by encouraging sharing of opinions, feelings and facts about our daily lives.

◆ It has motivated better listening habits.

◆ The activities have brought everyone into the action, especially working in pairs and groups. Children feel they are needed and sense their participation is valued.

Let's look at three different ways teachers can use the material in this book to create skill-building sessions.

EXAMPLE ONE:
HOW TO FOCUS ON LANGUAGE ARTS

1. Several times a week during regular language arts lessons, use activities from Chapters 3 and 4 which promote communication and affirmation: "The History in Our Hands," "Communicating Memories," "Story Drawings," "Anger Poetry," "Listening Pairs," and "Movement and Writing."

2. Begin and end the day with a Good News Board from Chapter 2 to give students practice reading.

3. During the latter part of the year, bring in more material from Chapters 5 and 6 which relates to conflict resolution and bias awareness through language arts:

"Name Celebration," writing essays about the "Please Touch Table," "Opposites Meet" and "Yes and No Drawings."

4. As a final unit for the year, focus upon the "Heritage Quilt Squares" (p. 163), using research and writing.

EXAMPLE TWO:

HOW TO FOCUS ON SOCIAL STUDIES

1. Begin the day with a Morning Greeting Circle involving objects that relate to social studies and geography.

2. Use the activities in the social studies section of Chapter 3, beginning with a Biographical Scroll.

3. Add material about stereotyping and Gender Peacemaking from Chapter 5.

4. End the year with some time travel! Take your students back 7,000 years to listen to "What the Spirals Say," and then focus on the future using the "Letter from the Future" role play in the unit, "Picturing the Future."

EXAMPLE THREE:

HOW TO USE ACTIVITIES FOR DAILY SOCIAL SKILLS PRACTICE

1. Select a time each day (half hour before lunch can work) to combine language arts work and social studies themes in lessons that let students practice cooperation.

2. Activities like "Cooperative Construction," "Communicating Memories," "Listening Pairs," and "Feelings and Conflicts" can be done in small groups. Allow each unit to go on as long as the class sustains its interest.

3. Introduce creative movement work with "Spider Web Hands" depicted on the back cover. Once students are secure moving in the room with awareness of each other, add the units "Discovery Dance," and "Storytelling Dances."

4. This movement work leads into conflict resolution skits. Begin with "Sharks, Turtles, and Kangaroos," then spend two weeks developing skits with "Heart Statements."

5. End the year with a "Talk It Out" night for parents and students.

DAILY PRACTICE

I recommend that you set aside 15–30 minutes each day to lead activities that develop social skills either as part of your language arts or social studies curriculum, or as a separate skillbuilding time. When I was a classroom teacher, I called this "Discovery Time." Feel free to call your sessions by whatever name works for you, but here is why I find the name "Discovery Time" useful.

◆ The name can be an umbrella for whatever you do — listening or poetry or conflict resolution skits. The way that the time is used is constant: group agreements are kept, people think about each other in a caring way, time is taken to handle conflicts, and students discover how to solve problems, take turns and collaborate.

◆ Using the word *Discovery*, which implies that students are explorers, is a fun, upbeat way to invite students to learn.

◆ As they work together, students will acquire new insights about how to interact effectively. They will also have difficulties, and we as teachers can help.

When I use the term "Discovery Sessions," I refer to a classroom session where the emphasis is on fostering positive interaction. If you decide not to adopt the idea of regular skill-building time, you will still find many specific lessons and specific practices to help build your classroom community.

HINTS FOR LEADING ACTIVITIES

◆ Pay as much attention to how the group works together, and how to guide students to learn the social skills involved in the project, as you pay to the work product or task at hand.

◆ Take time to help children when they have difficulties working together. For example, guide them through a method of dividing up work on a cooperative drawing. Or, listen to problems about "bossiness," and help change "bossiness" to shared leadership step by step.

◆ Let each unit have its fullness. Let the time be intentionally unrushed rather than driven by the need to complete a project by a certain date. This way you will feel freer to take time for teachable moments. Even if you are hoping Biographical Scrolls will be a one-week unit, let the project continue until it is completed.

◆ Supply sufficient closure time for each activity and each unit. Children enjoy sharing what they have made or written. Process what worked well and what was difficult. Share constructive affirmative feedback.

◆ Teach conflict resolution concepts apart from the heat of the moment. Provide time to work on understanding anger or learning how to engage with a problem when a problem is not erupting.

◆ Use activities like Cooperation Construction, Affirmation Drawings, and Story Drawings as a basic model, then modify and extend them over several days.

◆ Bring your own creativity. New ideas will emerge for you as you relate this approach to more of your regular curriculum and as you notice specific social skills that need more attention.

Building Blocks

A BROADER PERSPECTIVE
Our Common Flame

AS THIS BOOK BEGINS, I light a candle. Its flame honors the significance of work on the social curriculum in today's schools.

Children are learning interpersonal skills that previous generations were not taught. Ask any adult today, "Who showed you how to talk out conflicts when you were growing up?" and most will reply, "No one." Ask a child the same question, and they may answer — my teacher, my guidance counselor, my principal, my mother, my father, my camp counselor, my brother, my sister, or my best friend.

A groundswell of activity is building around the globe as teachers, parents, guidance counselors, and trainers counteract violence and bias by teaching peacemaking skills. Even while heartbreaking acts of violence by children shake us to attention, at the same time seeds of non-violence are being sewn through peer mediation training, conflict resolution programs, and daily efforts by teachers to strengthen the mutual respect practiced in their classrooms.

Most of this important work occurs away from the public eye. Here is a window into one local community. Third graders in a northern Minnesota town named Bemidji were invited by the town sheriff to provide training for his staff. These students had learned how to talk out problems by listening and by using "I statements" in their conflict management program at St. Philip's School ever since they were in first grade. They developed puppet plays to illustrate their skills and performed them for twenty-five police officers to convey what they had learned about constructive communication.

In October 1997, the citizens of Bemidji picked up their newspaper and found a story about this same group of students, now fifth graders, featured on the front page. At Lake Bemidji, where giant statues of Paul Bunyan and Babe the Blue Ox stand, these students went down to the water carrying four boats they had built themselves. Over three days they collaborated in cutting wood, wiring the wooden pieces,

applying putty, fiberglassing the seams, sanding, and adding braces. This project was the culmination of five years of developing cooperation and conflict resolution skills at school.

Conflict Management Director Sue Liedl explained to the newspaper reporter, "Boat building is a metaphor for the points we strive to make in conflict management." Sue volunteered for six years as a parent and social worker to create and teach a comprehensive program for kindergartners through eighth graders at St. Philip's School. Standing at the dock as students rowed in the dories they created, she was watching the fruits of her efforts. Sue commented, "Just like in life, the boat building taught cooperation, problem solving and getting along, the same skills we teach in conflict management. If we have the skills, the boats will float. If we don't, they will sink or leak."

In this era in education, pressures from test scores, state requirements, and keeping up with computer technology push teachers away from spending time on the social curriculum. Nonetheless, examples like this one from Bemidji illustrate that the skills of constructive communication and cooperation are fundamental to whatever we do. Our social fabric depends on people adept at cooperating for meeting group goals, communicating well with family and coworkers, and treating community members with mutual respect. Without the social curriculum, our boats will sink.

I light this candle for the valuable contribution of each person and for the tens of thousands of people working fervently to help children move toward community instead of violence. As I hold up the candle, I also praise the dark. Out of the mystery of darkness come unexpected creativity and strength to help us heal our traumatized world.

I have worked in elementary education since 1972. In 1986 when I started to teach a graduate course —"Cooperation and Conflict Resolution Skills: K–8th" — at the University of Vermont in Brattleboro, I had to seek the foundation of developing social skills and examine my goals afresh. I reflected that when we help children find words to use when they are upset, we aren't providing stock phrases to memorize. Rather, we are helping them find a reference point inside themselves they can carry into any situation. I felt we were awakening in young students their own inner force, one that is stronger than violence. Gandhi called it Truthforce, or *Satyagraha*. The word *discovery* encapsulated this experiential learning for me; I felt that for conflict resolution skillbuilding to work, each of us — student and teacher alike — has to contact, develop, and discover our own Truthforce.

When we work on conflict resolution and unlearning bias, evolutionary change takes place. After centuries of violent solutions, of "might makes right" and solutions using domination, we are teaching an opposite path. As the activity "What the Spirals Say" (p. 50) articulates, we must return to partnership skills that communities have practiced for thousands of years. Going even further back in time to the discovery of fire, we are reminded that our physically vulnerable species of humans survived because we developed cooperation skills. We shared discoveries like fire, planting seeds, and finding medicinal plants. Cooperation toward group goals made us strong. I light this candle to remind us that we and our students are making our own discovery of a kind of inner fire — a transforming power inside — that enables us to handle conflicts through Truthforce, not violence.

The students from Bemidji couldn't meet Gandhi face to face, but they did meet his grandson, Arum Gandhi. Sue Liedl brought him to Minnesota to train people of all ages in nonviolence. In fact, she helped write a part for him in a play the students created. The drama humorously contrasted the "No-Skills Family" — who mistreat each other as they emulate the characters they see on television — with the "More Skills Family" — who are trying to find better ways to communicate. At the end of the play, when children from each family argued at school, Arum Gandhi entered and showed them how to mediate their problem. As he walked on stage, the students could see the connection between a legendary peacemaker and a flesh and blood person. In his lectures he told students, parents, and teachers that we all have a spark of peace inside ourselves.

I believe that each person who teaches conflict resolution and bias awareness embarks on a journey. Although shelves of books that offer exciting methods now exist, in a sense each teacher has to head out into the wilderness. We need to try activities for ourselves. We change wording and revise activities to meet the needs of our own students, and in so doing, we engage in a creative ferment that increases our understanding of what is fundamentally at work. For all these reasons, each trainer or teacher of conflict resolution "remakes" the material into our own. We also enter into a process that is not only academic or cerebral, but personal. We are asked to look at the interpersonal skills we use with everyone we encounter — our colleagues, our partners, our relatives, our neighbors. Our students also need to make a journey and engage, with our guidance, in their own social discoveries. I invite readers to "remake" the material in this book: modify it and add your own insights and creativity.

An epidemic of violence rages through our world and through our culture. This is not only physical violence, but economic as well; it is the violence of racism, sexism, and classism; the violence of prioritizing those who already have privilege. These forces threaten true democracy, environmental safety, and economic equity. Together, students and teachers blow the whistle. As a community, we insist there is a different way to live.

I light this candle to share the important work in schools and families that helps us through our present-day evolutionary leap. The fire of this flame reminds us that we have a force stronger than violence within us, and it can prevail once we know how to tap into it. This candle is for the light of knowledge, for all educators who are building a sheltering culture where children can grow and discover this eternal force inside themselves.

—*Sarah Pirtle*

ACKNOWLEDGEMENTS

I WANT TO THANK Sue Liedl for her example that heart and common sense are the foundation of teaching social skills. I send appreciation to all the inspirational educators whose work is introduced in these pages. Three readers in particular gave close attention to the book and made invaluable suggestions: Thanks to Marcia Schuhle, Barbara Porro, and Jana Standish. In addition, this book would not have been possible without the expertise and good will of Potter Publishing Studio. Thank you to Jeff and Susi Potter, Linsey Kelch, and Abe Loomis for going above and beyond.

In 1988, a portion of these activities were published as *Discovery Sessions: How Teachers Create Opportunities to Build Cooperation and Conflict Resolution Skills in their K–8 Classrooms* by Franklin Mediation Services in Greenfield, Massachusetts. This manual was commissioned by codirectors Catherine Woolner and Judith Rubenstein at a time when student mediation training was a new field in the United States and peer mediators on the school playground were a rare sight. Today, Franklin Mediation Service, now called The Mediation and Training Collaborative (TMTC), is still going strong. With the help of a grant from the Peace Development Fund in Amherst, Massachusetts and the Carlisle Foundation, the activities I taught in my graduate course and the activities created by teachers who took the course were detailed in *Discovery Sessions*. The book was used as a manual to teach conflict resolution and mediation skills in the schools, and it was distributed by NAME, the National Association for Mediation in Education. Six other activities in this new edition first appeared in *Perspectives at Work,* published by Traprock Peace Center in 1984 with a grant from the Peace Development Fund.

I'm delighted that now the Children's Creative Response to Conflict Program (CCRC) is bringing this work to a wider audience and has made a complete update and expansion possible. Under the direction of Priscilla Prutzman, CCRC has been a pioneering force strongly affecting me, the teachers represented in this book, and thousands of teachers for nearly three decades. The material presented in CCRC's landmark book *The Friendly Classroom for a Small Planet* showed that developing social skills happens through concrete activities with experiential learning, and that if you dive in with conflict resolution work before establishing an affirming community you will get rote responses to conflicts, rather than a deeper understanding. This insight formed the foundation of the *Discovery Sessions* manual and is also at the core of *Discovery Time.*

Teamwork is another central theme. CCRC has set an example for teachers and trainers teaching social skills to see themselves as collaborators. I like to think of all the practitioners across the country as a team collaborating to create activities that affect the lives of young people. We are held together by work on the local level in classrooms and also by organizations who carry the banner nationally. I look to two national groups for inspiration and work with both of them: CCRC and Educators for Social Responsibility. They act as beacons holding out the importance of teaching children the social curriculum.

A final theme of this book is that it is critical to include bias awareness work in all conflict resolution training. In her essay "Bias Reduction and Mediation" (p. 133), Catherine Woolner of TMTC shares the insights she's developed as a mediator and a trainer of student mediators for ten years. Facing bias and committing oneself to changing bias is a powerful and important journey. I also want to express my appreciation to the director of Communitas in Northampton, Massachusetts, Andrea Ayvazian, an inspirational force in the lives of many people, for her leadership on unlearning racism. The bias awareness activities detailed in Chapter 6 are ones I created and collected while working as a trainer for Communitas.

ATTRIBUTION AND SOURCES

Whenever I know who developed an activity or who thought of an important concept, I have listed the source or sources. However, providing accurate sources can be difficult sometimes. In the past three decades many activities have passed among the overlapping areas of peace education, cooperative learning, new games, and improvisational theater in a kind of folk process. There is also, to use a Buddhist term, a kind of co-arising. For instance, Barbara Porro and I independently chose the phrase "talk it out" to describe the kernel of conflict resolution. You'll see references to her wonderful book, and you'll find that I wrote a song with the same title.

The activities I present as original are indeed ones I've developed, and where I draw upon other sources, I have listed them as I know them. I care a great deal about accuracy and welcome any feedback; errors and omissions will be corrected in future editions.

And finally, thanks to the many wonderful teachers, mediation trainers, and school counselors in this book for sharing the activities they've developed.

—*Sarah Pirtle*

AN OVERVIEW ON WORKING WITH GROUPS

THIS BOOK AIMS to provide educators with methods and activities for teaching social skills practice sessions. The next four sections provide background information to help build the classroom community during these group sessions.

The Magic of Groups

The self esteem of individuals develops not in isolation, but in community. A group is a place where students can make personal changes as they receive feedback on their ideas and their behavior, observe new possibilities, try on new outlooks, and feel valued.

When a group is "humming," when children are laughing together and noticing each other, they drink from the experience like drinking from an old, deep well. The activities in this book are based on assumptions about how groups serve students.

WHAT CHILDREN NEED IN A GROUP

What do we know about the social self, and how can this inform the way we lead our groups in the classroom? Individuals have these three needs when they are in a group:

CHILDREN NEED TO BE INCLUDED

Provide activities where each person explicitly is noticed on the first day of school, the first week, the first month, and the beginning of every day. (*Example:* Hold a "Morning Greeting Circle," p. 22.)

CHILDREN NEED TO HAVE CHOICE

Use open-ended questions and activities that incorporate their ideas. Encourage a love of learning by finding places within the curriculum where students follow their interests. Ask for input on which songs are sung and games played. Seek ways they can choose partners without excluding others. (Example: Use the "Fair Choice" method, p. 60)

CHILDREN NEED TO RECEIVE AND EXPRESS AFFECTION

Include activities that encourage age-appropriate friendly physical connection. Show your love for each child in your own way — smiles, hugs, pats on the back. Include processing time at the end of the activity session, when positive feedback is given and received. Use a good-bye procedure that builds closeness.

STAGES OF GROUP FORMATION

1. Agreements: *Students test norms and limits, and this solidifies the boundaries of the group.* Make group agreements together at the start and repeat them. Expect that they will be tested, and guide students in a non-punitive manner to keep the agreements.

2. Presentation of Self. *Every individual needs to present her or himself to the group.* Individual children discover that they are seen and included by having a chance to be the focus of the whole group. If you don't provide opportunities for this to happen constructively, some children will seek negative routes. Each child needs to have a turn as the center of attention. It's helpful, therefore, the first week and the first month of school to plan activities where students become acquainted, express their unique interests, share news, and feel noticed.

3. Group History: *By sharing experiences, the individuals sense that they are one group.* Group poems and other class activities show what can be accomplished through collaboration. Friendly class jokes and "running gags" are other ways that a class becomes one community.

4. Challenges: *As the group solidifies, it becomes able to deal with feelings, problems, and tasks.* As a group gets closer, in one sense more conflicts or issues may surface because unconsciously students feel that the class is ready to deal with them. Certain group meetings or group decisions may require extra time and can be seen as markers that the time has come when issues can be handled together.

Insights from CCRC

The Children's Creative Response to Conflict Program (CCRC) teaches that we need to make cooperation building the focus early in the year. A high number of conflicts stem from student low self-esteem. To address these underlying unmet needs, the class begins by developing cooperation, affirmation, and communication skills to build a foundation.. Conflict resolution skills can be introduced in September but will be strengthened as an affirmative atmosphere is established.

The goal is to encourage teachers and others who work with children to move beyond the treatment of isolated crisis situations by developing a positive dynamic which motivates children to respond to conflict constructively. We find that children develop positive self concepts and learn to be open, sharing and cooperative much more effectively when they become part of a community in which these attributes are the norm.

—The Friendly Classroom
for a Small Planet, *p.2.*

Our activities give people the skills to improve self-concept, communicate more effectively, and build a cooperative environment in which conflict resolution can be practiced and discussed creatively. [...] Sessions begin by inviting everyone to sit in a circle to emphasize equality and to encourage participation. [...]We usually begin with cooperation activities to establish a safe environment. Then we work on developing communication and afffirmation skills. This builds a positive atmosphere for conflict resolution. While the approach is developmental, the themes often overlap, and we find ourselves working with several at once.

—"What is CCRC All About?"

RECOMMENDATIONS FOR TEACHERS

◆ **Practice Time:** Build in daily or weekly activity time where children interact cooperatively.

◆ **Sequencing of Each Session:** Start with short activities and icebreakers that help bond the group and then build up to more challenging activities.

◆ **Diversity, Unity, and Bias Reduction**: Help children learn how to recognize and intervene when there is bias and unfairness.

◆ **Sequencing Across the Year:** Plan work on Bias Reduction after a groundwork of trust and communication is in place.

◆ **Problem-Solving Methods:** Set up clear, age-appropriate methods for talking out conflicts.

THERE ARE SEVEN BASIC THEMES OF CCRC.
THEY ARE, IN THIS ORDER:

1. Cooperation
2. Communication
3. Affirmation
4. Conflict Resolution
5. Problem Solving
6. Mediation
7. Bias Awareness

Detailed information on carrying out these recommendations is provided in this book. We recommend three companion books which amplify these same seven themes:

◆ *The Friendly Classroom for a Small Planet,* by Priscilla Prutzman, Lee Stern, M.L. Burger, G. Bodenhamer, (Children's Creative Response to Conflict, 1988).

◆ *Elementary Perspectives,* by William Kreidler, (Educators for Social Responsiblity, 1994).

◆ *Linking Up: Using Music, Movement, and Language Arts to Teach Caring, Cooperation and Communication,* by Sarah Pirtle. (Educators for Social Responsibility, 1998). This resource includes a 350-page book and a recording of 46 songs for ages 3 to 8 available in cassette or CD. Twenty of the songs are also recorded in Spanish.

Perspectives on Conflict

The experience of participating in a classroom community where mutual respect and responsiveness are taught has a lasting effect on each member of the group. Here are principles for helping children learn from conflicts.

1. Teach social skills experientially. Telling children how to behave isn't as effective as helping them learn by doing. Children need to have experiences where they can construct their own ideas about how people get along.

2. Work with human capacity to develop positive social skills. We awaken and develop ability that is innate within the student. Children can learn to read because our brains are encoded with the ability. Likewise, children can learn to cooperate, to include and respect others, to communicate constructively because they are also encoded as social beings to take part in a community as members.

3. Anticipate that developing new skills will take time. Acquiring any skill — whether riding a bicycle, hitting a baseball, or finding words when we're upset — takes an investment of practice time. When strong emotions are involved, change takes longer.

Since conflict is a normal part of human interaction, ironically, we teachers can welcome the conflicts that happen during Discovery Time. We are right there to assist. We can ask students questions to help students reflect. We can guide them through new behavior. We can observe, then make informed guesses about where children are feeling stuck. We can teach the next step a child is ready for, such as helping a student who is stuck in the need to dominate, experience new ways of being heard.

WHERE CONFLICTS COME FROM

Conflicts can stem from events at school:

◆ Disagreements over sharing belongings or space.

◆ Problems resulting from social interactions. These include accidents, misunderstandings, exclusion, unfriendly physical contact, and name-calling.

◆ Problems in group decisions relating to classroom events, or disagreements over group games

◆ Boundary violations — for example, play-fighting that evolves into real hurt.

Also, conflicts stem from situations that originate outside the classroom. Children come to the class upset because of a family illness or fight, or ill treatment at home. They have worries, unexpressed anger, or strong unmet needs, and these feelings affect the way they interact with others. Some children live in fear of mistreatment or abuse or are traumatized by its aftermath. This affects their resiliency in handling schoolwork and social interactions, as well as their ability to understand the behavior and motivations of others.

Since group safety is maintained, Discovery sessions help children who are hurt. Expressive arts activities in particular allow students to express and integrate feelings.

HOW CHILDREN CHANGE

Children change their social behavior:

◆ When the message they are sending through their anger, aggression, or withdrawal is received and heard.

◆ When children see new behavior in people they trust.

◆ When the norms and agreements in the classroom provide safety, and adults maintain this safe container.

◆ When they feel safe enough to take control of themselves and be at the center of their own lives.

◆ When they feel safe enough to take in new information and learn how to respond to social cues.

◆ When they learn how to solve conflicts themselves rather than counting on adults to control them. If we use punishment, we're not helping the child think about the problem. By guiding rather than punishing, we allow children to learn and make new conscious choices and try on new behavior.

METHODS OF CONFLICT RESOLUTION

Every classroom needs clear conflict resolution methods in place. These might include the following practices:

◆ A "peace place" can be set up in the classroom where students go to cool down or talk out conflicts.

◆ Students can learn the steps of talking out a problem: "Take turns saying how you feel and what the problem is," "Brainstorm ways you could solve the problem," and "Choose a plan you both like." Teachers learn to facilitate this process and post the steps on a classroom chart.

◆ Peer mediator programs train students in grades five and up to help other students resolve conflicts.

◆ Concrete methods of sharing, like using an egg timer, help children measure equal time when taking turns.

Discovery Time will show you how to lead sessions that introduce skills, give ways to practice skills, and offer problem-solving methods. For instance:

◆ Students use puppets or role plays to explore methods of handling conflicts.

◆ Students meet in a fishbowl format (listeners observe a small group in the center) to discuss group decisions.

A survey of sample methods is provided in "How to Make Your Conflict Resolution Plan," p. 101-102. Many excellent books detail a variety of practices, and the Resource List in the Appendix, p. 169, directs readers to them. Barbara Porro's book *Talk It Out: Conflict Resolution in the Elementary Classroom* (ASCD, 1996) is highly recommended for the methods it provides.

For School Counselors

In many schools the guidance counselor goes from classroom to classroom to provide direct group instruction on social skills. This book is designed so that school counselors can find activities to use.

PROFILE: JANA STANDISH

Jana Standish, school counselor at Colrain Central School in Colrain, Massachusetts, works with eight classrooms every week for 30 minutes to teach positive social skills. She is also in charge of the school peer mediation program. Two of the activities she has developed are in this book: "Know Your Neighbor," and "Make Assumptions." Here are some of her recommendations:

1. Start slowly:

Year One: Go into one class where the teacher is supportive or would like assistance with a difficult class. Lead a weekly session of thirty minutes. Work not only with direct problems but also lead activities to help students develop affirmation and community.

Year Two: Continue to work with the same class as the year before with their current teacher, and add two more classes, each thirty minutes a week.

Year Three: Go into eight classrooms to teach social skills for thirty minutes a week.

2. Ask teachers to stay in the room and be active members, joining in the activities.

3. Begin scheduling time in classrooms the first week of school. Setting up this schedule with teachers involves (a) getting the support of the school principal, and (b) asking teachers to select a thirty-minute slot before their schedules fill up. In larger schools, focus on a limited number of grades, such as all classrooms in the kindergarten through second-grade range.

4. Meet with every classroom on the first day of school. Jana Standish tells each group:

◆ "As school counselor, my biggest role is to be a listener. I'll be teaching you how to be better listeners, too."

◆ "We have a common school language . When any staff person in the school says, 'Freeze,' that will mean to stop and pay attention."

◆ "We say 'our school' instead of 'the school' because this reminds us that we have ownership in the school. This is our family away from home. We want everyone to feel welcome and included here."

◆ "We notice the positive in each other."

◆ "I'm in charge of the peer mediation program. Mediators are assigned to each classroom and they can help you talk conflicts out."

5. Provide classroom lessons on all aspects of social skills: how to take turns, how to handle bullying, how to recognize bias and stereotyping, how to respect other people.

Music For All of Us

One intention of this book is that teachers who don't yet think of themselves as artists will feel supported to integrate the expressive arts into their academic curriculum. Music can be infused many ways: exploring sound, discussing lyrics, hearing songs from many cultures, and learning songs related to historical periods. It doesn't have to involve leading singing. Throughout the book, I have listed recordings that can be played. Teachers are also invited to photocopy the lyrics provided for students to sing along. Chapter 4 includes a unit on songwriting for language arts lessons; these methods can be used to write either poems or songs. Each teacher is invited to find an enjoyable way of adding music to their year.

CHAPTER 2
Community Building

COMMUNITY BUILDING

Here are plans for assemblies, school contracts, and school-wide activities that unify an entire community with clear agreements for mutual respect. This chapter also provides daily classroom procedures that increase group cohesion through affirmation and communication.

❈ SCHOOL-WIDE ACTIVITY ❈

SOCIAL RESPONSIBILITY ASSEMBLY

ORIGIN

The idea for a Social Responsibility Assembly evolved from a brainstorm by the staff of Four Corners Elementary School in Greenfield, Massachusetts with principal Gail Healy. They asked the question, "How can our work on the social curriculum permeate through our building of 325 students?" As a team they have been conducting monthly assemblies for four years and have found that this practice consolidates classroom efforts on positive social skills, builds community, and involves parents in the school in a nonthreatening way. Four Corners School has an active mediation program. The staff incorporates ideas about the social curriculum from the Northeast Foundation for Children perspectives and from the William Glasser model of developing responsible behavior.

PROCEDURE

1. Monthly Themes: The Four Corners staff established these monthly themes:

> *September* — Respect and courtesy
>
> *October* — Safety and nonviolence
>
> *November* — Cooperation and compromise
>
> *December* — Diversity

GRADES: K–6th

FOCUS: A monthly school assembly celebrates the social theme studied that month by each classroom

> *January* — Nonviolence
>
> *February* — Kindness and forgiveness
>
> *March* — Honesty and fairness
>
> *April* — Tolerance
>
> *May* — Community
>
> *June* — Friendship

Although the staff reviews the themes each year, they have left them unchanged because they found that they effectively relate to the timing of the year. September's theme helps set agreements, October's theme relates to safety at Halloween, December's theme honors diversity in celebrating holidays, February's theme relates to Valentine's Day, and June's theme corresponds to graduation and summer good-byes.

2. Skill Development: Each class studies the theme during the month. The teacher leads skillbuilding activities, which may include songs, and talks about the meaning of the theme. Four Corners School has twelve classrooms spanning kindergarten through grade 5. One or two of the classrooms each month prepare a skit or song to share in the assembly. In addition, all students know that at one of the ten assemblies they will be honored for their work in that theme area. Each month two or three students from each class are selected by their teacher to receive a certificate of achievement. For example, the certificate for the December theme of diversity says, "For your knowledge and appreciation of diversity." Gail intends these awards to recognize individual students inclusively rather than competitively.

3. The Assembly Program: Assemblies take place the last Wednesday of the month, from 9:00–9:45 in the school gymnasium, where a microphone is set up.

a. The student mediators present a skit or song.

b. One or two classrooms lead a skit or song. For example, in November a fifth-grade class offered a skit showing that working together works better than trying to do something by one's self, and a second-grade class sang and acted out Red Grammer's song "Use a Word."

c. The music teacher leads a participatory song. The lyrics are displayed on a chart so all students and parents in the audience can sing along, while a child guides everyone by pointing to the words.

d. Awards are given to students in each classroom. Each rstudent receives a certificate signed by the principal and a coupon for an ice cream cone, provided by the P.T.O.

Teachers sign up at the beginning of the year for the month when each class will present. The principal draws up an agenda a few days in advance of each assembly, letting all participants know in what order they will appear. For example, the student awards might be first or last presentation in the program.

Assemblies often include a fifth component to build community. Each September, Gail Healy writes a rap introducing all the teachers and performs it in the assembly as teachers dance. Each June she honors the graduating fifth graders with a rap that celebrates characteristics of each child.

These traditions have become important to the students. Sometimes the fifth section of the assembly is an interactive dance or movement game. The humorous Chicken Dance and the Macarena were added to two assemblies. Parents and students stood up to try them out, illustrating that a group of more than 350 people could cooperate.

Principal Healy comments, "These assemblies are a team effort. Everyone is invested in this work on the social curriculum and it helps us feel inter-connected as a school community."

Parent Involvement: At every assembly, all parents are encouraged and welcome to attend. Two days before the assembly, all parents of children receiving a certificate of achievement receive a phone call alerting them about the award, but are asked to keep it a secret. Approximately forty parents each month attend the all-school assembly.

School Contract

GRADES: 3rd–12th

FOCUS: Set social agreements by using a contract throughout the whole school

ORIGIN

In Canada, at Horizon Alternative Senior School in Toronto, Ontario, staff and students worked together to create a school-wide contract . In addition to agreements about homework and assignments, they listed two interpersonal agreements and placed them first in the document.

EXAMPLE

Discuss this contract at your school and use it as a reference as you create your own agreement.

Horizon Contract

Horizon Alternative Senior School dedicates itself to the pursuit of the following goals:

1. *To provide an environment that promotes equity and safety for all students regardless of sex, race, sexual preference or degree of popularity.*

   ◆ *In pursuing this goal we recognize that it is necessary to educate our community about situations in our society that have led to an unequal distribution of power and rights. We will also help each other raise awareness of behaviors that make people feel unsafe.*
   ◆ *Teachers will provide opportunities for students to develop a sense of community.*
   ◆ *We will all work to create an environment that is free of harassment. No harassment or bullying will be tolerated. Students who harass or bully will be suspended unless they agree to work out a solution for this problem using conflict resolution.*
   ◆ *We will encourage each other to use what we have learned to help change the larger society in which we live.*
   ◆ *A student/teacher equity council will be established to hear complaints.*

2. *Whenever possible, conflict resolution techniques will be used to solve problems within our community.*

   ◆ *In pursuing this goal, students will be taught the skills of conflict resolution in their weekly guidance classes. Teachers will reinforce the use of these conflict resolution skills.*
   ◆ *Though it is not always appropriate to use conflict resolution to solve problems, the teachers and students should encourage each other to make use of these techniques whenever possible.*

The third goal in the Horizon Contract sets high standards for learning in all curriculum areas. It delineates ways in which teachers, students, and parents agree to act responsibly. Teachers agree to set assignments with clear and attainable goals, students agree to work at home for one and a half hours each night, and parents agree to keep themselves informed about their student's assignments through discussion and the use of a weekly time-management sheet.

This contract is signed by students, staff and parents.

EXTENSIONS

Rules for the School: During the first week in the fall, the public elementary school in Ashfield, Massachusetts, Sanderson Academy, asks all classes to create rules for the whole school. The Student Council helps the principal pool these lists to create common rules. Each classroom also has individual rules that pertain. This process helps students retain ownership of the agreements and to connect as one community.

Equity Council: For agreements on bias reduction to take hold, people must be clearly designated to collect and act on feedback. (See Appendix, item 14, p. 167)

✤ SCHOOL-WIDE ACTIVITY ✤
KNOW YOUR NEIGHBOR

ORIGIN

After reading that the number of people in the U.S. who know their neighbors is declining, Jana Standish, school counselor at Colrain Central School in Colrain, Massachusetts, created this activity to help children in her small, rural community of 1,700 understand the importance of maintaining and nurturing neighborly relations.

For "Make a Difference" day, each child identified one or two neighbors they would visit with the okay of their parents. Out of 156 students, 120 visited their neighbors, and all reported favorable experiences, handshakes, and smiles. Some students told of riding a neighbor's horse or feeding the neighbor's animals. Others in the community invited children and their families into their home for hot chocolate or cookies. As a result, students strengthened their connections to their neighbors and their small town.

This activity was developed for a rural school, but it can be adapted for urban and suburban settings. One way to do this is to introduce people who work in local stores as neighbors.

ORIENTATION

Tell the students: "Today we will be talking about neighbors."

PROCEDURE

SURVEY

Ask students to think about the neighbors immediately around them on all four sides, whether this means next door in their apartment building or miles away. Tell students:
◆ "Raise your hand if you know your immediate neighbor."
◆ "Raise your hand if you get along with all your neighbors." Notice that there will probably be several students who do not raise your hands on the second question.

DISCUSSION

1. Ask students: "What do you think is the importance of having neighbors?" Examples you might cite:
   ◆ Neighbors can help in an emergency such as a fire, a medical problem or being locked out of your home.
   ◆ Neighbors can lend things like eggs or ladders or tools.

GRADES: K–8th

FOCUS: Students reach out to a neighbor

◆ Neighbors are people you can be friendly to.

2. Discuss with students how contact with neighbors is decreasing in the United States. It used to be that people knew their neighbors and therefore everyone was looking out for each other and their children.

3. Discuss the meaning of the adage, "It takes a village to raise a child." How could a neighbor help a child learn?

4. Explain to the students that in order to really make a difference in our communities, we need to get to know our neighbors and try to mend problems if there is disharmony between neighbors.

MAIN ACTIVITY

1. Pick a Neighbor: Ask students to take a moment to think about a neighbor or shopkeeper they could visit with the permission of their parent(s). Ask the students to put a thumb up if they have thought of a neighbor.

2. Introduce the idea of a visit:
   ◆ Imagine knocking on the door or making a call on the phone to this neighbor.
   ◆ Think about saying something like this to your neighbor: "At school, we are visiting neighbors to help make a difference in our community. I'm just stopping in to say 'hi.' My name is _____."
   ◆ To get perspective, imagine what it would feel like if somebody dropped over to say "hi" at your own house.

3. List-making: Make the idea even more concrete by asking students to identify the name of the neighbor they would connect with. If they don't know the name, they can list a description of where the neighbor lives (for example, the apartment next door, the trailer across the street, the yellow house). Write the student's name next to the neighbor, and bring this list to the next session.

4. **Specify a specific weekend** for this activity; for example, use the national Make a Difference Day in October. Ask students to try this exercise as a social experiment and be ready to report back what happened.

5. **Have a Backup Plan:** Tell students that if the neighbor they were going to call on is not home or is busy, they should think of someone else to join them in improving their neighborly relations.

FOLLOW-UP SESSION

1. **Go to your list of students** and the neighbor they identified. Ask each student on the list whether the neighbor con-

nection took place, and, if so, what happened. Help encourage their stories. Affirm students in the risks they took. If the first neighbor they tried to contact was not home, reinforce what they did next to connect in a positive way with someone else.

2. **Return to the discussion** of the value of neighbors in session one. Ask: "Do you have any new ideas about the importance of having neighbors? If you needed to borrow something or needed help in an emergency, do you think you could go to the person you visited? Would they be able to turn to you and your family for help they needed as well?"

EXTENSION

Language Arts: Have students write a letter or make a card for a neighbor.

✳ SCHOOL-WIDE ACTIVITY ✳

TALK IT OUT FAMILY NIGHT

Bringing Parents and Students Together

OVERVIEW

Here is how I lead a participatory event in the evening for families. When families arrive, they are seated in a circle of chairs or at a table along with other families in groups of 12 to 16 people.

Students participate in the event in two ways:

a. Classes learn one song to perform or prepare a skit.

b. Pairs of third through sixth graders facilitate the Family Circles of participants.

This involvement gives parents an incentive to attend. For instance, at the Helen E. James School in Williamsburg, Massachusetts, 150 people (first- through third-grade students from six classes, parents, grandparents and siblings five years old and up) turned out from 7 to 8 p.m. for "Talk It Out Family Night."

PREPARATION

Train student facilitators to work in pairs, leading one of the circles. If attendance of 40 to 60 people is estimated, prepare twelve leaders to facilitate six circles. In advance, prepare clip-

GRADES: 1st–6th
FOCUS: Share cooperation and conflict resolution methods with parents at an intergenerational evening program
MATERIALS: recordings to learn songs, clipboards, name tags for student facilitators

boards and name tags for student leaders. During the training, student leaders practice reading out loud the directions they will use during the evening program and practice calling on people and listing their responses on the sheet. Pairs decide which person will read each section and decide who will be the "Recorder" and who will be the "Picker," the one who calls on people in the group whose hands are raised. It is best to schedule at least an hour for this practice.

Display student stories, poems, and drawings related to cooperation and conflict resolution. At Park Street School in Springfield, Vermont, students made videos of conflict resolution skits with their guidance counselor, Jean Korstange.

The tapes were playing as parents arrrived.

PROCEDURE

Create a coherent program that has variety. Start with songs and skits presented by students. Also, include activities led by the presenter and facilitated by the student leaders. These activities should involve parents and children in each small group.

Example:

1. Start with a welcoming song — "This Land is Your Land" or "This Little Light of Mine" — led by one class.

2. Next another class leads a thematic song: "Two in the Fight" (p. 85).

3. Icebreaker: Family Circle Activity One, "Affirming Our Differences — Listmaking."

One student leader reads these words to the group, "Please work with us to make a list. Our group will think of eight different answers to this question." The other student leader reads the question. Each circle is given a different topic that can be answered by children or adults: What things are you looking forward to doing when the weather gets warmer? What are your favorite kinds of ice cream? What are nicknames that people in the group have had? What kinds of pets have you had in your life? What kinds of jobs do you do now or you'd like to do in the future?

Share the lists: Ask a student leader from each group to read the items on the list out loud to everyone.

Option: A song leader or music teacher works with the list to create a verse of a song on the spot. Use the song "Under One Sky" by Ruth Pelham, from her recording of the same name (See Resources in the appendix, p. 169.) For instance, a group at the "Talk It Out Family Night" in Williamsburg, Massachusetts, created this verse about what they were looking forward to doing when spring came: "We're going to garden. We want to play soccer. We want to go hiking, and get our cars out of the mud. We want to bike. We want to swing on swings. We want to go fishing. And put our shorts on."

4. Student Skits: *Two Ways to Solve a Problem.* Students show a family argument getting worse, and then show what things family members could do to settle a problem constructively. *Note:* Sue Liedl in Bemidji, Minnesota, likes to name the contrasting families "The No-Skills Family" and the "More Skills Family" (p. 7).

5. Family Circle Activity Two: *Worse and Better.* Student leaders read these directions to their Family Circle: "Now we will think about a busy family in the morning getting ready for school and for work. Imagine that they have been getting into arguments and feeling upset." The student leaders ask for ideas to fill in two columns. The student leaders take turns picking someone in the group to say an idea for one list and recording the response on their sheet. *Sharing as a Whole Group:* Hear two items in each category from every group.

These things would make it worse.	These things would help to make it better.
It makes it worse when someone wakes you up by shouting at you or pulling your hair.	It helps when people go to bed on time and don't stay up too late watching television.
It makes it worse when sisters and brothers use mean words and tease each other.	It helps when you make a lunch the night before.

6. Song: "There's Always Something You Can Do" sung by a class (music on facing page.)

7. Family Circle Activity Three: *Multiple Solutions to a Family Problem.* Name a common family problem. Ask each circle to brainstorm as many different ways as they can to solve it. Then hear some examples and discuss as a whole group.

8. Closing Song: One class sings a unity song (I use my song "The Colors of Earth") to close the program.

HELPFUL HINTS

◆ Schedule one or two meetings of 45–60 minutes with student leaders to train them and explain their roles. One option if you have a peer mediator program, is to involve mediators as the student leaders of the Family Circles.

◆ Clue in adults to the plan of student leadership and explain at the start of the evening what to expect. Three times the student leaders will provide an activity with questions for the group to answer.

◆ You can learn "This Little Light of Mine," "Two in a Fight,"and "The Colors of Earth," on the *Linking Up* recording. (Resources, p. 169)

There's Always Something You Can Do

© 1989 words and music by Sarah Pirtle Discovery Center Music, BMI

Verse 1: There is al- ways some- thing you can do, do, do. When you're get- ting in a stew, stew, stew. You can go out for a walk. You can try to sit and talk. There's al- ways some- thing you can do.

Bridge 1: Whe- ther in a school or fam- 'ly ar- gu- ment, when you feel you'd real- ly like to throw a fit Don't be trapped by fights and fists and an- gry threats. Reach out for this or- di- na- ry plan. There is

Verse 2

*There is always something
you can do, do, do.
Yes, it's difficult,
but true, true, true.
See it from each other's eyes.
Find a way to compromise.
There's always something
you can do.*

Bridge 2

*You can use your smarts and
not your fists, fists, fists.
You can give that problem
a new twist, twist, twist.
You can see it 'round about
and upside down.
Give yourself the time
to find a way.*

Verse 3

*There is always something
you can do, do, do.
When you're getting
in a stew, stew, stew.
When you want to yell and scream.
Find the words for what you mean.
There's always something you can do.*

Community Building

MORNING GREETING CIRCLE

Special Objects for Affirmation

OVERVIEW

Each day children need to feel they are seen and welcomed as individuals. This activity provides that opportunity. Many choices are presented here so that teachers can craft a procedure that best fits their own class. This activity encourages appreciation of diversity.

ORIENTATION

Tell the class: "Please pick one of the special objects on the table and hold it as we gather in our morning circle to start the day."

PREPARATION

Set up a location in the room where special objects are spread out. One option is to place them on a cloth to designate where they are and to give them a feeling of respect. Collect a range of interesting or humorous objects, favoring natural materials over plastic figures. Examples: shells, acorns, chestnuts, gems, stones, driftwood, tiny stuffed toys, elf dolls, figurines, carved dolphins, dried flowers, doll sunglasses, toy trucks. Also include objects that relate to students' cultures, to history, or geography.

A rule of thumb in supplying the table is to have twice as many objects as students to give sufficient choice. Each week add more variety. Also, prepare a basket or tray that will hold the objects that students have selected during that day. At the end of the day, all objects go back on the cloth.

PROCEDURE

1. Focus. Sit or stand in a circle, each person holding an object. Take turns saying what your object is: "I chose this clamshell today." When you are doing the activity in the beginning of the year, students may need to ask, "What is this?" This response provides a chance to provide accurate names: mussel shell, hazelnut, amethyst. Also, ask the students to add anything about why they picked that object; for example, "I picked this rainbow because my Dad told me he saw a rainbow last week," or "I feel tired so I picked this turtle hiding in its shell. That's what I'd like to

AGES: K–6th

FOCUS: Select a special object to hold

MATERIALS: Collection of interesting objects, basket, cloth, optional candle

PREPARATION: Add new items frequently

do right now," or "I chose this green cloth from Tibet because a family from Tibet is moving into the apartment next to me." One way to describe the activity for older elementary ages is, "This object will represent you today. It will stand for you as a member of our class."

2. Skillbuilding. "Now hold your object behind your back." Encourage observation and listening by asking two or three questions at the end of the sharing. *Examples:* Ask the class, "Can you remember who chose the *molinillo* this morning? That's the wooden spoon from Mexico for stirring a chocolate drink. Which people had the same object today as they did yesterday? How many people chose Guatemalan dolls? What was Kisha's reason for choosing the geode?"

3. Sending Good Wishes. Add a wish for the day. Say words that encourage the values and social agreements of your group. For instance, "Just like these objects are special, each person here is special to us and we send a wish that we will notice what we like about each person today." Or, "We send good wishes around the circle for everyone here to have the support to do their best today." Ask students: Who wants to send a good wish today?

Two activities in this book have images you can call upon during the Morning Friendship Circle to help set a tone of affirmation. If your class has done the activity "The Web of Human Unity" (p. 159), refer to the nerve cell image: "Because we are connected just like the nerve cells of one body, we send encouragement to each person here."

If your class has learned "Our Whale Hearts" (p. 117), ask students to "stand in their whale hearts."

Candlelighting Option: If you like, you can also light a candle to add a feeling of warmth and caring. For instance, tell the class: "We light this candle for the light of friendship." Or, "This flame helps us remember that each of us can shine our light brightly at the same time."

4. Closure. Set up a procedure for placing all objects in a designated basket or on a tray where they will remain for the rest of the day, standing for each person. Make clear agreements: Can the objects in the basket be touched during the day? Can objects not chosen but remaining on the cloth be touched during the day? Ask that all objects stay on the table. Clarify that if children add objects themselves to the Morning Greeting objects, that this means any person in the class can now use them.

❈ CLASSROOM PRACTICE ❈
CLASS MEETING AFTER RECESS

ORIGIN

First-grade teachers M.J. Long and Johanna Korpita at the Helen E. James Elementary School in Williamsburg, Massachusetts, developed this practice after they had classes with many recess problems.

Each day they were faced with six to ten students in line wanting to talk about the "horrendous things" that had occurred at recess. They decided to do a joint meeting with both classes. Since then, they have continued this practice for four years. Now they meet with their own classes separately. They say, "Our commitment is to give these issues the time they need. Sometimes this takes thirty minutes, but it has a positive effect on the entire year. We watch children change. Later in the year, these meetings become a time of reporting how they solved the problems and a sharing of their success."

They stress that "this classroom group we share so much time with is like another family."

PROCEDURE

1. Sit in a circle and use a talking object (p. 97) to help speakers take turns without interrupting.

2. Establish that all statements need to be kept anonymous. Give students this example: "Somebody grabbed the ball from me and wouldn't give it back."

3. Focus on how to help the speaker deal with the problem. *Example:* A person reports to the teacher that "someone called me a mean name." Instead of focusing on how to

GRADES: K–6th: especially grade one

FOCUS: A classroom meeting following recess builds problem-solving skills

MATERIALS: none

help the name-caller make a better choice, help the speaker find words like "I don't like it when you talk to me that way because it makes me feel nervous and scared" to speak directly to the student involved.

4. This time is used as an opportunity to teach important skills. Focus on one skill during each meeting, as needed:

◆ Students learn how to use "I statements" to express themselves.

◆ Students distinguish between a recess problem that needs to be reported to an adult and a problem they can walk away from once they resolve it themselves. The problem of tattling is approached by discerning whose problem it is and by learning how and when to let go of an issue.

◆ Children learn how to approach a child who is playing alone and ask him if he'd like to be included. If a child with disabilities or special needs is being excluded at recess, assign a recess buddy so she will have a playmate.

◆ Schedule time to teach the class group games they can play together as a community. Also add recess toys and games that can be used either individually or that encourage cooperation in a group: sidewalk chalk, jacks, match box cars. Ask children to donate recess toys and games which can be used by anyone.

VARIATION

SAFETY OFFICER

1. Every child in the class has an opportunity to be the Safety Officer for a day. The position is rotated in alphabetical order. Names are recorded on the calendar. Children who are absent and miss their turn become the Safety Officer upon returning. The Safety Officer wears a badge all day.

2. At recess the Safety Officer is responsible for noticing if children feel safe. When a problem happens, here are the steps to follow:

♦ *Step One:* Children who have a recess problem try to work it out through constructive self-expression.

♦ *Step Two:* If this doesn't work, they ask the Safety Officer for help, and the Safety Officer goes with them to try again to solve it.

♦ *Step Three:* If this doesn't help, they are accompanied by the Safety Officer to the adult in charge at recess.

Example: A ball rolls out of bounds in a game. Someone picks up the ball and won't give it back.

♦ *Step One:* A child in the game speaks to the person who has the ball and says, "We're playing with the ball and we need the ball back for our game. Please give it back to us."

♦ *Step Two:* This didn't work. A child in the game finds the Safety Officer and asks her to come over and assist. The Safety Officer says to the child involved, "I understand that [student's name] has already asked you for the ball. Could you give the ball back and not get it again when it rolls out of bounds?"

♦ *Step Three:* It still didn't work. Together the Safety Officer and a child in the game find the recess aide. They say, "We have already asked in a kind and respectful way two times. We need help getting the ball back."

By using the Safety Officer method, children figure out which incidents are finished and don't need to go to the recess meeting where they'd be the focus of forty children.

MJ and Johanna comment, "This also helps them learn how to overlook minor incidents. They learn how to communicate and check out their assumptions. For instance, if someone says, 'He looked at me with a mean look,' that person may reply, 'I had something in my eye — I wasn't even looking at you, I was trying to get it out.' Petty disputes do end up being solved quickly and eventually ignored.

"In general, the Safety Officer Program offers the children the opportunity to take control and be in charge of circumstances where they can make a difference."

EXTENSIONS

Older Children Teach Games: Arrange for members of an older grade to instruct younger children in how to play a group game. *Examples:* jumprope, hopscotch, four square, freeze tag, hand-clap games, playing house. Make a structured plan for two to four individuals in grades 3–6 to teach a specific small group of two to eight younger children how to play a game. The goal is for the younger children to be able to play the game by themselves. This will help the children who play fight or chase find more options at recess.

Peer Mediation Program: The Safety Officer procedure would not be needed in a school that has fifth- and sixth-grade students trained to help children mediate their conflicts. The Safety Officer doesn't act as a mediator, but does try to be a neutral advocate for fairness who does not take sides in a dispute.

✼ ACTIVITY ✼
GOOD NEWS BOARD
Affirming Class Behavior

SOURCE

Sharon Vincent, first-grade teacher at Kittredge School in Hinsdale, Massachusetts, records positive actions of her students at the end of each day on a Good News Board.

PROCEDURE

1. Establish a bulletin board or chart paper on a stand where positive statements are recorded. Urge the students: "Tell me the good news from today." Explain that they give their response without saying the name of the particular person who did it.

   Examples:
   - "Someone helped me with my coat."
   - "Someone thanked me when I held the door open."
   - "Someone came over to help when I fell down."
   - "Someone told me that I did a good job."
   - "I saw people sharing."

   Model the activity at the start by writing down statements of behavior that you've observed, and then invite students to add their own.

2. At the start of the next day, the teacher reads the good news from the previous day, tears it off, and gives each child a turn to bring it home to keep.

3. Ask students to reflect: "What are positive statements you'd like to be able to make about our class? Think about moments of the day when you can search for good news."

   Examples:
   - "We picked teams for kickball at recess in a fair way."
   - "We shared board games during free choice time."
   - "We wrote songs by cooperating in groups and ideas

GRADES: K–6th

FOCUS: Keep a record of specific positive actions of the class

MATERIALS: Bulletin Board display or chart paper on an aisle

from every person in the class were included."
   - "We walked in lines to lunch all week without pushing."
   - "We worked together to solve a problem before we asked for help."

   Adapt the Good News Board idea to fit your age group and the schedule of your day. Give it a name that will work for your group, such as "Our Success Board" or "We're Great!" If you don't want to make it a daily activity, focus on news of the week on Friday.

EXTENSIONS

1. At the end of any activity where you are working in small groups, ask each group to come up with "good news" to add to the board or chart. Help them develop the ability to describe specific positive behavior; for example, "We listened well to each person's idea."

2. In the activity "Conflict Interviews" (pp. 92–95), older students ask students in a younger class questions about the problems they experience. They also ask questions about what their class is doing well and collect the "Good News" of the class.

3. Help students realize that learning to get along is a sign of growth.

❋ ACTIVITIES ❋
AFFIRMATION GOOD-BYE
Classroom Practice

OVERVIEW

Design an affirmative ending to your day that takes into account children's basic need to give and receive affection. Here are choices:

FUNNY WAVING

Pick one student each day to create a method for waving good-bye. All wave simultaneously. Look at each class member. For example, a fourth- through sixth-grade teacher might introduce the process humorously. "It's time for our amazing wacky good-bye wave. Kaylee, will you think of a wave for us?" Kaylee waves just one finger and everyone imitates her. Or, a second grade teacher asks Gerald to invent a way to wave. He selects one hand waving from the top of his head, and all wave like Gerald.

TEACHER BOND

At the door, say good-bye to each person by name and take a moment for physical connection, even in the flurry of calling groups of children for buses or whatever dismissal procedure your school uses. Each individual signals what he or she wants to do today: a handshake, a hug, a high-five, or a jump. (Hold one hand high. Kindergartners through second graders jump up and tap your hand.)

GOOD NEWS

End the end with an affirmative statement that refers to an event from the day or the overall tenor in the room; for example, "I noticed how hard you concentrated on your group projects this afternoon," or "I watched many people help each other this morning when you were working on your Biographical Scrolls." For a method of eliciting positive statements from students themselves, see the previous activity "Good News Board," p. 25.

GRADES: K–6th

FOCUS: Close the day with affirmation

CIRCLE UP

Stand and cross hands in a circle. Pass a squeeze around the circle from hand to hand. Then finish by saying a greeting in unison, such as "See you tomorrow, " or "I hope you have a good evening."

CLOSING SONG

Sing a song together. Use this opportunity to smile at students and create a feeling of warmth.

Traditional songs:
- ◆ "This Little Light of Mine"
- ◆ "The More We Get Together"
- ◆ "Kumbaya"

Composed songs —
"Under One Sky," by Ruth Pelham
"This Land is Your Land," by Woody Guthrie
"Adiós, Amigos," by Sarah Pirtle and Roberto Díaz

REMINDER SONG

Using the tune, "Fréres Jacques," work with your class to construct four lines that give reminders and affirmation:

Put your chair on top of your desk.
Take home the notice on yellow paper.
Have fun this evening, have fun this evening.
See you tomorrow, see you tomorrow.

CHAPTER 3
Core Curriculum
Integrating Cooperation and the Arts into Language Arts, Science, and Social Studies

LANGUAGE ARTS

Integrating Cooperation and the Arts into the Core Curriculum

✻ LANGUAGE ARTS ACTIVITY ✻

TRIBBLES

GRADES: 5th–8th

PLANNING: Place students in pairs

ORIENTATION

Establish a setting (the desert, another planet, the Amazon Basin, the ocean), and give one characteristic of a "Tribble," a creature discovered there.

You are a space explorer walking along a dry, dusty planet that seems deserted. Suddenly you hear a squawk. You turn around and glimpse a shy, odd creature with a piglike tail staring at you. You know that it is a Tribble. What does it look like?

Or,

You are rowing a dug-out canoe through a river in the Mexican rain forest. Long vines hang down in your face. Suddenly you hear the whoosh of large wings. You look up in time to see a Tribble swoop down to try to capture your hat. What does it look like?

PROCEDURE

1. Students draw a picture by themselves of the imaginary creature discussed in the made-up story.
2. Students describe their drawings in writing, and this description is passed to another individual. They take care to use "show" language—lots of detailed description.
3. Exchange writing with another student. Take a few minutes for each person to read over the description and then meet with the person with whom they exchanged to answer any questions about the words.
4. Using only the writing, each student draws the creature the other described.

CLOSURE

After processing together, with at least one positive comment made about each drawing, the group discusses what makes a good description. Students circle words in the descriptions passed to them which were particularly helpful or evocative.

SOURCE

Dave Johnston of Brattleboro, Vermont invented this language arts activity to introduce "show language" — parts of speech and language devices like adjectives, adverbs, similes, and metaphors — to students.

✳ LANGUAGE ARTS ACTIVITY ✳
ANGER POETRY

OVERVIEW

Poems are a place to tell the truth, our truth. Here are ways to work with the medium of poetry to express and discover the message anger is bringing.

FRACTURED ANGER POEM

Use this process as a jumping-off point for writing. Divide the class into groups of four. Photocopy these phrases and cut into eight strips of one line each. Give a set to each small group. Each member takes two. Students take turns laying down strips and rearranging. Emphasize that there is not one right way to assemble the phrases.

like a bonfire flaring in the dark

what will happen here

I see bright eyes

I follow my anger

in the cave where no one walks

anger comes now

looking for something forgotten

like a stone rolling down a passageway

After the group has arranged the eight lines in a manner they like, ask them to write more lines until they feel the poem is complete and expresses what they want to say. They can change any words on the strips of paper or omit any strips. Add a title.

ANGER QUESTIONS

Ask students to write their answers as you read these questions one at a time. Then have individual students use any of their words to build a poem.

◆ What color is anger?
◆ What sound is anger?
◆ What place or landscape is anger?
◆ What kind of weather is anger?
◆ What animal is anger?
◆ What shape is anger?

GRADES: "Fractured Poem" 4th and up.
Others: 1st and up

FOCUS: Encourage self knowledge.

ANGER SIGNALS

Discuss the different ways people appear when they are angry. Study facial expressions. Tell students: "We are going to show each other what our angry faces look like Cover your face with both hands. When I count to to three, reveal what your angry expression looks like." Discuss features such as tight mouth, scowling forehead, tight fist. Next, ask students to write a poem and/or draw pictures about the different ways they know that they are angry.

SILLY ANGER SOLUTIONS

Part of conflict resolution work is to help children create anger plans of recommended actions when they are upset. One plan might be to go to the classroom Calming Corner to scribble an angry drawing. Here is another plan. Create a Calming Down Book by assembling a list of silly actions with illustrations as a class book. List funny things to do that are not serious recommendations and not violent; for example, *I want to spray whipped cream in people's faces.* Reading the book becomes one of the choices students can make when they need help calming down.

SAFE WORDS, SAFE PLACES

If anger barrels in like a locomotive with no breaks, how can we make it safe to figure out what is upsetting? With students using the concept of the "Friendly Voice" (p. 115), give them these instructions: "Write a poem about what words you'd like someone to say to you or you could say to yourself when you are upset. Imagine yourself in a safe atmosphere where you have all the space you need to hear the message of your anger. Describe a helpful imaginary person or animal."

COMMUNICATING MEMORIES

Sounds, Smells, and Sights

ORIENTATION

Tell students: "We will explore how memories stay with us and how we can communicate them to others by sharing what we saw or heard or felt or even smelled."

PROCEDURE

Focus on different senses to help students search for memories through many avenues. Here is a five-day unit.

DAY ONE:
SMELLS THAT CALL UP MEMORIES

Materials: Assemble interesting and evocative smells such as spice jars of cinnamon, curry and oregano. Bring in objects with smells from home like rose perfume, or a balsam pine pillow.

Procedure: Pass an object around for the class to smell. Focus not upon guessing what it is but rather letting it call up memories of events or places. "This reminds me of ____."
Variation: Have each small group smell a different object and list all the events or places the smell reminds them of.

Next, each person writes a poem or story inspired by a smell.

DAY TWO:
HOW YOUR OWN MEMORY WORKS

Orientation: Tell students: "Each of us has our own unique way of holding memories. Some, but not all, people see pieces of a picture, while others remember feelings, smells, touch, movements, or a combination of these. Let's get a sense of how our own memories work."

Procedure: Select a situation that everyone in the class has experienced. Tell students: "Remember a time you played a game with someone that you really enjoyed. Notice how the memory comes to you." Students will return a variety of responses, like these: "I see grass and then bricks we used as bases and I'm playing kickball with my friends," "In my memory I'm feeling fuzzy, stuffed bears," or "I'm racing fast down the street."

GRADES: 1st–6th

FOCUS: Share important memories

MATERIALS: Paper, markers, sample photos of family events, objects to smell

PLANNING: Place students in pairs.

Other situations to use:
◆ "Remember a time you sat at a table eating food you liked."
◆ "Remember a place you stayed overnight that's different from your home right now and notice who or what was there around you."
◆ "Remember a place that means a lot to you."

Provide one situation and encourage students to seek as many details as they can find in their memory. Next, share in pairs. Help children describe to each other what they remember and also how the memory arrives. Talk about whether they experience memory visually, auditorily, or kinesthetically.

DAY THREE:
SNAPSHOTS AND STORYBOARDS

Orientation: Assemble picturebooks or snapshots from your own family album. Show an illustration or photograph that captures a moment of an event. Discuss as a class what you think was happening in these sample pictures and talk about what the people may have been feeling. *[Comment that people have both happy and unhappy memories.]* "Some moments — like a time we dropped an ice cream cone or broke a bone or saw a fight — may not have been photographed by a camera, but we remember them."

Procedure: Introduce students to the drawing activity: "We're going to do a memory search now to plan for our drawings. As you think about your whole life, which moments arise in your memory as important times?"

Remind them of that sense of snapshot — and ask them

to select the moment they want to show that conveys the event.

Example: In a fourth-grade class in Amherst, Massachusetts, each student divided a sheet of paper into four sections to describe four memories. The caption "I Remember" headed the paper, and children put captions on each drawing.

Katja Zelljadt of Amherst, Massachusetts created these words and drawings.

1. Katja drew children singing in rows with a caption giving the name of her nursery school, "Fort Hill."

2. She drew a baby tucked in with a blanket in a hospital bed labeled with her last name, captioned "My sister was born."

3. "Bit my chin" shows herself on the floor, crying next to a large table.

4. "Baby squirrel fell out of a nest" shows a tiny squirrel at the bottom of a tree.

Explain that some of our memories are private. "Select memories that you want to share with the class. They don't have to be happy memories." *Option:* Play music in the background if you think this will help students feel safe and focused.

Note: Our brains have built-in protection so that we remember only the portion of traumatic events we are ready to remember. While children are working, circulate around the class, looking for children who have described sad or painful events and ascertain what will be supportive to them. Find out if any children have drawn events that others may not be ready to handle. Plan how drawings will be shared based on what you observe. For instance, using pairs, you can place children with similar experiences together, or you can pair yourself with a child who has expressed a particularly upsetting event.

Closure: Provide adequate time to appreciate these drawings using any of these methods:

◆ Visit with every child to hear about his or her drawing.
◆ Help children meet in groups of two, three, or four to share their drawings.
◆ Gather in a circle and give time for everyone to say one thing about his or her drawing.
◆ Post the drawings on a bulletin board.

Extension: Follow up appropriately on any new infomation you have learned, taking cues from the child; for example, if a drawing tells you, "My brother is deaf," and you learn that the whole family has studied American Sign Language, ask the student to teach the class. If a child shares experiences from living in Israel, make room during the year to hear more information and to study Israel as a class.

Affirmation: Here is a method for extended sharing. Focus on three different children each day. The students share storyboards with drawings of events in their lives, and they also bring in family photos.

DAY FOUR:
MEMORIES OF SOUNDS

Procedure: Give your students a familiar setting, like "Riding the bus," "Midnight at my home," or "My kitchen before school." Ask students all the sounds in that setting, and list them on the board. Next, go back through the list, pointing to each item one by one, and ask students to make the corresponding sound using voices or objects.

Now, each student picks a place or event and uses sound memories to convey it with words and phrases. *More sample settings:* A walk down my street, Going fishing, In the lunchroom, Waiting for the bus, Going to the fair, Playing with my cat/dog, At the park.

Closing: Students present their writing without telling the title and listeners guess what place or situation is being described.

DAY FIVE: ## COMMUNICATING WITH MANY SENSES

Students search for a very pleasant memory. They are asked to convey it in at least two different ways — that is, with two different sensory avenues — so that the others in the class can imagine what it was like. Examples:

◆ They can lead the class in pantomiming the movement.
◆ They can bring in a smell or describe a smell.
◆ They can describe a taste.
◆ They can imitate the sounds.
◆ They can draw a picture of it.
◆ They can make a collage with many different colors, textures, lines.
◆ They can write a poem or story about it.

❊ LANGUAGE ARTS ACTIVITY ❊
COOPERATIVE DIALOGUE WRITING

ORIGIN

Seventh-grade teacher Ingrid Chrisco and fourth-grade teacher Flo Nestor, from Brattleboro, Vermont, taught *Alice in Wonderland* concurrently and brought their classes together for three lessons structured for cooperative learning. (Flo continues to teach in Brattleboro; Ingrid is now assistant principal in Keene, New Hampshire.)

PREPARATION

Arrange students in heterogeneous groups of three or four. If you are combining two classes, mix the ages in each group. Or use the lessons with one class.

LESSON ONE:
GROUP DRAWINGS

1. **Shared Reading:** In preassigned groups, students read orally from Chapter 2 of the book. Tell the group members that they need to share the reading and determine who will read and for how long.

2. **Brainstorm:** Provide a sheet of paper and pencil for each group. Ask the whole group to work together to brainstorm a list of the episodes in the chapter.

3. **Main Cooperative Learning Activity:** Small groups choose one episode to illustrate. They discuss what they could draw and what should be included in the scene. They work cooperatively to draw the scene they have chosen.

4. **Processing:** Evaluate the activity. Give each individual student a form to fill out with two reflection questions. Examples:

   ◆ How did you decide who would read and for how long?

   ◆ How did you decide which episode you would illustrate?

   ◆ How did you go about doing the illustration? How much do you feel you contributed to the group?

Give a chance for each small group to share and discuss their drawings of the scenes.

GRADES: 4th–8th

FOCUS: Literature study combines reading and grammar skills with drawing and creative dramatics

MATERIALS: Drawing paper, markers

LESSON TWO:
CREATING DIALOGUE

1. **Shared Reading:** The teachers create a synopsis of one chapter which they have divided into as many scenes as there are cooperative learning teams. Ask groups to share the reading of this synopsis, and set a target social skill for the lesson for everyone who will participate.

2. **Information:** Lessons from previous classes on the correct punctuation for dialogue are reviewed.

3. **Cooperative Learning Activity:** Each team is assigned one scene which they are to bring to life using dialogue. Members pick which role or roles they want: Timekeeper, Recorder, Encourager, Reader, or Orchestrator, who helps the group decide how they will approach the dialogue writing assignment..

4. **Presentation:** The reader from each group stands in a line in the order that their scene appears in that chapter. The scenes they wrote are presented orally in sequence to everyone.

5. **Processing:** Each student has an evaluation sheet to fill out with questions such as:

   ◆ How much do you feel you contributed to the group? (rating from 1 to 10)
   ◆ How did your group decide what you would write for your dialogue?
   ◆ What did you like about working with these people?

CONFLICT RESOLUTION AND LITERATURE

A New Perspective

USE LITERATURE to complement your conflict resolution program. Literature is about interaction and personal change. By focusing on any of the following six concepts, you can formulate discussion questions that will help students use their reading to increase their understanding of conflict resolution.

1. **Concept: Conflict exists.** All people have conflicts with others and within themselves every day. What matters is how these conflicts are approached.
   - ◆ "How does the book show that conflicts are a normal part of every human life?"
   - ◆ "What conflicts does the main character encounter?"

2. **Concept: People care about each other.** Human beings are social beings who have an innate interest in others. When we meet a character who is isolated, invariably we watch them come into increased contact with the human community over the course of the story.
   - ◆ "Who are supportive people in the life of the main character?"
   - ◆ "Pick one person and describe how they give help."

3. **Concept: Each conflict is unique.** Our intention and our perseverance will make a difference. Students will notice that there is not one script of words or a recipe of the right things to say that people use when they have a conflict. It is the overall intention of a person that registers and makes a difference to those who relate to her or him. Conflicts are solved by continued effort over time.
   - ◆ "Pick one conflict that the main character grapples with. What methods does the main character use to handle that conflict?"

4. **Concept: Violent solutions to conflicts may work temporarily,** but they won't resolve the underlying causes of the problem and don't create a stable resolution.
   - ◆ "If violent solutions are used in the book, examine them. In what ways are they effective or ineffective?"

5. **Concept: Conflicts have multiple causes,** and a lasting resolution involves handling several factors, when possible. Help can come from one's own efforts, from others, and from changes in circumstance.

   Write one problem that the main character faces on the board and draw a circle around it. Create a web drawing of all the different factors and forces that contribute to that problem. Put a check by factors which the main character has no control over. Circle aspects the person can work on. Take one of these factors and make it the center of a new web chart. Write down the actions the character takes to work on this underlying cause and write down any people or circumstances which also contributed to resolution.

6. **Concept: There is room in life for us to make mistakes and grow.** Characters in literature have difficulties, make choices they later regret, misunderstand other people, and get misunderstood. What we like about the characters in our books is not that they are superhuman but human. They have an enduring nature and a unique self, which we as readers grow to understand and affirm.
   - ◆ "Based on this book, do you think that people have to be 'perfect' or 'superhuman' to solve their problems? What things the main character did are things you could do?"

RECOMMENDED BOOKS

- ◆ *The Pinballs,* by Betsy Byars (HarperCrest, 1987).

- ◆ *The Hundred Dresses,* by Eleanor Estes, illustrated by Louis Slobodkin (Harcourt Brace, 1944).

- ◆ *Teammates,* by Peter Golenbock, illustrated by Paul Bacon (Harcourt Brace, 1990). This book describes the support Brooklyn Dodgers player Jackie Robinson, the first black player in the Major Leagues, received from his teammate Pee Wee Reese. For first through fourth graders.

- ◆ *Teaching Conflict Resolution Through Children's Literature* by William Kreidler and James Graham Hale (Scholastic, 1995). Here are activity suggestions and discussion questions for more than 25 books.

SCIENCE ACTIVITIES

Integrating Cooperation and the Arts into the Core Curriculum

❋ SCIENCE ACTIVITY ❋

PEACE FLOWERS

PROCEDURE

Pairs of students work together to create a paper flower large enough to fill a window. First and second grade teacher Susan Vegiard of Amherst, Massachusetts uses these instructions to help students step by step through the process.

1. She places a choice of four colors of paper. Partners discuss which colors to use and bring the paper to the desk where they are working.

2. They discuss how they want to make the center of the flower, and they cut it out.

3. They discuss how to form the petals, cut them out, and attach them to the center with rubber cement.

4. They discuss how thick and how long they will make the stem, and cut that out. They attach the stem to the center of the flower.

Here is an interview that Susan had with one of the pairs working on a Peace Flower. She spoke to Gabriel Bodin and Amir Baghdadchi.

> Teacher: *That's an unusual looking stem. How did you decide to make it?*
> Amir: *Well, I cut from one end and Gabe cut from the other end and we met in the middle.*

GRADES: K–2nd

FOCUS: Pairs collaborate on making a flower

MATERIALS: Colored paper, scissors, rubber cement

> Teacher: *I notice that your flower was the only one with a face. How did you decide to draw a face in the center of the flower?*
> Amir: *Gabe just said, "Let's put a face on it," so he drew the nose and mouth and I drew the eyes and eyebrows.*
> Gabe: *It's a peace flower, so I thought it should have a face.*

VARIATION

Science curriculum: Focus on learning the names of flowers of your region. Provide real flowers in a vase or pictures of flowers to use as models. Emphasize the scientific names of the parts of a flower.

❋ SCIENCE ACTIVITY ❋
TELL ME WHY

ORIENTATION

Ask the students: "Have you heard people ask, 'Why is the sky blue?' What is one of the things you wonder about?"

PROCEDURE

1. Students meet in groups of four. Each person contributes one question to their verses. At the Hilltown Charter School in Haydenville, Massachusetts, one group in Joe Colombo's third grade wrote:

> *Why do leopards have spots?*
> *Why are snakes so long?*
> *Why are slugs so slimy?*
> *Why are we made of atoms?*

2. As a group, talk together or do research to answer the questions.

> *Leopards have spots for camouflage.*
> *Snakes are so long so they can slither.*
> *The poisonous slime on slugs protects them.*
> *Atoms make everything.*

GRADES: 2nd–6th

FOCUS: Student questions promote research

MATERIALS: Science books, *Earthsong*

3. Illustrate each line to create a book. Use the research books to create accurate drawings.

4. Choose a melody you like, such as "Row, Row Your Boat," and turn the poem into a song.

RESOURCE

Use Sally Rogers' book *Earthsong* (Dutton, 1998) to sing her song, "Over in the Endangered Meadow." She skillfully wove her research on eleven endangered animals into the revision of the folk tune, "Over in the Meadow."

❋ SCIENCE ACTIVITY ❋
OUR SENSE OF SIGHT

ORIGIN

Patsy Mehlhop, Deerfield Valley Elementary School first- and second-grade teacher, created a six-session science unit on the senses, a unit that teaches cooperative learning. This activity from that unit focuses on sight.

PLANNING

Prepare an observation box for each group of three. Fill a small box or shoebox with a potpourri of common items (pine needles, crackers, celery tops, seeds). Cover the box with clear plastic wrap and tape it securely. Put the same objects in every box.

GRADES: K–3rd

FOCUS: Study the sense of sight using cooperation

MATERIALS: Boxes filled with common items

ORIENTATION

Tell students: "Our target social skill today in our small groups will be that everyone is contributing."

PROCEDURE

OPENER

Use a communication game with the whole class to introduce the theme of sight: "Guess What I See In Our Room."

Begin with the contrast of not having use of your sight:

"Close your eyes for a moment and try to remember what is around you in our room. Now open your eyes. Notice all the colors and shapes and all the information your eyes give you. I will pick an object in the room, and you will guess what it is using your eyesight."

Provide one clue about size or shape before each new guess, such as, "It's red." After playing the game several times, brainstorm the categories of information our eyes tell us: the color of objects, the size of objects, the distance of objects.

ICEBREAKER

Seat students together in teams of three. Ask each person to take turns looking around the room while the other two study the first student's eyes as they move.

Introduce vocabulary words about our eyes: *iris, cornea, retina,* and *pupil.* Ask children to locate, without touching, the part in the eyes of another member of their group.

MYSTERY NATURE PICTURES

Option: If you have access to nature pictures, such as puzzle pictures in *World* magazine, or photos in *National Geographic,* you can do this activity. Give each team a nature photograph (the top of a pinecone, for example), and have the three students decipher the identity together.

COOPERATIVE LEARNING ACTIVITY

Reminder of target skill: Everyone contributing.

Procedure: Each group is given an observation box. Students can shake the box but can't reach inside. The task is to compile a list of items your group can see in the box. Students should be prepared to share your list with the class.

Roles used: Recorder, Resource Person, Encourager. Teacher hands out cards with the name of the role. Resource Person gets the materials to be used — the box and recording sheet — and brings them to the teacher. Encourager encourages each person to participate. Teacher offers this simple question for the encourager to use with teammates: "What else do you see?" *(Note that these roles are used in other activities in this book and are common designations in cooperative learning formats.)*

Processing: The Recorder reads the group list out loud. Lists from all teams are merged, and the common list is used to reinforce how much more we can come up with many when many people work together. Emphasis is not on which team found the most. The encourager reports on how their group did on the target skill.

CLOSING

Evaluation: Say one thing you enjoyed about the lesson. Ask several students to contribute their ideas.

SCIENCE ACTIVITY

Cooperative Study of Animals

ORIGIN

Pat McGiffin, school library media specialist and consultant from Leverett, Massachusetts, developed this sequence of lessons for a third-grade class. The entire unit (with the creative dramatics extension) involved the class for thirty-minute sessions every day for a month. Teachers can adapt sections of the plan for shorter units.

ORIENTATION

Tell students: "Our study of animals is specially designed so that each member of the study group will help each other."

OPENER

Introduce the concept of classification using the various types of shoes that students are wearing that day. List the properties — tied shoes, Velcro shoes, etc. Ask students to classify their shoes into one of the groups. Next, apply this concept to notetaking.

Read a passage in a book with facts about a specific animal (earthworms, for example) to the whole class to show exactly what they will be doing during their research. As you read, ask students to take notes in specific categories. Explain that they will be classifying the facts. Use these categories: size of animal, its food, its habitat, its predators/enemies.

PROCEDURE

1. Assign a study group of four students one classification of animals: reptiles, birds, fish, sea mammals, or insects. Provide them with books in their subject area, and a sheet listing categories for their research. Ask each team member to choose an animal within that class and research it. (For example, a bottlenose dolphin might be chosen from sea mammals.)
2. Individual students report on their animal out loud with their team, referring to the categories taught. As they deliver their research, team members work on the skills of listening and asking good questions; for example, "I didn't hear you say what the animal eats."

GRADES: 3rd–6th

FOCUS: Cooperative learning techniques structure interconnection of group members

MATERIALS: Research sources on animals

PLAN: Study groups of four

3. Individuals write about their animals using the format of an animal autobiography. Pat McGiffin describes this phase: "They had to write the information from the animal's viewpoint, telling its life story and incorporating some kind of life-and-death struggle, building in the survival story so you could see what the animal is up against. And they could give words and thoughts and feelings to the animal. It had to be serious. They worked as editors for each other. They didn't ask adults for help, so if they had trouble spelling, or had any other problems, they asked each other."
4. Team members present their animal autobiographies to each other and receive positive feedback. Before presentations begin, each group brainstorms and comes to consensus about what criteria they will use as they give feedback.

INTERCONNECTED DRAWING

Each group constructs a "new animal" composite drawing using properties of all the animals group members studied. One person from each group is chosen at random to explain the fictitious creature to the class and the team process for creating it. Each student has to be prepared to speak because they don't know whom the teacher will choose as spokesperson.

CREATIVE DRAMATICS

Each group designs a play where their animals interact. They write dialogue, make animal sounds, and create costumes. This process takes one to two weeks.

❄ SCIENCE ACTIVITY ❄
THE DECISIONS OF CELL MEMBRANES

ORIENTATION

Tell students: "In conflict resolution training, we help people identify what they do or don't want in their interactions with others. This is called *setting clear boundaries*. Today, we're going to see how the cells inside one's body decide what they do and don't want. As we learn about the decisions that go on inside and outside individual cells, this may help us reflect on the decisions we make in the way we relate to people."

PREPARATION

The class will be depicting the interactions inside a cell and in the fluid the cells float in. To do this, students will need to be divided into five groups of roughly the same size. Prepare five types of cards, enough so each student will have one.

1. One fifth of the cards will say, "Outer Cell Membrane." Each person will be a different kind of "receptor" looking for a particular substance needed by the cell. Add different labels randomly to each Outer Cell Membrane card: "receptor of protein," "receptor of glucose," "receptor of oxygen," "receptor of antibodies."

2. Another fifth of the cards will say, "Inner Cell Membrane." These membranes have different kinds of receptors; they receive substances from *inside* the cell to let *out*. Label the cards: "receptor for carbon dioxide," "receptor for cell trash," and "receptor for ATP," the energy produced by the *mitochondria,* one kind of the cell's small organs. (One student will later be asked to portray the ATP itself.)

3. One fifth of the cards will say "The Space Between the Membranes." Students receiving these cards will portray the fat cells that create the Holding Tank area; their intelligence is very important.

4. One fifth of the cards name Substances that travel around the cell. Mark two of these cards "protein." Other cards should be labelled "oxygen," "glucose," and "antibody." On the antibody card, write, "Will take waste from the cell." Extra cards could say "hormone," or "enzyme."

5. The final fifth of the cards name the parts inside the cell: "ribosome," an organelle that seeks protein; lysosome, an organelle that gets rid of cell waste; "microtubule," a part of the cytoskeleton (the structure of the cell) that provides strength, and "mitochondrion," an organelle that makes energy through seeking glucose and oxygen.

PROCEDURE

1. Background: Explain that cells are like protein factories. Each cell has a very thin double plasma membrane around it. The outside of the cell isn't tough or closed off like a wall; it is a *membrane,* which is a word for tissue that can allow substances to pass through it. Another word to describe tissue that can decide to open or close in this way is *permeable.* For instance, since the cell is permeable, oxygen can come in and carbon dioxide can go out.

These two membranes protect what's inside the cell (the organelles and the cytoskeleton). The cell membrane does three things — it can let in what it wants, like glucose and protein; it can let out what it doesn't want, like cell waste; and it can keep out what it doesn't want. Add that what happens in the holding space between these layers is particularly important because it is where the changing, deciding, and waiting take place.

Explain that actually there are more types of organelles than are represented in this activity. (For example, the nucleus, which is the home of DNA, the substance that holds the "recipe" of yourself).

2. Planning meetings: After roles are decided by distributing cards, each of the five groups meets separately.

a. Ask the Outer Cell Membrane group and the Inner Cell Membrane group to decide how they will connect as they stand to form the Outer Wall and Inner Wall, respectively. (Linking elbows? Hands on shoulders?) Explain that there won't be enough space to completely encircle the organelles and cytoskeleton, so each student will represent only a section of the cell membrane. Explain that the Receptors will be saying their names and searching for substances that they receive. Students should create motions for how they will open.

b. The Space Between the Membranes group forms two lines facing each other with their outstretched arms, representing the short tails of the cells, interrelating like the teeth of a zipper. Clarify that they are fat cells that create a Holding Tank. They can store what the Receptors on the membranes bring them, and they make decisions about whether to bring the substances farther in or out. (This is one of the many reasons that fat is essential for our bodies.) Students in this group can practice how they will expand or contract in this formation.

c. Ask each student in the group of Substances to invent ways to move independently. Ask them to invent soft sounds to make. Explain that each student that represents a part of the Outer Membrane will be asking each Substance its name as the Substances pass by.

d. Meet with the students in the Parts Inside the Cell group and clarify their roles. Ask each Part to invent a motion to do while standing in place as the whole group helps chant the name of the part.

3. Placement: Set up the Parts Inside the Cell group — the organelles and microtubules — first. Watch them one at a time move while they chant their names. Next, place the students in the Inner Membrane group partially around them. Ask each Receptor to name the substance it works with and demonstrate how it will open in response like a door when it finds that substance. Now ask the Holding tank to be set up in the zipper-like formation and show how it will contract and expand as needed. Now add the Outer Cell Membrane. Demonstrate how the receptors will let substances in or out. Finally, ask each substance to keep its name secret until it whispers it to the Outer Wall.

4. Interaction: Establish a signal for silence so that you can lead students step by step through each process.

a. *Bringing in what's needed:* All the organelles move at regular speed but then start to slow down. They need protein. The Ribosomes tell their request to the Inner Wall. The Receptors see if the Holding Tank has any. Meanwhile, the Substances start to move. When they

reach the outer wall, they whisper their names. The receptors whisper back what they receive: for example, "I'm protein," says the substance. The receptor answers, "I'm a receptor for glucose. Keep looking." In this way both the receptors on the Outer Membrane and the Substances are perceiving and responding. When a protein receptor finds protein, it passes to the Holding Tank group between the walls; that group then helps the substance enter the cell, letting each Cell Part make its own decision. As the ribosomes receive the protein, all the organelles start moving again at regular speed now that they have enough nourishment.

b. *Releasing:* Inside the cell the Lysosomes go around collecting waste (students can pantomime or use props) from the other cell parts. A Lysosome brings the waste to the door. Only an Antibody (from the Substances group) can carry it away. The waste is stored in the Holding Tank while the Receptors hunt for an Antibody.

5. Sounds: After the interaction is familiar, ask each part to create a sound that works in rhythm harmoniously with the other sounds around it.

6. Closing: The mitochondria have made plenty of energy. They release this ATP (ask a student to be the ATP), and as the ATP moves out of the cell into the body, everyone feels increased health and well being.

EXTENSION

Use a book on anatomy and physiology to provide diagrams and further information about the human cell. Add other organelles and their functions to the role-play, or add hormones as referees who make observations like, "There's not enough oxygen here," or "More energy needed here."

REFLECTION

Use journalling to help this activity shed light on interpersonal communication. Ask, "How do you communicate your decisions about what you want to take in and what you want to keep out? How do you interact with the outer boundary of other people? Just as mitochondria call out for more oxygen, what are you calling out for? What would you like to put in the holding space for when you need it?"

SOURCE

I devised this dramatization based on what I have learned from Lenore Grubinger, a senior teacher of Body-Mind Centering®, the work of Bonnie Bainbridge Cohen. Lenore can be reached at Creative Bodywork®, 11 Arnold Ave. #1A, Northampton, MA 01060.

SOCIAL STUDIES

Integrating Cooperation and the Arts into the Core Curriculum

❈ SOCIAL STUDIES ACTIVITY ❈

BIOGRAPHICAL SCROLLS

PROCEDURE

1. Read a biography to your class to help them learn about the life of a famous peacemaker. Second and third grade teacher Idalia Morales at Marks Meadow School in Amherst, Massachusetts chose the book, *Mary McLeod Bethune,* by Ruby L. Radford (Scholastic, 1973).

2. Ask students to name all the important events in the life of this person. Put each event on a separate sheet of paper and tape the sheets to the board. Be sure to include events that took place during this person's childhood. Look also for moments of handling conflicts and making difficult decisions.

3. Ask students to move the sheets of paper around until they are in chronological order. Read them in sequence and ask, "Does this tell a complete story of his/her life? Are there any more events that you want to include?" When the order is set, number the pages.

4. Give one event to each student or pair of students. Ask them to illustrate with a sentence of description.

GRADES: 2nd–6th

FOCUS: Use art to explore the main events in the life of a famous peacemaker

MATERIALS: Paper, markers

Examples:
◆ Mary McLeod Bethune makes speeches to raise money for her school.
◆ President Roosevelt meets Mary Bethune.

5. Place all illustrations together in one long scroll. The scroll made by Idalia Morales' class was thirteen feet long.

Variation: Fourth- to sixth-graders meet in small groups and choose the same biography to read. Each group makes a separate biographical scroll about a different person.

SOURCE

The suggestion for this activity appeared in *Perspectives: A Teaching Guide to Concepts of Peace,* Educators for Social Responsibility, Boston, 1983, p. 87.

SOCIAL STUDIES ACTIVITY

Conflicts of Community Builders

Creative Dramatics

GRADES: 3rd–12th
FOCUS: Spotlight an important moment in the life of a person working for positive social change
MATERIALS: Biographical books, tape recorder (optional)

ORIENTATION

Tell students: "We will use drama to help us understand how a person we admire handles conflicts in her or his life."

PROCEDURE

1. Select a biography of a person who has made a social contribution. *Example: Rachel Carson*

2. Look for moments of conflict and difficult decisions. *Example: The decision to write* Silent Spring, *a book about pesticides.*

3. Find concrete data related to that decision which would be useful in a dramatic skit. *Example: The book quoted a letter Rachel Carson received from a woman named Olga Huckins backing up the need to expose the harmful effects of pesticides.*

4. Dramatizing: Tell students they will be using as much factual information about the person as possible, adding what they imagine might have happened during this moment of conflict.

5. Have students list facts that may help create the skit.

- ◆ *Rachel Carson wrote* The Sea Around Us, *which won the National Book Award.*
- ◆ *As a child she liked to listen to the birds in the morning.*
- ◆ *Chemical companies threatened to make her stop writing the book.*
- ◆ *DDT is the name of the pesticide she fought.*

6. Create guesses of what might be happening at the time of the decision. *People who knew Rachel Carson might have been worried about her writing this book.*

7. Think of a specific moment during the conflict. Where was the person? Who was with her? What were the circumstances?

8. Help students pick their own roles, talk about what their characters are like, and then create dialogue to fit the situation. On-the-spot improvisation can produce a script that shows understanding of the dilemma.

Option: As you go through the process, try to add in all the facts listed earlier. Keep a tape recorder running to capture their dialogue and transcribe the words later.

On the next page is a script I developed for students at Marks Meadow Laboratory School in Amherst, Massachusetts.

RESOURCES

Beatrice Siegel writes biographies for young readers, books that are outstanding in the way they bring people to life. Here are five about women:

- ◆ *An Eye on the World: Margaret Bourke-White, Photographer.* Frederick Warne, New York, 1980.
- ◆ *Cory: Corazon Aquino and the Philippines.* Lodestar/Dutton, New York, 1991.
- ◆ *Faithful Friend: The Story of Florence Nightingale.* Scholastic, New York, 1991.
- ◆ *The Year They Walked: Rosa Parks and the Montgomery Bus Boycott.* Four Winds Press/Macmillan Publishing Co., 1992.
- ◆ *Marian Wright Edelman: The Making of a Crusader.* Simon and Schuster Books for Young Readers, 1995.

RACHEL CARSON

Conflicts of A Community Builder

◆ **PROPS:** A Letter

RACHEL: Oh, no! My friends are coming over any minute and they've said they want to stop me from writing this book. *(Picks up letter.)* But this letter will give me courage. *(Knock on the door.)* Come in.

FRIEND 1: Rachel, we've been so worried about you.

FRIEND 2: We don't think you should write that book about pesticides.

FRIEND 1: This is all you talk about these days. You don't have time for anything but this. I think you're going to exhaust yourself.

FRIEND 2: You've won the National Book Award. Your book, *The Sea Around Us*, stayed at the top of the bestseller list. You could stop working now. Why do you keep pushing on?

RACHEL: You don't understand! This book fights for everything I care about.

FRIEND 1: But why must you write about pesticides? about DDT? This is such an ugly topic. Before this you wrote only about the beauty of the world.

RACHEL: This book is about beauty. It's about the beauty we must save. I will show that the use of pesticides is harming the earth.

FRIEND 2: But your specialty is the sea!

RACHEL: No, my first love was the woods and the birds. I grew up playing in the woods. I used to wake up at 5:30 and go outside to hear the birds sing. Such magic! And these — our woods, our birds — willl die from the pesticides.

FRIEND 1: Aren't you afraid of the companies that make pesticides?

FRIEND 2: They'll try to make fun of you to stop you from writing about what they do.

RACHEL: Someone has to have the courage to stand up to them! When I get letters like this one, I feel stronger. *(She reads.)*

> Dear Rachel,
>
> This summer a plane flew over our small town in Massachusetts and sprayed DDT. The chemical companies may call it a "harmless shower bath" but we found seven of our songbirds dead immediately, and the next day we found more and more. It was a terrible death for them. And these were birds who had come back to our yard year after year.
>
> Now when I hear that we have to choose between the pesticide of DDT or the mosquitoes it would kill, I say let us keep the mosquitoes! Won't you help by writing about this?
>
> Your friend, Olga Huckins

I will write this book! And I'll call it Silent Spring.

MYSTERY BAGS

PLANNING

Collect seven to ten special objects, enough for a third of the class. Each will be used by three students. As a classroom teacher, Richard Michelman uses antiques from his personal collection (like his 19th-century tool for smashing grapes before they are dried for raisins). Your selections might include spoons and dolls from Russia, rhythm instruments, shells, woodworking tools, or cooking implements; it is ideal to select objects with as much detail as possible.

PROCEDURE

1. Place students in random groups of three by asking them to draw slips of paper you have prepared. Each slip says: "You are in the (apple, plum, etc.) group. Your group will receive a bag with an object. Please look it over without taking it out of the bag." Give each person in the group a role. Use these descriptions:
   a. "Your role will be Recorder. You will write down on paper the description of the object that your whole group develops out loud."
   b. "Your role will be the Encourager. You will encourage everyone to participate and make positive comments about the work of group members."
   c. "Your role will be Question Maker. You will help your group think of features by asking questions like 'How long is this part?' or 'What does this look like?' "

2. Ask all the students to find their teams of three and arrange their seats together. Give each group two sheets of paper. One is for writing their group description. The other will be for making their drawings later. Hand out paper bags with hidden objects. As they create a description, indicate that they should not tell what it is, even if they have a guess. Instead, they should tell its size and what it is made of. Encourage them to use comparison, such as "The handle is the size of a quarter." Emphasize examining the object without lifting it up out of the bag.

3. Allow about ten minutes for the writing. Then, each group should pass its description to another group. (Even numbers of groups can do a simple exchange with a neighboring group; for odd numbers of groups in the classroom, the description can be handed to the next group, with the last

GRADES: 4th–8th

FOCUS: Writing and observation skills are linked to social studies

MATERIALS: Interesting objects related to social studies

group passing the description to the first.) Now randomly assign new roles to your groups of three:
   a. "Your role is Reader. You will read out loud the description you have received. If there are words you don't understand, ask other group members for help. If it is unclear to all three of you, you can ask the group who wrote it one question."
   b. "Your role is Artist. You will sketch the shape of the object. There is no wrong way to do it."
   c. "Your role is Encourager. Your job is to help the Artist when they feel unclear about how to do the drawings and tell them at least two things they are doing well."

4. After drawings are complete, each group takes a turn. The person who was Reader reads the description and the Artist shows the drawings. Afterward, the group who has the corresponding mystery bag shows the actual object.

5. *Option:* If you are using objects relating to your Social Studies unit, go back to small groups and ask them to answer a question such as "What is this object used for?" or "How would this instrument be played?" or "How is this Russian doll different from American dolls?" As Richard Michelman puts it, "Objects can help put students in a new cultural setting." At the end, when each group has had a turn, talk about the true identities of the objects. Place them in the center of the circle and discuss together.

6. *Closing:* The person who was most recently in the role of Encourager tells one thing his or her group did well.

SOURCE

Dave Johnston and Richard Michelman of the Brattleboro, Vermont area created this activity.

❋ SOCIAL STUDIES ACTIVITY ❋

AN ENCOUNTER OF CULTURES

SOURCE

Polly Anderson, art teacher at Buckland-Shelburne School in Shelburne Falls, Massachusetts, devised this activity for Marcia Schuhle's sixth-grade class to relate to their social studies unit about a village culture and a highly technological culture meeting.

PROCEDURE

1. Have students choose one cultural encounter as the focus of the artwork. For instance, sixth-grader Doug Paine chose to depict American and Japanese cultures meeting. Discuss examples of cultural encounters.
- ◆ Native American and European or Native American and Hispanic cultures meeting.
- ◆ The experience of being an immigrant in the U.S.
- ◆ An indigenous culture encountering an industrialized one.
- ◆ Two different groups of teenagers with different lifestyles meeting.

2. Have the class discuss what happens during the meeting. Do they learn from each other? Do they influence and change each other?

3. Students then establish what type of line will describe each culture. In pencil on scrap paper create two different types of lines —each representing the characteristics and values of one group.

GRADES: 4th–12th

FOCUS: An interplay of lines expresses an encounter of cultures

MATERIALS: Black and white construction paper, black marker

4. Tell students: "Now, make each line out of black construction paper and paste it on white paper."

5. "Using black marker, create patterns on each side of the lines, embellishing the basic shapes. Go farther out to the edges of the paper, but leave the space between the two lines open for the moment."

6. "Next direct your attention to the space between the lines, the place of encounter and influence. With black magic marker, show what happens when the two groups interact."

7. Students write a journal reflection. Student Melissa Griswold's example: "The loopy line is nice and even. They bend the rules. The other line is very strict. When they meet, they become more and more different."

RESOURCE

The Karuna Center for Peacebuilding (Nonviolence Resources, p. 169) leads intergroup dialogue.

Illustrations:

Jeffrey Bishop and Justin Butcher

PICTURING THE FUTURE

Social Studies Unit

OVERVIEW

Tell students: "The reason that we study the future is to understand that each of us helps to make the future. Everything we do is important because it affects what comes next."

PICTURING THE FUTURE

Help students envision a positive future: develop a local vision through whole group discussion, experience a positive future for the world through a creative dramatics role play, and examine an individual positive future with creative writing.

SOURCE

In the late 1960s Warren Ziegler began leading workshops on futures invention for a variety of community groups including schools and hospitals. His work was inspired by Dutch sociologist Fred Polak, who called the images a society holds about the future a "powerful set of magnets" affecting social behaviors that bring about the future that is imagined. In 1980, Elise Boulding, professor of sociology at Dartmouth College, began applying futures-invention to the problem of the nuclear arms race and with Ziegler created "Imaging a World Without Weapons" workshops. These had a strong impact on me and on many others working for peace, including Mary Link, from Ashfield, Massachusetts, who created these activities with me. In launching this work, Dr. Boulding noted the lack of believable images of peace. She showed that imaging work is important for empowerment; visions of peace can become magical thinking unless we take reponsibility for their realization. In the 1980s, Boulding, Ziegler, Link, and others brought this work to various parts of the world, extending the topic to be relevant to individual groups, such as "Imaging a World Without Hunger."

"Visioning the future is not based on prediction," Mary Link comments. "It asks people to find out what is there in

> "When you dare to dream a positive future and see possible pathways to that future, you relight the candle of hope and empower yourself with actions." —Mary Link

GRADES: 4th–12th

FOCUS: Students look at the present through the perspective of a positive future and see themselves as a creator of that future

their hearts to bring about." Many young people today don't feel that they have a future, and when they have participated in futures visioning they find new possibilities. As one student said to her, "This work has given me a hope for a future that I didn't think would necessarily exist for me."

For more information on Ziegler's work, contact Futures-Invention Associates, 2260 Fairfax St., Denver CO 80207. E-mail: warren.fia@worldnet.att.net.

✳ ACTIVITY ✳

LOOK AHEAD LOCALLY

PROCEDURE

1. Provide perspective on how much can happen in a span of years. List aspects of modern life that were unthinkable ten, twenty, or thirty years ago. *Examples:* exploration of space, the end of the Cold War, inventions like videocassette recorders or social changes (such as support for women and girls in team sports or creating accessible buildings for disabled people).

2. Pick an event known to the students in the school — a recent assembly, a change in policy, a school fundraising drive, a new local business — and work together to imagine the specific events that led to it coming into being. List them chronologically.

3. Say, "Now we are going to create a different kind of history: we will write a backwards history of a future event. We will imagine a positive event in the future and invent what led

up to it. Write the date ten years from today on the top of a list. Below it write each year in backwards order toward the present year — 2010, 2009, 2008, etc. You will use this timeline in step five."

4. Say, "Imagine it is now this date ten years in the future. We are standing at the opening of a building in our city (town, county) that has something inside that really helps the community. There is a party to celebrate it. Imagine what is inside this building. What happens there? Why are people excited? How will it help people in your area?" Hear different ideas from students, and select one vision that is compelling to the class. For example, one seventh-grade student imagined a factory making capsules to absorb the radioactivity that exists in the river near his school. Discuss the future image the group has chosen and elaborate upon it until the image is clear.

5. Tell students: "Now create a backwards history, imaging what events led up to the positive work that goes on in this building. List these steps as historical facts." One way to search for these is to ask students to see an image of something that helped this building come into being. "Connect this to your timeline, not by being strict about the years but by listing events in relation to each other. Ask which steps would occur before or after one another."

EXTENSIONS

Creative Writing: Thirty Years Ahead. Students search for another local positive image of the future in their region by picking an arena — such as schools, employment, entertainment, sports — and then searching for an image relating to that category, this time thirty years into the future. The purpose of the time jump is to help students break loose of thinking about the usual way things are, but at the same time to keep within the student's lifetime.

✻ ACTIVITY ✻

LETTER FROM THE FUTURE
Role Play

PROCEDURE

1. Photocopy the letter on the next page, fill in the correct year in the opening salutation, and pretend that you are holding a letter from the future. If you like, alter the date in the future: pick a date that is about thirty years ahead. Tell your class, "A most remarkable thing happened to me last night. I got a very unusual letter over the Internet. It's from the future." Read the letter to your class.

2. As a start, ask everyone to visualize themselves in this future time. The goal is to envision with many senses: what does this positive future feel like, look like, and sound like.

   Imagine you have been beamed forward to the year 2030. See where you have landed. Take a deep breath. What does it feel like to live in a time when there are no weapons and no poverty. Notice your shoulders relaxing because you feel safe. Look around. Who do you see? What are they doing? Where are you? Walk down a road to find a place where people will share food with you. What does this place look like? Walk to a place where children learn. What does it look like? Pick another place that you want to visit..

   Now write down the image that stays most vividly with you. Continue to catch in writing or draw in pictures as many images as you can. Afterwards, divide into groups of 3 or 4 and ask students to share their images with each other.

3. Take several periods to prepare for a day when the class will split into two groups to enact this visit between people of the future and the present. Ask students to select individually which group they want to be in during the role play of this time-travel visit. Have each of these groups meet separately. As a first step, ask each group to write questions for the other about what the past or what the future is like.

4. Brainstorm within topic areas: air and water conditions, respect for diversity, communication skills, war and weapons, food distribution, housing, schools, transportation. Ask each person to focus by themselves in one or two of these areas.

   Ask them to write about **a.** "What would a positive future feel like and look like where that problem was addressed?" **b.** "Thinking backward, write the events that led up to this. Consider what is happening today to work on that problem. What hasn't happened yet but could be a way to help with this problem?" Then divide the class into small groups based on similar areas of interest: for example, those who want to think about environmental issues meet together. When groups meet they may, but they don't have to, all agree. During the role play, these people will be experts on that aspect of the present or future. Ask each student to devise an identity they will use during the role play. *Example:* chief engineer in charge of fish farming in 2030, or pollution control expert in the present.

5. To begin the role play, arrange a circle of chairs and begin with just the students of the future seated. Ask two people to orchestrate the process of beaming forward the students of the past. They join the circle. As teacher, act the part of

moderator or River Listener facilitating this meeting.(See River Listening, p. 122.) People of the future speak in the present tense, not the future tense, and this can be very powerful. Help each group ask each other questions.

Allow students to say, "I don't know" or "I have to check" and hold a conference to think together about how to answer so that no one feels put on the spot.

Dear people of the year _____ ,

I am sending this letter through time-travel. I live in the year 2030 on your Earth, and through our amazing inventions I am able to tell you what it is like here in the future where I am. I have used a satellite from your time to receive my message and communicate it on what you call the Internet.

Here is why I am writing. I look back at you and know that you have many discouraging things happening on Earth like poverty, wars, violence, racism, and pollution. The future is very different. Teams of people all over the world have worked intensively on these problems. We are ending hunger. There are no more wars and no one uses weapons anymore. We are still working to end violence people have carried in their hearts, but we have made remarkable changes. People's diversity is enjoyed instead of feared, and we have found ways to live in partnership with each other. We are learning how to share resources. All the things you did to protect the air and the water took great effort, but they have worked. Most importantly, I want to thank each and everyone of you for the things you did to help us achieve the healthy, safe, and peaceful world we have today. What may seem like little actions to you, have added up to make important big changes.

We invite you to come and visit our time. We have developed a method of beaming up visitors. We hope you will come and talk about the things that were done by the people of your time did to create this future.

❈ ACTIVITY ❈
CREATIVE WRITING
Positive Personal Future

PROCEDURE

1. Students write an essay on how they see themselves helping to create this positive future. "Now you have a picture of how each thing a person does makes a difference. Select one area that we have been talking about and imagine yourself contributing to this area during your lifetime. What would you do?" Invent a history of your involvement as part of a team helping to work on one problem the world faces.

2. "Imagine yourself as an elder and decide what your age is. You are sitting in a room and you are happy in ways that

have nothing to do with fame or money. (For example, you live in a comfortable place, but you are not living in a mansion). You receive a letter from someone who asks you to tell them what things you are proud of doing in your life. Your answer can refer to accomplishing goals but not fame or wealth (*so that happiness is in reach for every student*).

Examples:
- ◆ They enjoyed playing sports regularly but they don't have to be in the Olympics or on a national team to feel satisfaction.
- ◆ They have a child they love, they have had wonderful friends, they have a husband/wife/partner they love, they accomplished goals relating to study, travel, skill development, helping their community. Ask the students to describe details of their life.

✳ ACTIVITY ✳

PARENTS OF THE FUTURE

Positive Personal Future

PROCEDURE

1. Help students get a concrete grasp of future time using a future family tree. Symbolically draw a basic family tree on the blackboard. Make a circle to represent a person the age of your students with lines representing their parents and then add lines to show the generation of their grandparents. Now go into the future two generations. Use lines to show that this person has a child, who in turn has a child. Choose an age that a woman might be when she gives birth, whatever age makes sense culturally to your students. Now use math skills to affix birth years. Invent the year in the future that this person in the future might write this letter.

2. Tell students, "I'd like you to imagine that you are receiving a letter from the future. It is from your own grandchild or godchild. *(Some students may not choose to be parents, and you can restructure this so that the person is thanking them for their influence on their life, or refer to the person as a Godmother or Godfather).* This letter has a question for you. Please write down what your answer would be and then we'll discuss this as a class.

Note: Focusing on a positive future can bring up buried feelings. Some students may consciously or unconsciously expect that they will not have a future. For example, economics and racism have produced a situation where African-American young males have a diminished chance of survival. This activity is intended to assist students to claim their ability and their intention to have a positive adult life.

Dear Grandparent [Grandmother, Grandfather, Godmother, or Godfather],

I am glad to have this chance to reach you and send you my thanks. I've grown up to be a wise leader, and many people turn to me for advice. Without all the things you did to be a

good parent, I would not be the person I am today. My mother said you were a wonderful parent and gave her lots of encouragement, and she passed your advice down to me. Can you tell me how you learned to be a good parent and what you did? I understand that the times you grew up in had a lot of violence. How did you learn not to be violent yourself?

Thank you, from your grandchild [or godchild].

Tell students that they can invent anything they want in their answer. Some students will be able to write, and others may draw a blank. If many students have difficulty, make a list first of all the different things that could happen to a person which would help them learn to be a good parent. Then ask students to take one of these events to use as their reason to invent details and to watch somebody else be a good parent, have a neighbor who gives helpful advice, take classes on parenting skills, travel to a different country and learn customs there.

EXTENSIONS

◆ **A Second Letter:** *Dear Grandparent, I want to let you know that there is much less violence now. Of course people have arguments and conflicts every day. What I mean is that we don't use guns or other weapons or violence to handle the problems. We get angry like you did but we have lots of ways of expressing it. We're learning what triggers our feelings. We help ourselves feel safe without attacking other people with words. Can you see a picture in your mind of what it is like to be in our* [schools/neighborhoods/families]*? What picture do you see?*

◆ **Asking Questions:** Write a letter to this person in the future and ask them questions about what their time period is like. Read the questions to the class. Class members take one and pretend to be the person of the future writing a response.

WHAT THE SPIRALS SAY

Art and Archaeology

OVERVIEW

Joseph Campbell helped to make the broader public aware of historical information about Old European culture from 7000 – 3500 B.C. that has a tremendous impact on how we think of ourselves today. Extensive evidence reveals this to be a period without warfare and suggests a time of partnership, not patriarchy, between women and men. Campbell points to the twenty volumes of research by Marija Gimbutas, professor of European archaeology at UCLA. He comments, "The message here is of an actual age of harmony and peace in accord with the creative energies of nature which for a spell of some four thousand years anteceded the five thousand of what James Joyce has termed the 'nightmare' (of contending tribal and national interests) from which it is now certainly time for this planet to wake." (San Francisco: HarperCollins, 1991, p. xiv.) This information is important for European-American students because it help them gain a more detailed and accurate picture of their heritage. It is important for all students to know of thousands of years of history when women were not subservient to men, and to perceive that the human story is not an unbroken line of aggression. Here the language of art becomes a means for the past to speak to the present. The pieces of pottery that are the focus of this lesson were excavated from the region that is present-day Bosnia.

Teacher's Note: The unfamiliar can be uncomfortable when it is so different from the picture of history one has carried. Campbell felt that this information was a crucial part of reclaiming human interconnection and transforming human warfare. It will feel new, unusual, and perhaps unsettling for many of us, both children and adults. The term "Goddess" is key to describing this historical era, and is not the teaching of religion, but an imparting of an historical period that has insights for us in our time.

ORIENTATION

Tell students: "Today we are going to step back in time 7000 years ago in Southeastern Europe and find out what life was like. We will use art to help us understand the people."

GRADES: 3rd–12th

FOCUS: Old European history of great significance today is revealed through art from a site in Bosnia

MATERIALS: paper and pencils, map of Europe

UNDERSTANDING THE HISTORICAL PERIOD

PROCEDURE

1. On a map, locate north of Sarajevo, Bosnia and tell students: "We will be talking about evidence from archaeologists at a site named Butmir. This settlement was excavated near Sarajevo from 1893 to 1896 and then in 1967 and 1968."

2. Describe the work of archaeologists. "They carefully unearth objects from the past, including tools, skeletal remains, and pottery. They date the material using a radiocarbon technique involving the radioactive decay of carbon 14, and then they double-check the date by counting tree rings. Then, based on all the information about that site and other sites nearby, the archaeologist reaches careful conclusions about the life of the people at that time in that location."

3. "Let's look at what our stereotypes are about life back then and compare our guesses to the archaeological evidence. The objects we will be talking about were dated to be 7000 years old; that is, from about 5000 B.C." Ask students these four questions to help them describe that they think life was like at that time at this spot in Europe:

a. "What kinds of dwellings did people live in?"

b. "What did they eat and how did they get their food?"

c. "Did they live in peace or fight with other people and have wars?"

d. "What kind of art did they do?"

4. Write the name of the archaeologist — Marija Gimbutas (pronounced *Maria Gim-boo-tus*) — on the board. Tell students that she wrote twenty books about her work as an archaeologist studying Old Europe. She excavated the Butmir site with Alojz Benac in 1967–1968, and it is her book that describes the life of the people and that gives us pictures of the art found at Butmir and throughout Old Europe.

Source: *Civilization of the Goddess: The World of Old Europe* by Marija Gimbutas (San Francisco: HarperCollins, 1991, pages 56–62.) Compare these conclusions from her work with the guesses made by the class.

a. People lived in houses made of wood with stone wall foundations. The walls of the house were coated with clay. The roof was made of wood and straw. Two-room homes contained a round bread oven and had deep storage pits for refrigeration of food. Grinding stones and spindle-whorls for spinning were also in the homes, and ash was used as a detergent to wash linen. They had stools, tables, and lamps.

b. People hunted wild bull, wild swine, red deer, and roe deer, and they caught fish such as carp and sturgeon with fishhooks made of bone and antler. In the forests they collected acorns, hazelnuts, strawberries, gooseberries, crab apples and cornelian cherries. They grew wheat and barley to make bread, and they raised cattle and pigs.

c. The archaeologists have concluded that for thousands of years there was no warfare. Here is the evidence — no lethal weapons were found, the villages had no fortifications, and the houses were built near rivers or streams. The people at Butmir lived in open villages in valleys and built ditches around their villages, not as moats but to drain off rainwater. If they had chosen steep hills for their houses, which are more difficult to live on, they would have known that the people were protecting themselves against an invader. A thousand years later than the time we're talking about, in about 4000 B.C., invaders on horseback entered this area from southern Russia, introduced the idea of war for the first time, and eventually destroyed the Old European culture. Knowledge of this civilization has been lost to us until recently.

d. The people made magnificent pottery vases. They decorated them with intricate designs and painted bands of red above a black background. They mined copper, and they traded with other people for obsidian, shells and painted pottery.

5. Butmir was called "the cradle of the spiral art" in Europe. We will be drawing the same spiral shapes that people back then drew onto their pottery. This will help us find out more about how the people thought. When they drew spirals on their pottery, they were expressing the thoughts most important to them. They also had a written language and the spiral S was one of the symbols.

LANGUAGE OF SPIRAL ART
PROCEDURE

Photocopy these spiral designs or draw them on the board.

1. Give each student drawing paper and a pen, pencil, or marker. Ask students to practice drawing simple spiral shapes. "Let your hand be guided by the momentum of the spiral. Can you draw without crossing over any lines?"

First, have them draw small spirals in both directions:

◆ *Outside to in.* Make a big circle and spiral farther and farther into the center.

◆ *Inside to out.* Start with a tiny circle and spiral farther out to about two inches.

Help students pay attention to the sensation of drawing. Say, "Notice how it feels to draw spirals. Do you like the feeling of going in one direction more than the other, or are they both enjoyable to you?"

2. Now work with an S curve to connect two spirals. Start on the left inside one spiral, let it get bigger, and then curve across to begin another spiral going farther into its center.

Sketch to sense the general feeling.

Then work carefully to make continuous spirals of equal size.

3. Tell students: "Professor Gimbutas discovered that the decorations people drew on their pottery all had a meaning. The people drew these spirals to give a message. What do you think they were saying as they drew spirals?"

After students have guessed, add the meaning that Professor Marija Gimbutas learned, not to contradict their guesses but to amplify what they were discovering. She said that spirals describe the force of life, such as the force inside the stem of a plant or the trunk of a tree to help them grow. Energy inside the human body moves in spirals. She also said that spirals have the forward motion of growing and becoming. She wrote, "The pulse of life demands an unending stream of vital energy to keep it going." (Gimbutas, *The Language of the Goddess,* San Francisco: HarperCollins, 1991. p. 277.) This means they are saying through their spirals, "We are part of nature, and we change and grow like every other part of nature."

4. Tell students: "Now we will work with more difficult forms. Try a simple S again, but give a thickness to it, like a coil of clay. Go from left to right and then double back, tracing from right to left without crossing over the lines. Who will discover how to leave space between the lines of the curves?"

5. Continue: "How do you make an ongoing run of spirals? As you go out on the S curve, you have to double-back. The design at the bottom of this page is one that appears frequently in the pottery. Decorations with runs of spirals were found on vases from Butmir dated 5100–4900 B.C. *[Gimbutas,* The Civilization of the Goddess, *San Francisco: Harper Collins, 1991, p. 59.]* Here the secret is to curve once around, twice around, and then curve back the other way. This is a metaphor for conflicts; when you are in a tight snarl, go back the other way and this gives dynamic energy to move forward."

6. Have the students examine how the spiral shape relates to two things they have learned about this culture.
   ◆ How does this meaning of the spiral reflect the fact that they had no warfare?
   ◆ How does it reflect the fact that women and men were equally regarded and lived in partnership? Have the class look, for example, at the dynamic interrelationship of opposites in the form of spirals.

To help get this idea across, approach it from another direction. If a person were sending a different message, he or she would use a different kind of line. Ask students: "What

line could you draw to say this message "I feel like a machine. I try to do everything the same and not make a mistake." *Note:* The activity "An Encounter of Cultures," p. 45, also helps students be aware of how lines communicate.

7. Lastly, try the complex shape which appears at the top of this page. A spiral-decorated Butmir vase from the 49th–48th century had a design just like it. Tell students—one way to experience the intelligence of the people is to draw what they drew.

Source: Figure 3-7, Vase 2 in *The Civilization of the Goddess* (San Francisco: Harper Collins, 1991, p. 57).

Hint: The secret of this shape is to draw the top curve first like a wave and then add the bottom line to nest in it.

EXTENSIONS

Language arts: "Create a story about a child living in these times. Decide whether he or she will learn to make pottery, spin, catch fish, hunt, or build houses. How do they feel to live in a time when there is no violence?"

Movement

1. Stand in place. Roll your hands in a decreasing inward spiral shape until you are curled up, then expand as you roll your hands with an increasing outward spiral.

2. Walk a spiral shape. Holding hands, the line leader takes the line spiralling into the center, then turning to double-back out again.

Songwriting: Write a song as if it were written by a person living at this time in Old Europe.

BACKGROUND

The term *Old Europe* applies to the civilization of 7000–3500 B.C. from the Atlantic to the Dnieper. Evidence of this culture is just reaching us because it was systematically destroyed by authorities of the cultures that supplanted it. The Indo-European tribes from southern Russia overran these people from the fourth millennium B.C. in three waves and ended Old European culture between 4300 and 2800 B.C. They brought cattle-herding, they introduced and imposed the practice of male domination, and they brought their language, which became the basis for English. They buried important males and their weapons in round barrows, called *kurgans* in Russian, and Professor Gimbutas refers to them as the Kurgan Culture. She writes, "We are still living under the sway of that aggressive male invastion and only beginning to discover our long alienation from our authentic European heritage — gylanic, nonviolent, earth-centered culture." (Gimbutas, *The Language of the Goddess,* San Francisco: HarperCollins, 1991. p. xxi).

The Old Europe people had other symbols in common besides spirals: eggs, zigzags, streams, chevrons, rams, deers, bears, and snakes, all of which were life-giving symbols. They also invented a written language and had a common script of symbols 2000 years earlier than the Sumerians, previously thought to have been the creators of the first complex written communications. Joseph Campbell compares Professor Gimbutas' extensive study of pictoral motifs that undergird Western civilization to the discovery of the Rosetta Stone that unlocked the meaning of Egyptian hierogylphics.

SOURCE

The 500-page *Civilization of the Goddess: The World of Old Europe,* San Francisco: HarperCollins, 1991, by Maria Gimbutas, is out of print, but you can use Interlibrary Loan or an out-of-print book search service (like www.amazon.com) to find a copy. The book shows drawings of the excavated houses and extensive illustrations of pottery. Students can create designs using other motifs in the illustrations, and learn the basic signs of Old European script on page 308.

❋ SOCIAL STUDIES ACTIVITY ❋
COOPERATIVE HISTORY FAIR
A Research Project

SOURCE

Full Circle School in Bernardston, Massachusetts involved thirty-one students in bringing American history to life. Students worked in cooperative teams to focus upon a period of history. They could select any person within that time period. As parents visited each display, they met these historical people — or, as the program announced them, "Historical Guests" — seated at tables, or in covered wagons, or panning for gold at a real trough of trickling water and conversing about their lives. The students talked in the first person, becoming that figure and answering questions. The experience for parents of travelling from display to display, passing from the 1600s through to the present, was like walking along a living timeline. One moment they met Anne Bradstreet, then Peter Stuyvesant; as they turned the corner, they saw Emily Dickinson, then Andrew Jackson, then Mary McLeod Bethune.

PROCEDURE

1. Begin preparation at least one month ahead, for example, starting in February for a history fair in March. Plan to involve students one and a half to two hours per day to complete each phase of the work. Arrange students in five study groups of five to seven students, and assign each study group to a different time period in American history such as 1600–1750 (with an importance of studying both Native peoples as well as European settlers), 1750–1800, 1800–1850, 1850–1900, 1900–1940, and 1940 to the present.

2. Help each child identify with a person during the chosen time period. Students can pick any person who interests them who made a significant contribution. Provide library books and photocopies of articles, taking special care to have examples of women.

3. Students decide how to portray their person. They research all they can and write down facts. They especially

GRADES: 1st–6th
FOCUS: Students portray a person in history
MATERIALS: Displays, costumes, food
PREPARATION: Month-long involvement toward presentation for parents

look for clues to their subject's personality — not just what they accomplished, but the decisions they made, the chance encounters that changed their lives, the details about quirks and habits. Students write an autobiography and from this create a short oral version of the autobiography, which they memorize. They assemble a costume and think about what props they want — books, a hat, music — that will help this person come alive.

4. During the history fair, students sit or stand by a table where they have a visual display of artifacts. They select an important quote by the person and write it on a poster. Additional materials such as maps, pictures, or drawings they have made are posted on the wall behind them.

5. The whole team studies their time period. For the night of the History Fair they select and work with parents to cook a food that is representative of some of the experiences: grits, for example, or hard tack, corn pudding, or journey cakes. They also learn a song — like "The Erie Canal" — to perform from their time period.

6. On the day of the history fair, parents are instructed to treat each child as if he or she is that historical figure. They kneel or sit to be at their height, ask respectful questions, and enter into the figure's life with questions like, "Jane Addams, was there any experience you had as a child that made you want to help the poor?" Parents must avoid questions that pop the kids out of the time frame — questions like, "How did you die?"

7. One parent wrote a letter to the editor of the local newspaper about the event: "Each child selected a person who fascinated them, and studied them so thoroughly that first and sixth graders alike were comfortable speaking with us adults to describe 'their' lives. The miracle for me was not only how knowledgeable they were (one high school teacher remarked they had a deeper grasp than his students), or how comfortable they were with public speaking, but also how history became transformed. Suddenly the life of each person, the choices they made, the chance opportunities they encountered, became illuminated and dignified. We walked away from the evening uplifted, with more perspective and more hope."

E X T E N S I O N

Yearly Themes: Each year, in the fall, the Full Circle School selects a new theme for their cooperative fair. Here is how the various themes were handled:

◆ **Science Fair:** The words *science fair* conjure up a room of exhibits where students compete for prizes. At Full Circle, the science fair means students come dressed up as actual scientists in history. Each person shares a replica of an invention or does an experiment attributed to the scientist the student is portraying.

◆ **Music Fair:** Study groups are assigned to a type or a period of music such as indigenous folk music from around the world, classical European music from 1700–1800, or twentieth-century American music covering jazz, blues, rock, and popular musicals. For instance, one student studying the Rennaisance/Baroque period discovered that Anne Boleyn (1507–1536) was an accomplished lutenist, singer, and composer. Other girls chose to portray Clara Wieck Schumann, a gifted composer in her own right (her husband was Robert Schumann) and Francesca Cassini, a composer in the Medici Court. Resources on women musicians in history include contemporary recordings of music composed by Hildegard Von Bingen eight hundred years ago. Also see *The Pandora Guide to Women Composers,* by Sophie Fuller (Great Britain: Pandora, 1994).

◆ **Art Fair:** Students selected an artist within their time periods and did a copy of their work: Rosa Bonheur's studies of horses, Leonardo DaVinci's "Mona Lisa," Claude Monet's paintings of changing light, Georgia O'Keeffe's powerful flowers.

◆ **Geography Fair:** Instead of time periods, study groups were assigned to regions of the world. Instead of portraying individuals, students made maps, provided music of the region, and shared history and food. Six study groups covered one continent each.

◆ **Math Fair:** Study groups were assigned time periods stretching back to classical Greece. Each student demonstrated an experiment or game related to math. From the ancient era, a student portraying a Mayan priestess explained base five. Another student demonstrated a formula related to edges and faces of geometric forms as eighteenth-century Swiss mathematician Leonhard Euler. For the twentieth century, a student taking the part of Amalie Emmy Noether, a colleague of Albert Einstein, dropped a Ping-Pong ball into a glass fish tank set up with mousetraps ready to release other Ping-Pong balls; this illustrated a nuclear chain reaction. Other mathematicians they chose to portray included Sophie Germain, Sir Isaac Newton, Archimedes, and Einstein.

Co-director Michael Muir-Harmony commented, "Each year the hardest thing is to find enough material about women in history. We uncover phenomenal women doing parallel work to male scientists, musicians, mathematicians, or working against great odds and doing more outstanding work, but the story of their lives has been eclipsed instead of preserved."

Resource: Amy Dahan-Dalmédico has an article about an extraordinary French mathematician, Sophie Germain, in the December 1991 issue of *Scientific American*. This article cites other women mathematicians in history to research — Hypatia of Alexandria, the Marquise de Châtelet, and Maria Gaetana Agnesi.

V A R I A T I O N

Schools can apply this basic method to where they want to put the spotlight — Latinos over a 500-year history, African-Americans in science — and structure the theme to be of importance to the school community.

✳ SOCIAL STUDIES ACTIVITY ✳
LOCAL WOMEN IN HISTORY

SOURCE

Marcia Schuhle and Wanita Sioui Laffond created this activity when they were sixth-grade teachers at Buckland-Shelburne Elementary School in western Massachusetts. They arranged for five women to be portrayed, including the first woman in the region to cross the Rocky Mountains, and also Mary Lyon, who grew up in Buckland, Massachusetts, and founded Mt. Holyoke College.

GRADES: 3rd–6th
FOCUS: Community members are historical guests

PROCEDURE

1. *Community members depict women in local history.* Working with the local Historical Society, each participant researches an actual woman from the region, or in some cases represents a woman in her own geneological line. They use artifacts and costumes to portray the woman they select.

2. *Learning Stations.* Each historical guest sits at a separate table and converses with students as they visit their station. If possible, they read from an actual journal, show photographs or share food prepared in the manner of the time period when they lived. *Example:* The great-granddaughter of the first woman doctor in the county told the true story of how her great-grandmother disguised herself as a man at her interview to be accepted into a medical school in England.

EXTENSION

1. *Discussion.* Help children reflect on the experiences of these women in history. Pose questions that relate to the women they met. *Example:* "What do you think it felt like to be told you couldn't be a doctor? How does this relate to experiences women and girls have of oppression today?"

2. *Reflection and Journaling.* Ask all the students to pick one of the women and think about the decisions she had to make and the bravery she needed to summon. Have them invent an inner dialogue of this person.

CHAPTER 4
Discovery Units
Exploring Cooperation with All Our Senses

DISCOVERY UNITS
How to Lead Daily Cooperation Groups

DISCOVERY UNITS provide lesson plans that teachers can repeat daily for one or two weeks or more. They are specifically designed to build cooperation, communication, and affirmation. Here is the basic model:

FAMILY GROUPS

◆ Divide the class into small groups of four students. These groups will stay the same for the whole week. This provides opportunities for members to improve their skills of collaborating over the course of five days. Then make new groups each Monday. In this chapter, small groups of four will be referred to as Family Groups.

◆ Each day for a week, the groups cooperate on a similar task. For example, for one week they focus on creating a tower or building together.

◆ Cooperative learning formats are employed to help children learn how to work interdependently.

◆ Time is taken to give direct instruction on social skills. Through a repeated focus on cooperation, children learn how to work together — how to make decisions, how to consider options, how to encourage each person to contribute. Groups that have difficulty receive assistance in handling conflicts.

◆ CCRC recommends that children be allowed to "pass" on any activity and choose whether to share what they create. Participation is voluntary. However, if a child chronically doesn't participate or makes fun of those who do, give appropriate guidance to the child and make an individualized agreement.

◆ Processing: Each day, time is provided at the end to ask what went well in your group and focus on the positive behaviors and contributions. *Variation:* Each individual fills out an evaluation form using these questions from Nancy Schniedewind and Ellen Davidson, authors of *Cooperative*

COOPERATIVE TEAM APPROACH
Discovery Sessions are facilitated by the teacher but they belong to the entire classroom community. In a very real sense, the whole group becomes a cooperative team. Three factors build teamwork:

◆ Guidelines and ground rules — making them together

◆ Evaluation and feedback

◆ Student input

GUIDELINES OR GROUND RULES
It is important for you to pick the guidelines which fit for you and for your class. The CCRC program suggest these two ground rules:

◆ Everyone has a chance to participate

◆ Everyone respects the contributions of others

Learning, Cooperative Lives:
◆ How much did I contribute to the group?
◆ How well did I listen to the ideas of other people?
◆ How much did I ask other people for their ideas?
◆ How well did our group work together?
Marcia Schuhle, At-risk Counselor in the Mohawk School District in western Massachusetts, recommends after debriefing that each group set a social skill goal for their next work period. Then the next Discovery Session begins by remembering — "What was it we were going to work on today?"

DIVIDING THE GROUPS

If the number of students in your class doesn't divide exactly into groups of four, plan groups of four and three, but not five. Here are methods for forming small groups.

- *Clothespins:* Write the names of every student on a clothespin and place them in a hat or basket. Randomly draw four clothespins at a time and clip them to a card.

- *Puzzle Pieces:* Prepare sets of interlocking puzzle pieces out of cardboard, one for each student. Make a geometric cardboard shape for each group — diamond, circle, triangle, rectangle, oval, square — and divide this into three or four puzzle pieces. Now mix up the pieces and put them in a box. Ask children to pick a puzzle piece out of the box and silently find the other members of their group. This method is used by Susan Vegiard, first- and second-grade teacher at Marks Meadow Laboratory School in Amherst, Massachusetts. She calls it "Peace Partners."

- *Fair Choice:* This method allows students to make choices while insuring that no one will be excluded or put down. Arrange the room so there are clearly designated work sites — one for each small group. Push desks together or, if you are working on an open floor instead of at tables, use masking tape to designate the meeting spots; for example, if you have 23 students, make six work sites. One group will have 3 members.

Tell students, "This is a silent choice. No calling out. No motioning for someone to choose your group. No frowning at who arrives. Stand up and line up, using a fair method. One by one, according to the order in line, children walk over to join any of the work site locations. As the selection progresses, each person can go to any spot until it is full. Whenever four children have chosen the same site, that group is now closed.

Example: I used the Fair Choice method every Monday for a year to make groups for Discovery Dance with first graders when I taught in Cleveland, Ohio. The makeup of the groups turned out differently each week. Once the method of selection was clear, no one groaned as people selected their groups. In fact, the choices were often surprising. For instance, a person might pass by the location where her best friend was already sitting in favor of being the first at a new spot waiting to see who else would arrive.

HOW TO DEVELOP COMMUNITY

1. Set clear ground rules using student involvement. Make agreements together and simplify them to two or three. Empower students to intervene whenever these ground rules aren't followed. *Example:* In our first grade, anyone could call out "contract" if somone got pushed or hurt. We agreed to stop and talk together when the word *contract* sounded.

Expect that whatever your agreements are, they will be tested. Having a set of guidelines means teachers need to speak up each time an agreement is not kept, especially when the infraction is hazy. For example, if you have agreed that everyone's contributions will be respected and you hear snickering when a student is taking a turn, you might say, "We've agreed that the way each of us participates will be respected. I hear laughter. No one wants to feel laughed at in here," and continue from that opening in any way that is appropriate to the situation. Persistent vigilence, friendly and clarifying rather than punishing, helps build a safe atmosphere. What consequences do you need if the contract is not kept? After a clear reminder, I stopped the activity and gathered the group together to talk when the contract continued to be broken, or I asked individuals to skip a turn and observe while they cooled down.

Also, agree upon a "zero noise signal" that calls for quiet. This might be a visual signal like a raised hand or an auditory signal such as a bell.

2. Evaluation and Feedback: Since one of the things that makes Discovery Time so special is the feeling of ownership that students have, it is important for us as facilitators to listen when we hear the class say they are not enjoying the activities. I recommend building in a method of feedback so that from the beginning there is an avenue for evaluative comments to be made constructively.

The CCRC Program offers four methods of evaluation. One of these I have found particularly effective is "Thumbs Up, Hands Out, Thumbs Down."

"One at a time, name activities the group has recently completed. If children liked an activity, they put their thumbs up. If it was just okay, they put their hands out extended. If they disliked it, they put their thumbs down. Some children at first may put thumbs down or up just for the fun of it. But if you take it seriously, eventually they will see it as an important way to communicate their likes and dislikes. If there is unanimous disapproval of an activity, take the time to ask the children why they didn't like it."—*The Friendly Classroom*, p. 75.

What is central here is believing that feedback is healthy to the process and helping it to be brought forward, offered constructively, and considered with respect. Two other methods for feedback are:

- **Daily Feedback Person.** I draw a name of one class member from a hat. This person agrees to meet briefly after the session and discuss it with me. Other class members can tell them feedback to convey. They also may offer amendments to activities or other feedback during the session.

◆ **Planning Group.** A small group of self-appointed or randomly chosen class members agree to meet with me as needed to discuss how the sessions are going and look ahead to review the next things I have planned. This can happen informally: "I hear a lot of grumbling today. I'm going to finish what I have planned but I want to know what you are thinking. Anyone who is interested can talk to me for five minutes after Discovery is over." Or this can be formal: "As you know, the Discovery Planning group meets every Friday for fifteen minutes during lunch recess. If you want to join, you can talk to Juanita who heads the group."

3. Student Input: Set up specific ways students can offer their own suggestions and give input.

◆ Ask for suggestions of favorite games.

◆ Ask for new topics for a familiar activity like cooperation drawings or affirmation notebooks.

◆ Create a suggestion box where students can anonymously suggest the conflicts they want to explore.

◆ Ask for the group to bring in songs or records or tapes which they want to use for singing, listening, or dancing. Set up certain days where class members choose the music.

◆ Create a suggestion box of topics to discuss or questions.

Discovery Sessions can also be structured to respond to general areas of interest. Personal events, such as the injury of a classmate, or community events (food collection, a fire, needs of homeless people) can become the focus of a session.

It is also possible for students to lead sections of Discovery Sessions. For example, "Maria and Jack are going to teach a rap song today for our gathering," or "The planning group will be leading a cooperative mural project they've designed for our main activity today."

PLANNING

Here are strategies you might find helpful:

◆ Select a general category (such as story drawings) that can be repeated over a series of days.

◆ Make opportunities for students to suggest or lead activities.

◆ Keep a folder of interesting activities. Add a photocopy of the table of contents of books you review, and check the activities relevant for your class; they'll be quicker to locate later.

Working with your lesson plans: As I plan, I jot down my major theme or goal. I also write notes such as "Be ready for testing of the guidelines today," "They might need calming activities after the class trip," "Welcome Robin back."

After Discovery, I make any notes which will be important the next day. I use a quick system, putting stars by activities that went extremely well, and bracketing those we didn't actually have time for. I also write down any observations about individual children in a few words.

Here are six components you can use when you write the lesson plans:

1. *Orientation:* a brief and friendly review of your guidelines or ground rules for participation. If appropriate, include a statement of the goals or themes of the session or describe how the activities relate to what you are studying. CCRC suggests that you post and review the agenda for the session.

2. *Opening activity:* a short gathering activity which helps to focus the class.

3. *Preparation (optional):* a short activity that lays the groundwork for the main activity to follow. This could be a game that's fun and helps to break the ice. It could be practice of a listening skill necessary for what is to follow. It could be a cooperation activity that helps to build trust.

4. *Main activity* or pair of activities.

5. *Evaluation and feedback.* Processing of the activity.

6. *Brief closing activity:* a clear ending rounds out the experience.

This sequence can be thought of as an arc.

1   2   3   4   5   6

See "Our Sense of Sight," p. 36, for an example of how these components can be used.

✳ DISCOVERY UNIT ✳
COOPERATION CONSTRUCTION

OVERVIEW

Each day Family Groups work with a different type of building material. The activity "Will the Castle be Build?" (p. 94) is an excellent way to introduce this unit.

AGE: K–6th

FOCUS: Develop collaboration skills by building or designing cooperatively

MATERIALS: Building materials

PREPARATION

Assemble a wide assortment of construction materials: Legos, pattern blocks, wooden block sets, marshmallows and toothpicks or dry spaghetti, index cards and cellophane tape, dominoes, tangrams, 12–24 sticks from trees, a ball of twine, scissors, cloth, thumb tacks, stones, acorns, modelling clay, toothpicks and clay, wooden Popsicle sticks and glue, shoeboxes and other small boxes, scissors, markers, cardboard tubes and masking tape. To make floor plans of buildings, pass out graph paper and markers or decks of cards.

make. Use a Zero Noise Signal (p. 60) to gather attention. Now let the Family Groups take turns sharing something about the structures they made and their identities ("This is an ice cream store.") Also, process how the group did at cooperating: Ask students to "name one thing you did well today as you worked together."

PROCEDURE

1. Explain any collection of materials that is unclear. For instance, if a group receives a basket of sticks, a ball of twine, scissors, cloth and thumbtacks, explain that you can tie four sticks together with the twine, making a frame work that can be built upon, and that cloth can be attached to the walls using the tacks.

2. Help students think together about *how* they want to collaborate before they begin. Provide these possibilities, and ask them to choose one method:

- ◆ *Rotation:* Each person in the family group can add one item, taking turns in a circle.
- ◆ *Switch:* People will take turns holding sections steady while others attach tape or glue, and then they will switch, letting others do the holding, until everyone has taken both roles.
- ◆ *Sections:* Each person can begin at a different section.
- ◆ *Freestyle:* Students will all begin randomly, and if the situation starts to feel unfair, any of them can say, "Wait, let's pick a different way to work."

CLOSURE

Give the groups a five-minute warning before the time is up so that they have time to add the last details they want to

EXTENSIONS

- ◆ Have a silent day. All building takes place without talking.

- ◆ Once the groups are adept at group work, put all the possible building materials in one location and allow "Resource Runners" from each group to come up to the table and take any materials their Family Group desires.

- ◆ Work on a unified theme. "Today all groups will make stores." Or give each group a small stuffed toy or puppet. Ask groups to make homes for their animal.

- ◆ Continue for several days on the same constructions. Add materials such as pipe cleaners and thread, to create little people or animals who live in that location.

- ◆ Read the picture book *Roxaboxen,* written by Alice McLerran and illustrated by Barbara Cooney (Picture Puffin, 1992). Provide groups with pebbles to outline yards for houses similar to those in the book. Or create tiny houses of sticks.

- ◆ Tape paper on a long table and draw out roads to create a town. Ask each group to create a small structure in that town and to decide what that building will be used for.

- ◆ Tightly roll pieces of newspaper diagonally to make long tubes. Build huge constructions by taping the tubes.

✳ DISCOVERY UNIT ✳
STORY DRAWINGS
Visualization and Cooperation

UNIT PLAN

Set up a different cooperation drawing each day for a week. In each activity, children close their eyes to visualize the story as you read it, then they tell each other what they imagined and combine their images into a single picture. Each successive activity requires an increased level of collaboration skill.

ANIMAL APARTMENT HOUSE

Story: *Once upon a time a bird called out to all the animals around: "Apartment House is opening! Who wants to come and live there?" Now imagine an animal who hears this call and decides to move into one of the apartments. See this animal moving into its new place. What does its furniture look like? What decorations does it put on the wall? What food does it put on the shelves? What games or books does it like? Now open your eyes.*

Drawing: Cooperate on drawing one apartment house together. Each person says what kind of animal they chose. Together they draw a pattern of a house with a roof, deciding if any parts need to be underground for the needs of that animal. Individual students each take one section to draw the separate apartment for their animal, showing its food, furniture, and activities.

ANIMAL SPORTS TEAM

Plan: Ask the group to pick one sport that will be the basis of their drawing.

Story: *Once upon a time the animals came running to join in a sport. They travelled from the woods, the river, the rain forest, or wherever they lived, and they magically appeared on one playing field. Think of the sport you have chosen and imagine an animal playing. Does it help its teammates by running fast? Does it help by kicking or catching or flying? See your animal with any equipment it might need. Now open your eyes.*

Drawing: Cooperate on drawing the game. Individuals draw the animals they chose. Talk together to arrange where each animal will be placed. Plan how to draw the action of the sport. Example: octopus as baseball outfielder.

GRADES: K–6th

FOCUS: All members of the group make contributions to one drawing

MATERIALS: Large paper, markers, crayons

ANIMAL MIX-UP

Story: *Once upon a time, there was a magical creature who had the abilities of many different animals — the head of one, the body of another, the wings of still another, the legs of another, and the tails of yet another. This creature has a special magic — try to guess what it can do. Now open your eyes.*

Drawing: The students cooperate on drawing this magical creature. Each person chooses one part to draw. Together, the class decides what the special magic is. Tell students: "Give the animal a name if you like. Draw the background of where it lives."

WHALE RIDING

Story: *Imagine that everyone in your Family Group is in a boat going to a magical island. The people who live there know how to talk to whales. As you get close to the island, a whale appears and leads your boat to the dock. The people called Whale Listeners thank the whale. They take you to swim in the waterfalls that tumble down to the sea. They tell you that you will meet a special whale friend who will teach you how to ride on its back. Imagine this whale comes to you and you travel safely on its back. Where do you go?*

Drawing: Each person tells one thing he or she imagined. Talk together about how to create one drawing that will include what everyone said. On a large piece of paper delineate all the locations that the class will need to show.

This is a two-day activity.

✳ ACTIVITY UNIT ✳
LISTENING PAIRS

OVERVIEW

Spend fifteen minutes each day for a week on listening activities. Explain: "Listening is how we reach out and connect to the world."

WARM-UP

"Clap on Moose": Present the class with a list of animals. Students clap whenever they hear "moose." *Example:* whale (silence,) monkey (silence), moose (*clap*).

ONE: AWARENESS LISTENING

Diana Mazzuchi of Brattleboro, Vermont, a teacher and educational consultant, offers these topics. She has developed more than sixty questions in each category.

Awareness Tasks

◆ My Favorite Story and Why

◆ A Worry of Mine

◆ A Hiding Place I Like

◆ My Favorite Time of Day

◆ A Way I've Grown Up Since a Year Ago

Mastery Tasks

◆ Something I Can Do All by Myself

◆ A Way I Got Over Being Afraid

◆ A Tough Problem for Me

◆ A Decision That Turned Out Well

◆ Something I Think Is Unfair That I Can Do Something About

Social Interaction Tasks

◆ A Time I Felt Left Out

◆ What I Look for In a Friend

◆ How I Got Someone to Pay Attention to Me

◆ Someone Who Really Understands Me

◆ Someone Felt Hurt by What I Did

Choice of formats: (a) Pairs take turns speaking on this topic and paraphrasing what their partner said, or (b) A few students speak in front of the whole class, or (c) The teacher meets with just one small group and listens as each person shares.

Option: Follow this activity with Affirmation Drawings (p. 70). Students draw their responses to the topic.

GRADES: K–6th

FOCUS: Work in pairs to provide listening practice

TWO: LISTENING WITH STORY QUESTIONS

Here is a method that combines interviewing and paraphrasing. Describe the roles in each pair as "interviewer" and "speaker."

Select a topic. *Examples:*

◆ A time someone surprised you.

◆ A time you felt very angry.

◆ A birthday you really liked.

Using the following four categories, devise a list of questions that best apply to that topic, providing at least one question in each category.

1. *Setting:* "Where were you? How old were you?"

2. *Inner State:* "What did you feel? What was your concern? What did you want?"

3. *Action or event:* "What happened?"

4. *Result:* "Then how did you feel? What was the result?"

Note: These are categories of information contained in stories. Usually, if we hear these units clearly, we can remember a story more easily.

Give one list of story questions to each pair. The first interviewer holds the list and asks the questions one by one while the speaker responds.

Example: "Think of a time you wanted something very much."

Questions:

◆ How old were you?
◆ What did you want?
◆ What happened next?
◆ Then, how did you feel?

After hearing the answers, the interviewer repeats back the story. Switch roles and give the interviewer a turn as speaker.

THREE: SEE A PRESENT

1. Tell students: "Here is a game of the imagination that you can play anytime by yourself to help yourself calm down and feel comforted. Close your eyes and hold out your hands. Imagine that there is a safe, helpful, magical being who wants to deliver a present to you. Imagine that this present is now placed in your hands. Know what shape the box is and how big it is. Open it up and see what is inside. Imagine who gave it to you."

2. Choose a method to share: (a) students first write down what they imagined, (b) students describe what they imagined to a partner, or (c) ask for any volunteers who would like to share with the whole class.

Note: Sometimes students say, "My imagination is what makes fears at night." Explain that it's important to listen to messages that you're worried, and you can talk to someone to explore what you feel afraid of. Find a time to talk to that student later privately. Convey that our imagination can create and send friendly, helpful messages. That's the way we're working with it. Help students feel comfortable with visualization.

GENERAL HINTS FOR WORK ON LISTENING

1. *Topics:* With any of the listening topics, make sure each person in the room will be able to answer and modify the question as needed. For example, instead of using the topic, "My Pet" modify it to "A Pet I Have, I Used to Have, or I Wish I Could Have."

2. *Dividing Into Pairs:* To avoid arguments about who will speak first, give two names such as "apple and orange," and ask partners to pick if they are "orange" or "apple." Assign them their role using that designation; for example, "Apples will speak first while oranges listen."

3. *How To Listen:* Demonstrate with a partner in front of the class what listening looks like and sounds like by modeling first ineffective and then effective listening. Demonstrate how to show that you understand by the way you listen, nod your head, or ask questions. Illustrate how to respond with questions such as, "Tell me more," or "How did that happen?" Clarify that good listeners don't tell their own stories until the speaker is finished.

4. *Listening Check-in:* How do you check on whether students are remembering and accurately paraphrasing? I like to do a spot-check. After each person has had a turn as speaker and listener, I randomly check in with three people and ask them to repeat what they paraphrased so that the whole class can hear. For example: "Marta, tell me what Geraldo said." Marta paraphrases and Geraldo comments on whether she remembered accurately. Pick people from different areas of the room. This element of surprise gives added incentive for listening and remembering.

✳ DISCOVERY UNIT ✳
MAKING COOPERATIVE BOARD GAMES

ORIENTATION

Tell students: "We are going to invent a board game together that a small group of children can play. What board games have you played before? Is there always one winner? In this game everyone will win at the same time."

SKILL-BUILDING

This activity places a value on imagination and home-made materials. It shifts the emphasis from, "Look at the games I can play on my computer" to "Look at what I can create from my own imagination." It also develops planning skills, teaches sequencing, and promotes collaboration.

CREATING THE STORY

1. Assemble figures that will be used in the game such as rubber dinosaurs, rubber animals, tiny cars, or Lego™ figures. Select figures that aren't scripted for fighting. Place a rectangle piece of poster board on a table where everyone can see. Line up the figures along one of the shorter sides of the board.

2. Tell students: "We are going to make a board game that was never invented before today. [Option: *show a sample game like Chutes and Ladders or Candyland as an example of the way that figures move along a path.*] Help me think of a story for our game. These figures will move step by step across the board to get to the other side of the board Let's think of a reason for their journey. Where are they trying to go? Instead of having one winner, the goal of the game will not be who can get there the quickest. The goal will be to get all figures over to the other side of the board. That is how it is different from Candyland or Chutes and Ladders."

Examples:

◆ Four cars are the figures. Look for a story where everyone wins. *Not recommended:* Race cars try to win a road race. *Recommended:* Cars are bringing supplies to a town after a flood.

◆ Four whales are the figures. Make one side of the board

GRADES: 1st–6th

FOCUS: Create a win/ win board game

MATERIALS: Poster board, makers, figures, optional sample board game, dice or spinner

their summer feeding grounds and the other side the-warm winter location where their babies are born. For instance, humpback whales in the Atlantic swim from Georges Bank off of Cape Cod in Massachusetts down to the Caribbean. They have different potential hazards to avoid like nets, and oil spills. They follow the shapes of the undersea rock formations.

◆ Four dinosaurs are the figures. The story is that they have to make a difficult journey through swamps and mountains to get to a new area that will have more food.

MAKING THE BOARD

Once you have a shared image for the game, talk about the different tasks involved in creating the game — some groups will make pictures that will be pasted onto the board. Help them visualize the completed game. Make measurements and do planning first as a whole group:

◆ Decide how big the starting section will be where the figures are located at the beginning of the game.

◆ Decide how big the ending section will be. This is the destination. Where will it be located on the board?

◆ Measure the middle and decide how many hazards or roadblocks can fit on the board. Decide the size requirements for these drawings.

Divide into four work groups:

1. *The Starting Place:* Group 1 begins work on the board itself. They draw circles where each figure will begin. They measure each step of the path to fit the whole figure. Ask

them to draw only two steps forward for each figure. They help decorate this section.

2. *Roadblocks:* Group 2 uses the size requirements that have been established for the hazards and roadblocks and draws pictures on separate paper, which can be glued in place.

3. *Ending Place:* Group 3 draws the end spot, the landing place. They use the measurements decided earlier. Working on separate paper, cooperatively they create this location and then paste it on the board.

4. *Paths:* Group 4 is given another activity — like selecting books from the library corner — until the drawings are pasted in place. Then they create crisscrossing paths for each figure. Place some of the paths near the hazards and roadblocks.

Variation: Using the instructions above, create a game by your-

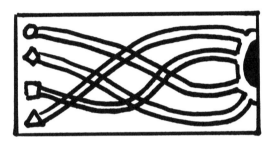

self or with a small group of students and present it to the whole group.

HOW TO PLAY

Setting The Rules: Once the board is completed, get out the dice or spinner. Brainstorm as a group about all the different ways the game could progress. Explain that there will be a choice of rules, but that first they will want to pick the easiest rules as a way to get familiar with using the game. Start a rule book where each page can have a given set of rules and players can point to which set they want to use that day.

Examples of easier rules:

◆ Each player can move any of the figures because they belong to the group and not any single player. Take turns. Roll one die. Select which figure you want to move forward during this turn and move it the number on the die. When all have reached the ending place, the game is over.

◆ Use the rules above, but add that if a figure lands near a hazard picture that figure is stuck there until a player rolls a 4, 5, or 6.

Variations:

◆ Players aren't freed from hazards until another figure

passes by them.

◆ In order to get to the home location, you must roll an exact number.

◆ When you get to a hazard, you have to make a sound that relates to it.

◆ Have a special spot that is where you pick up a card from the pile. Create cards that send the player to different locations on the board.

◆ Have a special spot where you draw cards that give you actions that you have to do before the game can proceed. To add interest to the game, these cards give directions for making sounds or pantomiming. These can be random, such as:

—moo like a cow

—pretend you are eating messy spaghetti

—pretend you have glue on your hands and they are stuck together

Or they could relate to the story of the game:

—move your hands like a fish

—think of the name of a fish beginning with G

—say a word rhyming with fish

EXTENSIONS

Once the basic method is modeled, divide into small groups and give each group a different set of figures. Ask them to create their own game. Help them through the planning steps: agree upon the story, measure and plan the space, draw in the pictures on the board, make the paths, decide the rules. Help the class be aware of sources of variety:

◆ The path could progress not straight across, but in a spiral

◆ They can create cards for the game

◆ They can add an extra magic figure who lives in a location and comes out when someone lands on that spot.

Example: Maya and Margery Winfrey, sisters from Shelburne Falls, Massachusetts, invented a game they called "Funny Garbage Pail Pickup." Out of clay they made garbage pails that were the figures that progressed around a spiral path. They also made "litter" like old bottles out of clay and scattered these objects over the path. To win, all the litter had to be picked up by landing directly on that spot; a player could move forward or backward until it was collected. Next, the garbage pail figures progressed to the center, where the litter was deposited. Maya and Margery also used cards with pantomime directions to add extra interest for the game.

❊ ACTIVITY UNIT ❊
PEER TEACHING

ORIENTATION

"Each person here is a teacher. We all have skills that we can teach and ways we can learn from each other."

PREPARATION

Help each person see themselves as skillful. "Think of something that you could teach, offer to do, or help with." First, brainstorm a long list so that children can see possibilities. *Examples:* braid cornrows, tie fishing flies, make fudge, play a G chord on the guitar, draw a cartoon figure, lip synch, write a name in fancy letters, put on face paint, knit, describe how to babysit, imitate the way a famous person talks, say a tongue twister, fold origami paper, assemble a complicated Lego construction, enter the World Wide Web, identify herbs or flowers, show a collection (shells, baseball cards, puppets) and explain it.

Select a person who is having trouble thinking of something and demonstate the process of searching. With the help of the class members, ask this person questions until they do indeed discover something they could share. Make sure this is an affirmative experience that helps show everyone more possibilities.

Now help each person search. Use the format that will work best for your class: (a) go around the circle and help each person identify a skill, (b) schedule private meetings with each student, (c) give a homework assignment to think alone or with family, (d) arrange students in pairs to help each other.

SKILL-SHARING

Explain: "We can all be resources for each other. Let's take turns sharing something we know how to do."

PLAN ONE:
SMALL GROUP PRESENTATIONS TO THE WHOLE CLASS

Group students with similar skills together. Ask them to give presentations to the class. Provide time in class to prepare. Ask each group to identify specific questions they can answer. For example: "We collect baseball cards and we're going to explain what we think is a valuable card, talk about the different companies that make the cards, and give advice about how to collect."

GRADES: 3rd–12th

FOCUS: Students teach other students about a skill or hobby to build self-esteem

PLAN: Help students assemble additional materials they will need

PLAN TWO:
INDIVIDUAL PRESENTATIONS WITHIN A SMALL GROUP

Devise groups of four or five students. Ascertain which students would be most ready to present a skill or collection first; distribute these kids among the groups. (Likewise, those who will need the most assistance are also distributed among the groups.) To build in support, make it possible for two children to work together. *Planning:* Help small groups have a planning meeting. Allow at least 30 minutes. Give each group four cards with the four roles. Each person takes a turn being Person #1 and the cards rotate in a circle as the turns shift.

Roles for the Planning Meeting:

1. Tell what you could teach or share

2. Be an Encourager. Ask Person #1: "What would you like to teach or share?" This person encourages them supportively as they select something to teach, and helps draw them out until they have a decision.

3. Be a Checker of Plans. Ask Person #1: "How would this work? Tell me step by step how this would happen." This person helps them examine whether the plan is realistic or needs any modification. They encourage the speaker to talk through the steps and see if there's any extra support or planning needed.

4. Be a Recorder of Materials.
   ◆ Ask Person #1: What materials will you need to have? This person asks them to say what materials they would need to have and writes what they say on a list.

◆ Ask Person #2: What support do you need?

◆ Find out if a teacher or parent needs to be involved.

◆ Find out if they want the members of the group to do certain things to feel supported.

Next, the students who recorded the list of materials give these pieces of paper to the appropriate speakers. As a review, ask each person to copy a reminder list of what they will need in their own handwriting.

Forming plans: A child wants to show how to cook fudge, but there is not easy access to a stove. During the planning meeting they realize that they need help from the teacher to talk to the school cafeteria and find out if the stove could be used. If not, they decide to just bring in the recipe and some of the ingredients and show how it is done. If special treats are brought in — like the fudge — arrange for enough not only for the members of the small group but for the whole class.

Scheduling: Two children present each day for 10–15 minutes each, just to their small group. Ask everyone to bring in their materials in advance.

EXTENSIONS

Classifieds Activity — "Help Wanted/Help Offered": Create a resource bulletin board. Ask each person to write down or draw one or two subjects they could teach, help with, or demonstrate. On a second index card ask each person to write down two skills they would like to learn.

Ask students to read their cards to the class; faciliate discussion and maintain an affirmative atmosphere. Post the cards on the bulletin board.

Journal Writing: Ask the students: "Reflect upon two of the presentations. Summarize what was demonstrated, and describe what you enjoyed about it. What specific things did they say that helped you learn?"

SOURCE

Mara Sapon-Shevin, professor of education at Syracuse University, devised these activities, which will appear in her forthcoming book, *Because We Can Change the World: A Practical Guide for Teachers Who Care* (Allyn & Bacon, 1999).

Mara says, "Asking people to teach one another is the best way I know to affirm that each person brings gifts to the classroom. Acknowledging other people's expertise affirms who they are. It's particularly exciting when students who haven't been 'shining lights' get to show themselves as capable, admirable people — this can really help to reverse some of the typical classroom hierarchies which can develop in a classroom. Peer teaching allows students to experience that everyone is smart at something and that it doesn't make sense to compare students along a single continuum as if this were their real or only value."

✳ DISCOVERY UNIT ✳

THE HISTORY IN OUR HANDS

Affirmation Drawings

ORIENTATION

Tell students: "Today, I'll ask you to remember a time you learned to do something new with your hands."

PROCEDURE

Warmup: Help children explore their hands:

1. "Touch each of your fingers to your thumb."

2. Open your hands as wide as you can, then close them.

3. Wiggle your fingers slowly and look for the way your bones are moving.

Pantomime:

1. Show that you are holding an apple. Take a bite from where the outside of the apple would be.

2. Hold a sandwich tight so nothing inside will fall out. Take a bite.

The Memory Game: Explain that you will describe things they learned to do when they were very young while they pantomime to remember what it was like to learn with their hands. *Note:* Think about the children in your class and adapt instructions if necessary to include any member who because of physical or cultural differences had a different experience.

◆ When you were a baby you wiggled your fingers and watched them moving.

◆ When a toy was put into your hands you learned how to hold it. Pretend you are shaking a rattle.

◆ You learned to pull yourself up on a crib and look around.

◆ When you knew how to sit, maybe you held toy cars and moved them back and forth along the floor.

◆ Later, you held a crayon or marker and made marks on a piece of paper. Try lines. Now try circles. Which do you think were more difficult to do?

GRADES: K–3rd

FOCUS: Remember a time you learned to do something new.

MATERIALS: Paper and markers.

PLANNING: Place students in pairs.

◆ You learned how to hold a cup and drink.

◆ Think of other things you learned. Tell us your ideas and we'll try them in pantomime. *Example:* "I learned to tie my shoe/dial the telephone/bake cookies."

Option — The Memory Song: Make a verse with the actions children remember. Sing it to the tune of "London Bridge." *Example:* Once I learned to write my name/Write my name/write my name/Once I learned to write my name, and this is how I did it. (Pantomime.)

MAIN ACTIVITY

1. *Draw:* Tell students, "Pick what you would like to draw." Pose this open-ended question: "What is something you remember learning to do with your hands?" Ask the group to close their eyes and picture their answers. "Think what you want to show. Will you be in the drawing? Are other people or animals with you? Will you show how you felt? How will you show what you did?"

2. *Sharing After Drawings Are Completed:* Help the class pair up and ask each pair to sit together with their drawings. Lead each student through a process of showing a drawing, describing it, and answering any questions the partner has. Divide the time so that each person has a turn of an equal length and each person is encouraged to talk.

CLOSING

After cleanup everyone sits in a circle. Each person takes a turn holding up his or her drawing. The partner then speaks, saying: "She's proud of how she learned to _____," or,

"One new thing I learned about my friend is that he_____."

When Carol Jacobs taught at Four Corners School in Greenfield, Massachusetts, she added a final listening component. She randomly chooses one student and asks the class, "Who can remember what [name] was proud of?" Carol also hangs the pictures which her students make in Discovery Sessions on tree branches set up in her classroom. The students call this their "discovery tree." Currently, Carol is a school principal at Green River School, also in Greenfield.

EXTENDED UNIT

Each day for a week, have kids create affirmation drawings with a new partner. Here are more topics:

◆ Can you remember something that a person taught you how to do? Draw how they helped you learn.

◆ What is your favorite place in your neighborhood?

◆ What is your favorite place to be when you feel sad?

◆ What is your favorite summer activity?

◆ What animal would you like to be for a day? Show the animal doing what you would like to do.

◆ What does the table look like when you sit down to eat with your family for a party or special celebration?

◆ What family holiday is your favorite? Show something you like to do on that holiday.

✺ AFFIRMATION ACTIVITY ✺
SEND A RAINBOW

SOURCE

Clare Green, kindergarten teacher at Warwick Center School in Warwick, Massachusetts, created this method of sending affirmative thoughts to children who are absent. She reports that as a result of teaching her students this custom, they have brought it to their own families. Parents have said, "The children send a rainbow to everyone at dinner."

GRADES: K–3rd

FOCUS: Acknowledge absent children

ORIENTATION

Tell students, "Today we're going to send a greeting to our friend who's absent. We're going to send them a rainbow."

OPENER

Ask: "Who's out today? Let's think about them." Here's how Clare Green introduces the procedure: "Where do you think a rainbow lives? We each have a little magic, and it lives right inside our hearts. We're going to think together about our friend who is absent and send him or her good wishes as we make a rainbow with our hands."

PROCEDURE

1. Rub your heart until it feels warm. Now, catch the rainbow. (Pretend to pull a rainbow from your heart). Rub your hands together until they feel warm. The rainbow is growing as you feel the warmth and the heat. Get ready to open your palms.

2. Ask a child to lead the counting: "One, Two, Three"

3. "On the count of three, open your hands and stretch like you are extending a rainbow. Leave your palms open and sense that the warmth is still there. Feel it go from palm to palm."

4. "Put a little back inside your heart. It's always there when you need it."

EXTENSIONS

◆ *Science:* Relate the themes of friction, prisms, and a review of color names. Place a prism or crystal in the nature center of your classroom.

◆ *Movement:* Explore how you can make a rainbow shape with a friend.

◆ *Language Arts:* If a child has an extended absence, make rainbow cards with pictures and greetings with affirmative statements. ("I miss playing on the swings with you.")

❄ UNITY ACTIVITY ❄
SPIDER WEB HANDS

OVERVIEW

This activity is an excellent lead-in to any of the following Discovery Units which employ creative movement.

ORIENTATION

Tell students: "We are studying in our class the fact that people are connected to each other and matter to each other. Today, we will explore this with creative movement."

AGREEMENT

Use a drum or bell as a Zero Noise Signal (p. 60) to request silence. Introduce this signal at the beginning of the lesson. This is a noisy activity, and the noise is part of learning through interaction.

PROCEDURE

SPIDER WEB HANDS

1. Hold up the picture on the back cover of this book and ask students to study the shape the four children have formed.

2. Help them get into groups of 4 to 6 students and ask them to connect their fingers in the same manner as in the picture. If floor space isn't possible, work at desks.

3. Use your signal for silence. "While I count to five, hold your shape silently as if I were going to take your picture with a camera."

   Introduce the word *snapshot* to describe the moment of holding still in a group shape without talking.

UNITY SHAPES

1. "Stand up and make the same spider web shape with your fingers. Hold your shape still as a snapshot. Get ready, now hold it for five counts."

2. "Find another way to connect your fingers like a spider web."

GRADES: K–6th

FOCUS: Create interconnecting group shapes

PLAN: Establish small groups of 4 to 6 students, and clear sufficient space for movement in the room

3. Use your arms to connect in a shape.

   Examples:

   ◆ Put one hand in the center like a wheel

   ◆ Touch palms together

   ◆ Reach both hands high like making a roof

   ◆ All stand backwards and stretch your arms up to touch in the center

4. As needed, use the Zero Noise Signal for silence, and talk about any problems that developed — pushing or squeezing hands too hard.

5. If possible, discuss and apply the vocabulary of "unity" and "win/win." How is this an experience of win/win?

6. Each group picks its favorite shape and shows it to the class for everyone to try.

EXTENSION

Share the image of people interconnected like nerve cells from "The Web of Human Unity" (p. 159) and ask students to create a shape that expresses this web. Try the Spider Web Hand Squeeze from that activity as a closing.

❉ DISCOVERY GAME ❉
MAGIC PEBBLES

SOURCE

Sharon Edwards, first-grade teacher at Marks Meadow School in Amherst, Massachusetts, created this game. Karen Schweitzer elaborated on the activity for her first/second grade class at the Helen E. James School in Williamsburg, Massachusetts. Here is the version that Karen leads.

GRADES: K–3rd

FOCUS: A short game using creative movement.

PROCEDURE

1. *Safety:* Establish safety agreements, such as "watch out for other movers." Arrange space for movement in your room and specify where in the room it is okay to go.

2. *Preparation:* All children curl up into balls on the floor at the start. They are the Magic Pebbles. Explain that the story will ask them to transform into Magical Beings. As they move, they will need to keep their own bubble of space around them. When the story asks them to become Magic Pebbles again, they curl up wherever they are. They don't have to return to their starting location.

3. *Begin the story:* "Once upon a time there was a day very much like today. It was raining/sunny/windy." Describe the weather outside the window. "A sister and a brother decided it would be fun to go for a walk." Add embellishments of any outdoor clothing they put on, describe where they are walking to fit environments familiar to the students, or establish the mood of an unfamiliar but interesting place in the woods. Lead the children to walk to a house or to a store where they look in and see a magical old woman who has a velvet bag.
Examples: "It was a cold but sunny March day just like today. They put on gloves and zipped up their jackets. As they walked, they passed maple trees with sap buckets. They followed along a path lined with stones that headed deeper into the forest. They both knew where they were walking. They got to a little stone cottage. They looked in the window just in time to see the magical old woman take the magic pebbles out of her black velvet bag." Or, "It was a hot September day just like today. The sister and brother could smell the salty smell of hot pretzels for sale as they walked down the blocks of their neighborhood. They passed the drugstore, to a shop so very tiny that many people missed it when they walked by. They looked in the win-

dow just in time to see the magical old woman take the magic pebbles out of her purple velvet bag."

4. *Change:* The pebbles were so still and quiet. She said:
Magic pebbles on the table.
Become _____ if you are able.
And that's just what happened. (Children become whatever is said and move in place or around the classroom.)

5. *Return:* The teacher decides how soon to make the transition back to pebbles. Comment first on the reasons why she wants them to go back in their bag. Example: The dolphins began swimming around. They enjoyed leaping up and carefully gliding. But the water was splashing all around her. And so, the old woman said:
Dolphins, dolphins, if you are able.
Become magic pebbles again on the table. And they did.

Karen recommends to start with images that stay in place:
◆ Become trees blowing in the wind.
◆ Become tulip bulbs in the ground. They didn't open up quite yet. They stuck out one leaf, then another. Slowly a stalk with a bud rose up and the bud began to open.

Karen advises, "If students need guidance, speak to the class through the story and stay within the story framework." For example, say, "But some of the snakes began to climb on the others, so she made sure each snake was by itself." Here are other favorite images of Karen's class:
◆ Become frogs hibernating. The old woman saw them slowly start to wake up as the water got warmer.
◆ Become snow flakes floating around.

6. *Close:* Keep repeating the game using different transfomations. For the ending: "And then she put each of the magic pebbles back in her velvet bag and put the bag away."

Discovery Units

73

⁜ DISCOVERY UNIT ⁜

Discovery Dance

SOURCE

After studying dance therapy at the American Dance Festival with Linni Silberman, I created this method to allow children to explore movement freely, to express themselves, and to learn how to cooperate in a group. As a classroom teacher at the Independent School in East Cleveland, Ohio, I led these sessions daily, for 30 minutes before lunchtime, with my first-grade class for an entire year. This plan is designed so that many teachers, not only those who are dancers themselves, can lead it.

GRADES: K–4th

FOCUS: Children move creatively alone and in small groups

MATERIALS: Drums, costume basket with cloth, scarves, masks

PROCEDURE

- **Make Small Groups:** Use the "Fair Choice" method described in the opening essay of this chapter (p. 60) to select small groups. Each Monday the class lines up and one by one selects one of the designated locations on the floor until everyone is a "family" of three to four students. These Family Groups keep their same makeup for a whole week.
- **Keep Agreements:** Children select the group promises they want to make at the beginning of the year and are reminded of them each day. *Example*: No bumping. If someone gets hurt, stop and see what they need.

1. *Opener — "Together and Apart":* Groups start in a shape, then individuals go apart and move their own way independently to a drum beat. At the drum's signal, they come back to rejoin their family group and freeze in a connected shape, making physical contact with each other. Try the sequence of away, then back, several times.

   Establish two different messages from the drum:

   a. Use one sound to mean go apart from your family group and move anywhere in the designated space. Keep a steady beat as children skip, dance, join hands and travel or in any other way they like explore free movement.

   b. Use a sharp definite sound to mean — come back, rejoin your group and freeze together in a shape.

   Teach what it means to "freeze together in a shape." The Spider Web Hands activity (p. 72) helps to teach this. Ask all members of the same small group family to connect to at least one other member. As they are learning this, specify body parts to illustrate the wide range of options: "Freeze in a shape touching with elbows, or noses, or knees, or heads, very low, with one foot off the ground, any way you like."

   At the beginning of the year help children explore the range of ways they can move as they travel independently around the space.

   - Locomotor suggestions: jump, walk backward, touch your hand to at least one person, skip, zoom.
   - Suggestions from the natural world: you're a monkey, you're a fish, you're a star.
   - Imagery suggestions: move as if it's a very cold day, as if you're moving through peanut butter. as if you're a tree blowing in the wind.
   - Work to the point where they can choose their own kind of exploration.
   - Each day watch the mood of the group. Do they seem particularly interested in connecting with each other? Do they need a longer time to explore movement on their own? Let their needs that day guide your decisions as to (a) how soon you will call them back from free exploration to freeze in a shape, and (b) whether they need suggestions for movement. As a surprise, you can vary how soon to call them back: very quickly after a short interval of dancing, and then very slowly, after a long session.

   Variation: If you prefer not to play a drum, you can use taped music while students move.

2. *Family Dances:* The whole group comes back together. Set up an array of materials that can be used for costumes, such as pieces of cloth, scarves, masks, and simple props in-

cluding rhythm instruments. The purpose, as in "Together and Apart," is to provide an avenue for them to explore and express what they need to do.

◆ *For K–1:* Each group takes a turn making up a dance on the spot. Each member may choose one or two costumes or props to use. This provides practice in collaboration. Children pick a role for themselves and then interact.

◆ *For 2nd–4th:* Divide the costumes and props, and have all small groups work simultaneously to create a quick scene, skit, dance, situation. Children this age are able to sustain a story: they can work on it from Monday to Thursday and present their scene on Friday.

Option: Relate the scenes to your curriculum — for example, pretend you are a family in North Carolina after the Civil War, or create a scene in the life of a person you are studying in your social studies unit.

If a particular group is having trouble collaborating during the course of the week, each day a different member of the family group can be the one who takes leadership and picks the story framework. ("Let's pretend we're in a house/in a school/at the circus/on a boat.")

Sharing the Dances: Every group has the chance to present. Limit the time, giving a warning signal such as, "Now it's time to make an ending." *Option:* Use a timer. *Feedback:* At the end of their dance, the group stands together facing the other class members. Each dancer/actor selects one observer to say a specific thing they noticed or liked about what they did. This way each person receives immediate positive feedback and the rest of the class has an incentive to watch closely.

3. *Closing — "Goodbye Dances":* The group lines up on the farthest side of the room. To go across to the door to leave, one by one each person invents their own movement sequence across the floor, while the teacher drums or plays taped music and then lines up at the door.

❊ CREATIVE MOVEMENT ❊
MOVEMENT AND WRITING

OVERVIEW

Have paper ready for writing. Prepare a clear space for movement, and use one of the following methods.

1. MOVING WITH EYES CLOSED

SOURCE

Janice Steinem, director of Silver Birch Dance Studio in Shelburne Falls, Massachusetts, developed this method. It is related to the authentic movement process developed by Janet Adler.

PROCEDURE

This kind of dynamic meditation allows children to go inside themselves and sense their bodies kinesthetically.

1. Tell students: "Start seated on the floor. Close your eyes and

GRADES: 1st–6th

FOCUS: After creative movement, children do free writing

MATERIALS: Paper and pens

focus on your hands. Move slowly and experience your hands. Allow your hands to move however they need to move, but slowly so that you can be aware of yourself. Keep your eyes closed as long as you can. If your eyes open, try to close them again." Use a short span of time, like two or three minutes.

2. After moving, students go directly to their writing. Janice says, "Move your hand as quickly as you can on the page and allow whatever you want to say to arise. Don't worry about grammar and spelling. The writing won't be checked for neatness or for content. The writing won't be criticized.

You can share it later as you wish. Keep that sense you had in moving of being in your body and let your writing be born through your body." If writing is difficult for any student, he or she can draw with oil crayons, dry pastels, or markers.

3. When this becomes familiar, increase the range of movement. Ask students to find a spot on the floor that is their own "space bubble." where they can move without touching anyone. Again, have them move with self-awareness with eyes closed, then write, allowing the movement and the writing "to roll out of you without checking it," as Janice describes it.

EXTENSION

A further step would be to allow students to move anywhere in the room. Janice Steinem was able to do this with a small group of ten students she worked with weekly over a period of months. They were able to close their eyes for five to seven minutes. Janice watched for safety and gave support as witness to the movement. Here is writing from one of these students:

"THE BUBBLE OF LIFE"

A bubble of life and wisdom holds us all. I sit at the far corner of the bubble. The bubble is not soapy like your world's bubbles. This bubble is rich and thick. It smells of lilacs and butterflies. My favorite food is daisy nuts and pickled daffodils with a little sprinkle of rose-blossom. It smells like a song I once heard at a lullabye fire. Our ocean is not like your ocean. It is not salty but sweet. And it is not clear like your ocean, but a magenta color. Our land is not like yours. It is purple and sometimes blue. We do not live in houses. We live under patches of berry nectar. — Addie Berard, age 10, Conway, Massachusetts

2. FREEZE IN A CHARACTER

PROCEDURE

1. Play "Three to Freeze." Standing in a circle, students jump three times and then freeze in place. Give them one direction at a time like "One, two, three, freeze very low." Here are other directions:

◆ *Locomotor:* "Freeze reaching high. Freeze on one foot. Freeze twisted up."

◆ *Different emotions.* "Freeze as if you are angry. Freeze as if you are frightened. Freeze as if you are wildly happy."

◆ *Favorite activities:* "Freeze as if you playing your favorite summer sport. Freeze as if you are lifting something heavy."

◆ *Imitating different people:* "Freeze as if you are a baseball player. Freeze as if you are a musician in a band. Freeze as if you are a dentist. Freeze as if you are at a surprise birthday party."

2. Let this movement be the impetus for writing. Take one of your directions and allow students to linger and explore it. Let the movement lead them to a character and help that character come alive. Establish in advance that individual students will stay in their own space bubbles and not move around the room.

Examples

◆ "Freeze as if you are frightened. Now take a moment to become this character who is frightened. Find out what they are frightened of. Listen to their story. See if you can make a wish so that what they are afraid of will not happen to them."

◆ "Freeze as if you are gathering something that is important. Now become this character who is collecting something important to them. Find out what it is and why they need it. Make a wish so that they don't lose it. Invent what happens next in the story."

◆ "Freeze as if you are finding a magic hat in an old chest. Put the hat on and become the character who wears this hat. Imagine they are eating breakfast. There is something special they need to do today. Find out what it is."

Writing: At the end of this exploration, say, "Now go to your desk and start to write about this character."

SOURCE

As a member of the Living Poem Theater in Greenfield, Massachusetts, I learned "Three to Freeze" and "Magic Hat" from director Mark Bluver and extended it into writing.

STORYTELLING DANCES
The Return of Unity

OVERVIEW

Theese stories are designed to contrast disconnection with connection. Use this activity after you have practiced Spider Web Hands (p. 72). The teacher reads the story narration as students act it out. The lesson works with either format:

◆ One large group in a circle.

◆ Small groups of four to six children.

ORIENTATION

Tell students: "Do you remember when we made shapes where everyone was connected? Today we are going to do story dances where we change from being connected, to going apart, to coming back together again. After we do the story we'll talk about how this relates to us being a supportive class that includes everyone."

PROCEDURE

1. Practice the contrast of connection and disunity. Each story follows this sequence:

a. Unity Shapes procedure from Spider Web Hands, p. 72.

b. Move away — no connection.

c. Change occurs. They start to return. Count to ten.

d. Children move back to their shape and arrive by the count of ten.

Practice this first with your fingers and hands:

a. Make a connected shape with your own hands. Hold your hands facing palm to palm with your fingertips touching.

b. Hands go apart and hide.

c. The time of change comes. Start to return. Count to ten.

d. Fingers reconnect again by count of ten.

Follow the same sequence of transformation standing:

a. The whole class or small groups stand together in a shape where they are all connected. This is easier to do if instead of holding hands, you touch palms or join hands in the center, or another variation of unified connection.

GRADES: K–6th

FOCUS: Use storytelling with creative movement to contrast disconnection and connection shapes

PLAN: Clear the room for sufficient space to move

b. Move apart and each become a tight ball sitting on the floor alone.

c. Get ready to change back to the unity shape you were before. Move while I count to ten.

d. By the count of ten, all need to be back in the first connected shape. When children are able to do this basic movement, add a story framework.

STORY CHOICES

Each of these four stories on the next page shows a group of people becoming disconnected and then returning to unity. Select one story that will work best for your group. To prepare, read the story out loud first so that children can visualize it before they act it out. If you like, expand upon the words and embellish the story your own way.

Now ask students to move as you read the story. Repeat the same story so that children have another chance to explore it. Afterward, ask if they would like to take turns watching the way other groups move and let half the class perform for the other half, with several group moving at the same time, and then switch and watch the other half. During presentations, you may want to invite other students to read the narration or tell the story from memory.

STORY ONE:
CHANGING ISOLATION

Unity Shape: Touching palms

The Story of the Hidden People: "Once upon a time there were people who were neighbors in a city, and they liked to stand together and look way way up at the tallest building. They stood palm to palm to steady each other. But one day a spell of grouchiness and grumpiness was cast over these neighbors. They shrunk and shrunk until they were shriveled up in tiny tight balls. They felt so far away from each other. The spell made them cover their eyes until they had no idea that there were actually other people nearby, only an arm's length away. They thought they were all alone until one day a star in the sky began to send them some help. They began to feel starlight on their heads. They opened their eyes a little bit and peeked out. That was the day that the change began and the spell could not hold them any longer. Very slowly and gradually they began to uncurl themselves from those tight balls, and connect to the other people — *[Teacher counts to 10 as they return to stand palm to palm]* — until they were back, and someone said, "Let's look up at the sky the way we used to." So they did. And another person said, "There's that star that helped us break the spell." When they looked back at each other they realized they were standing in a shape like a star.

Variation: Repeat the story and add the name of a person in history your students admire. "The voice of Harriet Tubman (or Cesar Chavez) spoke from the star and said 'You need to stick together and help each other out.' "

STORY TWO:
CHANGING DISHARMONY
AND SUSPICION

Unity Shape: Cross arms and shake hands

The Story of the People by the Well: Once upon a time there were people in a circle around their village well. They each held a bucket. *[Show these actions in pantomime.]* They tied a rope to their bucket and they threw their bucket down the well. Splash! The bucket hit the water. They each dipped their bucket in and pulled it up. It was heavy and hard to pull, but they got the bucket to the top. They drank the water and found it delicious.

They turned around and gave their bucket to their daughter or son to carry home (let these children be imaginary) and then they crossed their arms and shook hands with their neighbors on both sides. "Good neighbors," they said.

But suddenly someone called, "Watch out! I bet there isn't enough water for all of us. Someone is going to take too much water." They let go of their hands and drew them

back. They held their hands close to their chins and looked with suspicion at their neighbors. They drew themselves up very tall and tight and separate. Their mouths were tight and their eyes bugged out. They even held their breath. They let out their breath and looked around. They stood that way night and day, day and night for a week, afraid that someone else would get all the water.

Finally the children sent an old woman and an old man to help them. *[Options: imagine these two characters or have actors.]* The old man and the old woman explained, "This well goes to a deep, deep, endless underground stream. There will always be plenty."

"We don't believe you," they said.

"Then send a magic frog down to investigate." That's what they did. They sent a magic frog to hop around in the well. *[Ask one student to do this and have them hop around in the center.]* The frog was gone so long they had to call that frog, "Come on back."

"Gleep, gleep" said the frog. "What does 'gleep, gleep' mean?" they asked. The children explained, "It means that the water goes on and on so far that if they hadn't called the frog back it would still be gone today." That was the day of change.

They asked the frog to stand with them in the circle. They wanted to make peace with their neighbors again. They realized there would always be water for everybody. To the count of ten, they slowly returned to that neighborly greeting. They crossed their hands and shook hands on either side once more.

STORY THREE:
CHANGING METHODS

Unity Shape: Form a tree

Read this quotation:

Peace cannot be kept by force.
It can only be achieved by understanding.
— *Albert Einstein*

The Story of Keeping Peace: Once upon a time there was an old tree. Be that tree by standing back to back. And now turn around and face each other in a circle. You are no longer the tree. You are grouchy, angry neighbors standing in a circle. They woke up one morning. The tree was gone, and they all blamed each other. They squabbled a long time and brought out long lists of things the others had done that they found upsetting. They shook their fingers at each other with blame, and they said, "Were you the one who hurt our tree?" They made mean faces at each other, but the mean faces just made it worse and worse, until one day they looked down and saw a new young tree growing up in the center of the circle, getting larger and fuller by the moment. Each of them became entranced with that beautiful tree. Their faces changed and softened as they looked at it. When they looked at each other, they saw the goodness in each other's eyes, goodness that had also been there all along. Apples began to grow on the tree, they picked them, and they started to hand them to each other. That was the day that change began. *[Teacher counts to ten as students turn around and put their backs together like one tree trunk, bringing their arms up, crisscrossing together as if they were the branches of one tree.]*

STORY FOUR:
CHANGING POWER OVER

Unity Shape: Individual gestures in a circle

The Story of The Discovery of True Power: Once upon a time there were people who thought they were exactly the same. They all stood in a circle, and everyone stood the very same way. When one person moved their head, the others did, too. When one person moved their arm, the others did as well. They looked around and they said, "We are happy because we are all the same."

But it wasn't true. And when things aren't true they have a way of shifting. One day a bluejay came flying overhead. The people called out, "Do you see how we are all the same? "No, you are not the same," said the bluejay, for that was the case. But then the bluejay added a terrible lie: "That person there is the best." The bluejay didn't even look where it was pointing. But that person nearest to the bluejay's wing believed the lie and that one puffed up with pride.

That person stood with their hands on their hips tossing their head and lording it over the others. The others began to shrink down until they were on the ground, while the one in the center flexed muscles and acted very superior. "I am the best, I am the very best," they called. The others kept silent. The one in the middle looked around and began to feel very lonely. "I don't want it to be this way. I miss my friends. I wish that bluejay had never come along." And this one, too, sunk down in despair.

All the people were now low to the Earth. Right where they were, each found a hole in the ground and they called into it for an animal to come and help them. They saw a nose and whiskers, and a mole popped up. "I will help," the mole said.

"Tell us, are we different from each other?"

"Yes, just as I am different from the snake or the blue-

jay or the whale. Here are the words the Earth says to each of us each night:

> *You are strong, you are smart, you are powerful, and so are all the other animals, each in their own way.*

"You need to take up the strength of the Earth your own way, just like we do. The bluejay holds strength in its wings. The whale holds strength in its song, and I hold strength to smell and to claw tunnels in the earth. When you stand again, stand up in a way that says — I am strong and smart and powerful, and so are all of you."

That was the day of change. Now, as you hear the count to 10, slowly stand up again, finding the kind of power from the earth that all can have at the same time. Stand powerfully in a way that says, "I know that you are powerful, too."

Prepare first who will take the part in the center: Just as the bluejay declares who is best by chance, use an arbitrary method to decide who will stand in the center. For instance, the student whose first initial is closest to A will stand up in the center and make an unfair gesture that says "I am the best."

Note: The ending of this story examplifies Joanna Macy's description of "Power-with" in "The Web of Human Unity" (p. 159).

UNITY IN OUR OWN LIVES

1. *Discussion:* What are experiences that children have of exclusion, disharmony, disunity? What helps a group return to unity?

2. *Brainstorm Story Topics:* Brainstorm story topics that relate to students' lives like exclusion from a party or disunity among a team. Ask small groups for a topic as a basis for their dance or skit, or make up a story as a class.

3. Creating Story Dances: Small groups invent two contrasting shapes.
Shape 1) They are disconnected
Shape 2) They are connected.
Start with the first shape, and then slowly move into the second. Use ten drumbeats during the transition. Now ask each group to invent a story to go along with the movement.

EXTENSION

My song "The Sun Inside Us" on *The Wind is Telling Secrets* (Resources, p. 169) relates to the "Story of the Discovery of True Power." The chorus of the song says, "We're so strong, we're so smart./We were born with the loving heart."

❋ DISCOVERY UNIT ❋

COOPERATIVE SONGWRITING

OVERVIEW

Songs that have repeating patterns were named "zipper songs" by Lee Hayes, a member of the folk quartet The Weavers. One set of words can be zipped out and new words zipped in. You can use song patterns cooperatively to involve all children in building a song together where every voice will be heard. Each pair or trio contributes a verse to a single song. These three activities can be used either to create group poems or songs. They are from my book and tape of 17 song patterns, *Songwriting Together* (Discovery Center, 1989). (If you would like to hear the tunes for the songs "I Talk to My Food" and "That Quiet Place," they are both on the recording *Two Hands Hold the Earth* (Resources, p. 169).

❋ ACTIVITY ❋

I TALK TO MY FOOD

ORIENTATION

Pose this question to your students: "If you could talk to your food, what would you say?"

ICEBREAKER

Share this true story.

"Once I met a boy who was talking to his food. I was at a spaghetti supper, and he was sitting across from me. He had a big, crusty hard roll in his hands that was so hard, it looked like even if you hit it with a hammer, it wouldn't move. He tried to squeeze it, but the roll wouldn't fit into his mouth, so he began talking to it. I became very curious, and finally I said, 'Excuse me. I notice that you're talking to your food. Could you tell me what you're saying?'

" 'Sure,' he said. 'I'm telling my hard roll that I wish it would have babies!'

" 'Why?' I asked him.

" 'Because then the babies would fit into my mouth.' I asked if we could write a song together and he and his sister said yes. Their names are Eric and Kristen Mann.

GRADES: K–6

FOCUS: Songwriting patterns allow small groups to create new verses

Chorus:
I talk to my food, to my food, to my food.
But it doesn't listen to me.

Here is the verse about Eric.
I talk to my hard roll, and this is what I say.
I'd like to meet some baby rolls,
my mouth's too small today.

"Here is the verse his sister Kristen made up. She worked hard to find words that would make a near rhyme. *Mediocre* means inferior, not good enough.

I tell my eggplant, you're so mediocre.
I tell my yogurt more strawberries, less yogurt.

PROCEDURE

1. Begin work as a group. Use this song pattern:
I tell my _____

_____

I tell my _____

_____

Make one verse together on the board. Select two foods. Brainstorm all the things that could be said about them. Then ask students to craft the ideas into the pattern and help them find a rhyme for the last line. What makes this song work best is to explore a variety of ways of thinking about the food, going beyond knowing you like or dislike it, to discover its qualities. Model this exploration during the whole group brainstorm.

2. Illustrate how two students can work together on one verse. Interview them using these questions: "Is there a food you really like a lot or a food you can't stand? What does it taste like? What about it exactly do you like or dislike? What does it remind you of when you look at it? If you could change the food, how would you change it?" Engage the class in using these ideas to make one verse.

3. Expand the possibilities in any of the following ways. Provide additional sentence starters:
   ◆ I wish that _____ would _____
   ◆ I think that _____ looks like _____

Do a guided visualization: "Picture the food you have chosen and imagine yourself shrinking to the size of an ant. You are walking up to the food. What does it look like? What does it feel like to you to be the size of an ant? What textures do you discover? How does it smell?"

4. First, students write by themselves. Then they meet in pairs and take turns reading their writing to each other. They select one idea from each person and put them together into one verse. If writing is difficult, pairs can work out loud together and remember what they create. The verses don't need to rhyme.

I tell my dumpling
you're a baby in a blanket.
I guess you're very warm
because you're wrapped up in dough.

(from Barbara Pontecorvo's class)

5. All pairs have a chance to read their work to the class. They don't have to sing alone. After hearing their words, the whole class sings together. *Note:* If learning the melody below is difficult, subsitute a familiar tune. Sing these sample verses with your class:

I tell my brussels sprouts,
you have a cute green face.
You look like little round balls
that come from outer space.
—Third grader Jason Dudley, Greenfield, Massachusetts

I tell my hot chiles
Ah! Ah! Ah! Ah! AH!
(wave your hand to fan your mouth)
And I tell my Jello
Blah, blah, blah, blah, BLAH!
(wiggle flat hand, palm down)
—From a classroom of first graders in Barrington, NH:

EXTENSIONS

Bill Ackerman, a classroom teacher from Halifax, Vermont, suggests addressing other things besides food: "Talking to your food can be changed to, 'I Talk to My Pet,' or 'I Talk to My Chair,' or my pencil, or my radio."

I TALK TO MY FOOD

© 1989 words and music by Sarah Pirtle, Discovery Center Music, BMI

❈ A C T I V I T Y ❈
THAT QUIET PLACE

ORIENTATION

Tell students: "Each of us has the ability to calm ourselves down and feel more collected. Sometimes it helps to go to a special place where that is easier to do. Or we can journey to a place inside us."

PATTERN

(How do you feel?)
Sometimes when I feel _____
(Where do you go?)
I _____
(What happens there?)
and _____

Chorus:
In that quiet place where nothing can harm you.
In that quite place we carry inside.
The heart of the world, the heart of the world.

PROCEDURE

1. Write the pattern on the board and provide an example of how you or someone you know might fill in the pattern.
Sometimes when I'm feeling rushed and hurried,
I go by the stream to find the willow trees
and I hug them when no one is looking.

Sometimes when I feel mad at my brother.
I climb to the top of my top bunk,.
and I rest while I draw.
An additional verse to the song below says:
Sometimes I know that there is a whale/Calling me out to ride on her back./We go rolling high and low.

THAT QUIET PLACE

2.. Teach the chorus to get into the mood of the song.

3. Ask a volunteer to be interviewed and work as a class to create a poem or song with their words.

   a. Ask, "Why do you want to go to your special place?" The response goes on the first line.

   b. Ask, "Where do you go to feel safe?" The response goes on the second line.

   c. Ask, "What happens there? What does it look like? How do you feel then?" The response goes on the third line.

4. Provide questions to help students search: "What do you do to be able to listen to yourself? Is there a special place where you live where you feel particularly happy or safe or comforted? Is there a special place at someone else's home — like your grandparents'? Do you have a favorite place outside — such as on the playground? What's your favorite spot in the school? Is there someone's lap you like to go to? Did you see a place once before — a spot you visited? Is there a favorite book that has a special place? What about a special place inside you?

5. Here are formats for the writing:

   ◆ Ask students to write as much as they can about their real or imagined special place, what it looks like, why they go there, and how they feel when they are there, and to create a verse or poem by themselves.

   ◆ Ask students to tell a partner their thoughts about a special place and make a verse together.

   ◆ As a whole group, work with several students, one at a time, to create a song verse and sing each verse.

6. Be sure to also explore a safe place created by your imagination. Invent exactly what it would be like. The verse above (#1) about riding on a whale's back is an example.

❋ ACTIVITY ❋
OUTSIDE MY WINDOW

ORIENTATION

Ask students: "What do you see outside of the window you look out of most often? And what would you never see?"

PROCEDURE

1. Write the pattern on the board or on a worksheet.

   Outside my window I see _____

Outside my window I see _____
Outside my window I see _____
But I never see _____
And I never see _____
And I never see _____
outside my window.

2. Place students in groups of three. First have them talk together, each person taking a turn to describe several things they see outside their window. Next, students write down their ideas by themselves, adding adjectives to create vivid phrases. Now, each person chooses one thing from their list to put into the first half of the song.

3. For the second section, students collaborate to create interesting or humorous ideas about what they would never see outside their window. *Option:* Promote cooperative learning by using roles. Ask children to choose one of these three: The Recorder who writes the group's ideas in the second part of the song, The Turn Helper who assists in making sure each person's ideas are included, and The Reader who reads the completed work to the class.

4. If possible, engage students in creating a tune for this song. Use a piano or Orff instruments to find a melody, or work out loud and record the melody ideas on audio tape. Create the melody either by working in the same small groups or as a whole class.

5. Students also enjoy pantomiming the words they have created.

Sample verse:

Outside my window I see tall trees like soldiers.
Outside my window I see my sad neighbor's dog.
Outside my window I see people carrying groceries.
But I never see parachutes dropping.
And I never see circus clowns.
And I never see bugs playing baseball
outside my window.

EXTENSION

Write a verse using sounds instead of sights.

   Outside my window I hear _____ .

Instead of pantomiming the completed verse, assemble rhythm instruments or objects that can be used to make sounds. Create sounds to match the words of your verse.

THE SONGS
WE CARRY INSIDE

"**W**HOEVER asked *us* to write a song when we were kids?" bemoaned children's songwriter Michael Ekster as he thought back on the support he would have liked as a child. Let's look at why songwriting is an important activity in classrooms that are working on peacemaking skills and how we can add it to our language arts programs.

- -

THE SONGS THAT LIVE INSIDE OF US

All of us are born with musical intelligence. Songs come from a place inside that for many adults feels mysterious, unpredictable, or unreachable, yet researchers report that at age two and three we all combine words and tunes in our language play.

> *I go outside and then I play in the sand*
> *Strumming on the old banjo.*
> *I come in and I have a cookie.*
> *Strumming on the old banjo.*
> — Lucy, age 2½

> *Daisy, stomp stomp*
> *Daisy, stomp stomp*
> *Twirl around, twirl around,*
> *Run in place.*
>
> *Hop on one foot.*
> *Click your fingers.*
> *Daisy, stomp stomp*
> *Daisy, stomp stomp*
> *This is the end of the song.*
>
> — Amy, age 5

Encouraging songwriting is encouraging thinking. In making their songs, both Lucy and Amy worked within a pattern. They constructed their idea of what makes a song — like ending each section with "strumming on the old banjo" — and employed that structure in their writing.

What would it be like in our classrooms if we encour-aged children to keep developing their innate songwriting ability, just as we encourage children's first words or first poems? We would help them access an overlooked mode of exploring the world and processing information. When I interviewed a dozen adult songwriters of children's songs, I learned that each one had received painful criticism of their songs at some point in childhood from family, peers, or teachers. Many also felt they had been pressured to perform in ways that felt hurtful or disrespectful.

Here is what songwriting looks like when a child has been supported to find a river of songs moving inside. When I met Katie Ellison at age six and a half, she had already spent hours entertaining herself writing songs about the Earth. She often wrote riding in the car. Her mother provided space for Katie to reflect and sing; she didn't turn on the radio and she didn't evaluate, judge, or gush over her daughter's songs. This helped Katie's songs flow.

I met Katie at a farm when by chance we were both picking blueberries. After we discovered that we both liked songwriting, Katie said she was going to create a song on the spot. She sat quietly on the grass for many minutes. Then, when she was ready, this song tumbled out, one line and then a halt; more, then silence, then the rest of the song. The melody rose and fell as she focused upon capturing her exact feelings and the pictures she saw:

> *In the hills at night*
> *the deer is chewing up the grass*
> *and the owls are making their home.*
>
> *The sun settles down in her new foundation*
> *getting all her things done,*
> *getting ready for the things to come up.*

Later, as we walked along a trail, I asked if she would sing some of that song again. "I don't want to write about that anymore," she replied "I want to write about all I can see right now." She sang with a new tune:

> *The hawks are everywhere*
> *going hawk, hawk, hawk.*

This window on Katie's songwriting shows that when we write songs an important and vulnerable interior voice is revealed. Yet most people let this innate ability go, because it's not culturally encouraged. It's significant for the development of our society that this resource has been cut off. The voice that comes out in songwriting taps an inner wellspring that our traumatized society needs. This voice connects to feelings, and increases self-awareness. In writing songs we can come in contact with a part of us that connects cooperatively with our surroundings.

SUPPORTING CHILDREN'S SONGWRITING IN THE CLASSROOM

Children in our classrooms will be on a continuum: some will have facility with writing like Katie and others feel more comfortable participating in group songwriting. Offer support and acknowledgment for those who prefer to write alone, and provide cooperative songwriting opportunities for others who enjoy having song patterns supplied to guide their work.

1. Let students know that you believe all of them have the potential to write songs.

2. Assist students who like to write songs:

◆ Provide a tape recorder and a blank tape that is designated for "catching" songs. Songs are slippery. Remembering a song is like remembering a dream. If children know they can hold onto their words and melody by singing into a tape, they will feel encouraged to value their fleeting creations.

◆ Provide times of silence for writing. Songs need space. Help children understand that sometimes classmates want to be alone to think and feel and create.

◆ Make the sharing of songs optional. Songs can be private. Rather than assuming that the best way to honor a song is to comment upon it or to find an avenue to have it shared, let the writer take the lead. Query the writers to see whether they want to perform. Putting a song forth in a school assembly may not necessarily feel like affirmation. Let the writer be in charge of what happens to the song. Let the song belong to the songwriter.

◆ If a child shares a song they have created, provide only positive feedback. Receive a song creation instead of evaluating it. When you talk to a child about a song, talk about what stays with you and let the writer feel you have heard it. We, the listeners, can't know all that went into that song. For instance, a friend created this song, which was a turning point in her inner dialogue. Yet an outsider hearing it, might notice only its simplicity:

Walking out of there
I'm walking on air.

3. *Provide opportunities for group songwriting:* Writing songs in a group is an age-old human experience. Look for important events in the class as a starting point for songs. Here is a zipper pattern (p. 80) that can be used to relate to conflict resolution and making anger plans.

LISTENING TO THE MESSAGE OF OUR ANGER

Question: What could help you when you're angry?
Melody: "When you're Happy and You Know it"
Song pattern:
    When you're angry and you know it, _____.
    When you're angry and you know it, _____.
    When your anger is sizzling,
    there's a way that you can listen.
    When you're angry and you know it, _____.
        Examples: *hug a pillow, scribble on paper, find a friend,*
                breathe deep.
The activity Writing Conflict Resolution Songs (p. 99) provides additional zipper song patterns using familiar folk tunes.

Here is a song written with second graders in Bellows Falls, Vermont recommended for "Talk It Out" Family Night (p. 19). Use the same tune as "There were Two in the Bed."

TWO IN THE FIGHT

There were two in the fight
and the little one said, "I'm angry, I'm angry."
But the other one started to run away.
"Come back and hear what I have to say.
'Keep talking, keep talking.
"Come on back, come on back.
We can figure this out. (2x)
There were two in the fight
and the other one said, "I'm angry, I'm angry."
But the little one did not run away.
"Tell me what you have to say.
Keep talking, keep talking.
Talk it out, talk it out, we can figure this out." (2x)

✳ MUSIC ACTIVITY ✳
SONGS FOR COOPERATION

ORIENTATION

Tell students: "We're going to use song games to practice co-operation skills."

PROCEDURE

Use familiar songs as a basis for group games with singing and movement to give children an opportunity to cooperate. If you don't want to lead the singing, ask students to help start the song. Here are seven different ways to structure cooperative movement with any favorite song.

1. *Pass A Movement:* Sit or stand in a circle. One person starts a motion with hands and arms and then faces the student next to her and "sends" the motion sidewards for the next student to repeat. While the song is sung, one at a time each student in turn does the motion around the circle until it comes back to the beginning. *Example:* To the song, "My Bonnie Lies Over the Ocean" make a wave motion to fit the theme of "over the ocean." *The value of the game:* Each child receives a turn as the focus of the whole group.

2. *Stop and Go Practice:* At the end of each line of a song, add a word that indicates "stop" to help students alternate moving and pausing. Pick a motion such as rolling hands, stretching, wiggling, or jumping that will be done during the song except when the word (such as "hold") is said. *Example: My Bonnie lies over the ocean (hold). My Bonnie lies over the sea (hold).*

The value of the game: This pattern helps children practice self control.

3. *Exploring Movement:* Invite children to each move their own way to a song while concentrating on finding motions that feel delicious. If you select a slow song, this will have a calming affect. *The value of the game:* Students contact their authentic movement expression rather than following a movement set by another.

4. *Group Mirroring Game:* Ask if anyone wants to lead his motions while the others follow along. Ask the rest of the class to mirror the movements of the leader while one verse of the song is sung. *The value of the game:* Children feel affirmed when their movement idea is followed by others.

GRADES: K–4th

FOCUS: Seven methods are presented of using song games to develop cooperation skills

MATERIALS: Songs of your choice

5. *Mirroring with Pairs:* Arrange students in pairs, standing and facing each other. Ask one person in the pair to lead movements for the length of one verse while a partner follows. Next, the other leads. *The value of the game:* Children move in synchrony in a friendly, safe manner.

6. *Cooperation Small Group Dances:* Divide the class into small groups of three to five students. They invent movements during the song. Example: They act out motions to match the verses of "She'll Be Coming Round the Mountain." *The value of the game:* Children make decisions and collaborate.

7. *Story Game Dances:* Using the setting of a boat on the ocean, ask students to choose characters and act out a scenario while the song is sung. Example: Change the word "Bonnie" and sing: "My boat lies over the ocean." or "The dolphins lie over the ocean." First, students discuss what character they will be. For instance, first-grade students in Johanna Korpita's classroom in Williamsburg, Massachusetts, chose to become a diver swimming around the boat, a sea horse, a shark who doesn't eat people, and a magic rainbow fish.(This extends the activity Creating a Boat, p. 99). *The value of the game:* Children enter a story framework together and interact

RESOURCE

The book and recording, *Linking Up*, provide new songs that explicitly set up cooperation games. (Resources, page 169.) "Shake, Shake, Freeze" asks students to shake their hands in the air, then stop and freeze. The song "Cloud Hands" spells out the partner mirror game. It says, "Wave your hands like clouds in the sky" three times and then, "Look each other in the eye. Now the other one leads." "Under the Bridge" leads children in forming bridges with their arms.

✳ DISCOVERY UNIT ✳
CHILDREN'S PEACE STATUE

ORIENTATION

"If you were building a peace statue, what would you want it to look like? We will make our own statues in small groups and find our about a real statue that young people designed and raised money to build."

PROCEDURE

1. *Background:* An old legend in Japan says that if you fold a thousand paper cranes you will be granted the wish of your heart. Read *Sadako and the Thousand Paper Cranes* by Eleanor Coerr (Putnam, 1990), which tells the true story of twelve-year-old Sadako's struggle to fold a thousand peace cranes. She began folding them when she was in the hospital, completed one set, but died from radiation sickness. Sadako was exposed to radiation during World Wat II that resulted from the atomic bomb detonated by the U.S. over Hiroshima when she was two. Explain that children who were friends of Sadako raised money to build a Children's Peace Statue that stands in the Peace Park in Hiroshima.

Next, explain that elementary students in Albuquerque, New Mexico, who heard this story decided that the United States should have its own Children's Peace Statue. With the help of their teachers and adult advisor, Camy Condon, they raised money, and collected 900,000 names of children from 50 states and 46 countries who supported the statue. They organized a contest for children to submit their own designs and received more than 300,000 drawings. The finalists in the contest had their designs made into models; these were then judged by a panel of children and adults who met at the Los Alamos Museum, the city where the atomic bomb was created.

Keep the rest of the details secret until students have had a chance to make their own models, but tell them that in August 1995, fifty years after the bombing of Hiroshima, the statue made of the winning model was installed in front of a museum.

2. *Peace Statue Models:* If you could build a Peace Statue, what would it look like? Divide into Family Groups of four students to create models. *Option:* To form the groups, use a method related to symbols of peace, such as paper doves

marked with different colors. *Day One:* Ask the groups to talk together about symbols of peace and about what they would like their statue to communicate. Have them start making sketches. *Day Two:* Ask them to decide how to convey their design. "Will you draw a picture? Will you make a model? Will you put different symbols of cardboard and create a mobile? Write down a list of materials you will need and plan how to get them." *Day Three:* Students begin work on their drawings, models, or mobiles.

3. *Peace Process:* Emphasize that each stage of the work needs to be done in a way that illustrates peacemaking. Help students work on collaboration skills. For instance, on Day One suggest a way of going around the circle and hearing each idea. Talk about how to combine ideas and work consensually. Discuss the importance of having both the product and the way it was created exemplify peace.

4. *Sharing Peace Statues:* Members of each group show what they created, explaining how they worked peacefully to make decisions.

5. *The Children's Peace Statue Story:* A design called "The Peace Garden" by Noe Martinez, a Mexican-American from Texas, was chosen for the statue. When sculptor Tim Joseph carried out the plan, he asked the help of children to mold flowers and animals from balls of wax. More than 3000 children from around the world formed wax sculptures, then Tim cast the turtles, salamanders and other forms into bronze and used them to form all the continents and land masses on a huge stainless steel globe. Efforts to place the statue at Los Alamos were rejected by the Town Council there, so the statue was placed outside the Albuquerque Museum, at 2000 Mountain Ave. NW.

Paper cranes are hung on the Children's Peace Statue in New Mexico, just as they are hung in Hiroshima. Fold 50 or 100 paper cranes, or a thousand. String them on strong fishing line, and send them to be placed on the statue.

To contact the Children's Peace Statue group or Camy Condon, write New Mexico Conference of Churches, 124 Hermosa SE, Albuquerque, NM, 87108. This is where you can mail paper cranes for the statue.

✳ DISCOVERY UNIT ✳

COOPERATIVE BOATBUILDING

SOURCE

This activity, described on p. 6 as a metaphor for the entire concept of building cooperation in education, was created and led by Conflict Management Director Sue Liedl (St. Philip's School, Bemidji, Minnesota) with a fifth-grade class who had been working with her on communication skills since the first grade. She comments, "This project was a strength exercise for our conflict management program. It also became a unique family event." A project of this magnitude is done best in small groups that have a lot of experience working together as a unit.

Where To Order Boat Plans: Write Mark Kuleta, New Paths, 502 Beltrami Ave. NW, Bemidji, MN 56601, *or call* (218) 751-4345. Materials cost approximately $150 per boat

SUMMARY OF PROJECT

Groups of four worked with parents to create dories big enough to carry all four of them. The young people were part of every step. In advance, parents cut the boat parts out of wood according to the plans. When the students arrived at the woodshop, all the parts were distributed into four different areas and each team started work on one of the four boats. Students helped assemble the parts and wire them in place. Next the seams were fiberglassed. Students sanded the seams smooth with sandpaper. After sanding was complete, the wooden ribs were placed side by side for bracing. The whole team had to work together to hold the ribbing in place be-

GRADES: 5th and up

FOCUS: Teams of students, with adult support, build actual boats

MATERIALS: Tools, fiberglass and other equipment as delineated in plans

PLAN: Wood shop, parent volunteers

cause of the curved edge. Wood putty sealed the seams. When the center seat was installed, all students signed their names inside. This assembly process took two days. On the third day, students painted their boats with bright colors and gave them names like "Rascal" and "Toothpick." The students reported that the hardest part was working together to carry the boats down to the water to launch them. Balloons added to the festivities as students and parents were on hand to celebrate the launch.

PROCESSING

Sue Liedl noted, "At the beginning I overheard the boys state that certain parts of the construction should be the boys' job, and as a result, one all-girl group had reservations about their ability to do the assigned work. But when the hands-on building began it was clear everyone carried his or her own weight." If gender issues surface, talk this out. Respond and discuss: "Why do you think only the boys can do this part?"

CHAPTER 5
Awakening the Peacemaker
Conflict Resolution Activities

HELPING STUDENTS WITH CONFLICTS

WHAT ARE the conflicts that the students in your class encounter? Namecalling? An older student who tries to take money or food from others' lunches?

The scenarios may vary widely from encountering threatening strangers on their street, fearing violence from older siblings, to arguing over lunch boxes that look alike. It's important that we as teachers are realistic and informed about what our students are dealing with, and that we give them tools as we can.

The activities in this chapter provide ways that students can practice handling difficult situations. Naming a social reality greatly assists children. For instance, at a K–3rd grade staff meeting, teachers articulated a subtle but important problem students were experiencing at recess. After efforts were made to handle a situation, some students couldn't let go of it. It wasn't over yet for them. The teachers gave this a name — "finishing a problem." Naming it was the first step to helping students work on it. Then they could say to a child, "We've done a lot of talking about this problem. What would help this feel finished for you?"

Here are examples of key conflicts in different third-grade classrooms and how teachers addressed them.

◆ A group of third graders in a rural/suburban Minnesota school ganged up each day during recess and chose one person in their class to scapegoat. Their teacher and the conflict management coordinator addressed the problem by leading a workshop about exclusion that addressed the topic but didn't single out the children who were the leaders. They helped the children see that harm was being done. After this workshop using the "Open and Closed Circles" activity in Chapter 6, the scapegoating behavior stopped.

◆ Third graders in an urban school in Massachusetts, some having parents in a gang, escalated fights at recess as buddies jumped in to help buddies. Their teacher explicitly led role plays on what to do if friends ask you to defend them in a fight, and worked to change the classroom norm — it

---

TEACHER REFLECTION

Write down all the conflicts that you know your students are facing. Put the conflicts in categories according to where they occur: within the classroom, at lunch, at recess, in the hall, on the bus, in the neighborhood, at home. Put a check by three that you feel you can help with, the situations where you have the skills and resources to assist, including helping students seek out student mediators.

---

is not being a disloyal friend if you don't fight for them, because fighting isn't allowed at school. By naming this reality, the situation was reframed, students were given permission not to join in a fight concerning a friend, and this took everyone off the hook.

◆ In September a third-grade teacher in rural Vermont noticed with concern that her students were "decidedly individualistic" and unaware of other's needs. She began ongoing work on cooperation in practice time and used cooperative learning structures in academic lessons weekly. In November a girl in the class had a few personal items stolen from her purse when she accidentally left it in the school bathroom. The teacher called a class meeting to brainstorm how to assist. The students themselves decided to raise money so that she could replace her things.

When we step in as teachers, we can make a difference. What about the conflicts that you don't think of as manageable? Involve other teachers in solving problems that affect all students at recess, in the lunchroom, or on the buses by raising these issues at staff meetings. When cruel name-calling on bus rides was traumatizing some students, a rural school in Massachusetts appointed and trained student bus monitors to provide social protection.

Students need to know that the adult world is aware of the upsetting situations they face, and that adults are not ignoring their plight, but have tools to help them deal with problems.

✳ ACTIVITY ✳
CONFLICT INTERVIEWS

PURPOSE

The purpose of the interviews is for upper-grade students to gather information about the needs of younger students to increase student involvement in the conflict resolution program. Caring older students model for the younger students so that they take the work of learning conflict resolution skills seriously. During the interview the older students show that they are concerned about the kinds of conflicts the younger children are having. Also, problems may surface that adults aren't hearing. This interview process is helpful at the beginning of conflict resolution training and as a check-in at the middle and end of the year.

PLANNING

Teachers divide the younger class into four groups. Pairs of interviewers from an older grade interview one-quarter of the class. Interviews take place simultaneously. The recommended length is fifteen minutes. Photocopy the *Instructions for Interviewers* section (p. 93) and the *Conflict Interview* form (pp. 94–95) for each interviewer.

PROCEDURE

Prepare Interviewers: Select eight older students who are good listeners and will help draw out students. If you have a peer mediation program, mediators can be the interviewers; add additional questions to the survey, which will help younger students to be more aware of what mediation offers.

Explain that they will find out how students handle conflicts now, and encourage them to reflect on what's working and what help they will want. Ask interviewers to be open and accepting of every response so that the younger students feel free to be honest. Talk about body language that shows neutrality; for example: "If students tell you something aggressive they did and you laugh, it may seem that you approve of that solution. If instead you listen openly and help them think about it, they have space for growth."

Use of the Interview: It is important that the information gathered in the interviews be taken seriously by adults at the school. Children need to know that the information they share is being heard and acted on. Here are examples of feedback that can come out in the interview: "Someone put a rock in

GRADES: 4th–6th grade students interview K–3rd graders
FOCUS: Pairs of older students interview small groups of younger students about conflicts
MATERIALS: Interview sheet, clipboards, pencils

a snowball and threw it at recess," or "Someone waited for me in the hall and tripped me." Look for information that needs to go to the adults who are responsible for safety at recess. Distribute the results of the interviews to classroom teachers, guidance counselors and other conflict resolution trainers. See the section below on how to use the information you have gathered.

How to Prepare Younger Students for the Interview: Tell students: "Everyone in our school is learning about talking out problems and getting along with each other. Today students from *[name the class]* will be talking to you to find out what kind of help you would like. They want to know what kinds of problems and arguments happen, and what are the hardest ones to solve. They will also ask what is going well for our class. We realized that if the whole class had the interview at once, not everyone would get a chance to speak, and so they will be talking to you in small groups."

Ground rule: "We need to make a promise before the interview that we'll talk about the kinds of problems but we won't tell the names of the people involved. This means you can say, 'This is what happened to me at recess,' or 'Somebody pushed me,' but not 'So and so did this at recess.' Do you see the difference? Can you guess why we are making this rule?"

The interviewers will write down what you said and then they will meet with *[tell which adults are processing the information]* to tell them about it. This will help us give you the help you need.

INSTRUCTIONS FOR INTERVIEWERS

1. Both of you will take turns asking questions. In addition, one of you will be the timekeeper and one will be the record-keeper.

Timekeeper's Job:

a. *Stopping on Time.* Write down the starting time and ending time. Let the group know when there are only three minutes left. Let them know when it's time to stop.

b. *Fair Turns.* Pay attention if someone is taking a long turn and in a friendly way let them know that you need to hear more from other people, too.

Recordkeeper's Job: While they are talking, jot down words and checks on the Conflict Interview form. Try to keep listening to and looking at the students. Listen for the most important things. When the interview is over, write down anything else that you remember.

2. Directions for the Interviewers

a. *Step 1 — Greeting.* Ask the group to sit in a circle so that everyone can be seen. Thank them for talking with you. Tell them your names. Ask students to introduce themselves.

b. *Step 2 — Establish Three Ground Rules.* Ask students: "Do you agree to stay in your chairs during the whole interview? Do you agree to take turns talking so we can hear what you have to say? Do you agree — as your teacher explained — to tell us the problems but not tell names? You can describe the person, like saying 'a friend' or 'someone in sixth grade,' to help us understand what happened."

c. *Step 3 — Explain Sharing Time.* "When we ask a question, we want to give everyone a chance to answer. If you are taking a long turn, we'll let you know that we need to move on to another person."

d. *Step 4 — Include Everyone.* "Give everybody a chance to talk. It's not important that you use all the questions. The most important thing is that no one be left out. When there are three more minutes, go to question five if you haven't started it."

- *Listen!* — "Look at the person talking. Nod or in other ways show them that you are hearing them."

- *Encourage!* — "Thank each person when he or she is finished speaking. Draw them out if they give a short answer but you think they have more to say."

- *Remind!* — "If they start to use names and talk badly about specific people, remind them about the agree-ment and move on to another speaker."

e. *Step 5: At the End, Thank Them.* Use the ending question — tell something really good about your class — to close positively. Explain that you will share what they've said with adults who will help with the problems.

FOLLOW-UP

Meet With Interviewers Afterward. Schedule 30–45 minutes to process this experience:

- Ask students: "What was it like to do the interview?"

- Each pair of interviewers will have a chance to tell what they learned. Ask them: "What kind of help do you think the children in your group need? Did you find out about any problems that you think the classroom teacher or principal might not be aware of?"

- Tell students: "Let's appreciate the work you did. Can you say something you or your partner did well?"

How To Use the Information Gathered

- Adults read over the interviews, look for new information, and think how to best handle it: for example, work with staff in charge of recess? talk individually to a student? inform a guidance counselor or teacher?

- Make a list of all the key problems mentioned. Eliminate problems not relevant to school ("My sister yells at me and she goes to tell my Mom"). Look for problems that may be happening to several people.

- Designate an adult to handle situations privately if one individual needs help and it would be less productive to address the situation as a group: for example, "Someone threw rocks," "Someone pushed me down at recess."

Plan Follow-Up Skillbuilding:

- Ask the younger class to select one problem that they will work on first. Brainstorm ideas of what will help at a meeting. Write down their action plan.

- Include time to focus on the strengths of the group and acknowledge them. Use methods in the activity Good News Board (p. 25) to post positive news about behavior.

- Select one of the social skills that needs attention and plan skill-building sessions within Discovery Time.

- Use the information for planning conflict resolution role plays and puppet plays.

CONFLICT INTERVIEW
Questions To Ask

Name of Teacher of the Class:

Grade:

Names of Interviewers:

TIMEKEEPING

Starting time:

Warning time
when 3 minutes are left:

Ending time:

GO OVER THE GROUND RULES: **1.** Stay in chairs **2.** Take turns talking **3.** Don't use names

TELL THEM: "We want to find out if you have the help you need to handle the problems that come up at school."

1. Which of these times or places at school do you want to talk about? Circle what they pick:

- ◆ Before school starts
- ◆ While you're at recess
- ◆ Lining up
- ◆ Working in the classroom
- ◆ The lunch room
- ◆ Others:

Tell us what kinds of problems have happened there this year for you where you'd like more help or you think teachers don't know what happened. (Work with only 2 or 3 so you have time for other questions).

◆ List Problems:

2. What ways have you tried to deal with these problems? (Check any they say.)
- ☐ walked away? ☐ yelled? ☐ threatened them? ☐ teased them back?
- ☐ hit or kicked ☐ talked to them yourself
- ☐ got help from a teacher or recess aide? ☐ got help from a student mediator?

3. Which of these methods worked? What differences or changes did they make?
   If it didn't help, why do you think the problem didn't get better?

◆ Any Comments?

4. Have you ever been in an argument with someone and you were able to talk things out with them instead of hitting or pushing? How many people could remember a time of talking it out? ___ out of ___ people in the group.

◆ Any Examples:

5. We know that every class is really good at some things. We're going to name things your class might be good at.

◆ **Check how they feel their class does on these things:**

☐ Good at playing group games at recess?

☐ Good at sharing?

☐ Good at listening?

☐ Good at not hitting or kicking?

☐ Good at not teasing?

☐ Good at helping each other?

☐ Good at talking and finding words to solve problems?

Ask if there are other things they want to add.

6. What ideas do you have about how to help kids get along with one another and solve their problems?

ENDING THE INTERVIEW: **a.** Tell them you will pass on this information so they can get more help. **b.** Thank them.

- -

Please write more here after the interview.

1. Where do you think their class needs the most help?

Check if help needed here:	a few students need help	a lot need help
not hitting, pushing, shoving	☐	☐
not threatening	☐	☐
not name-calling	☐	☐
stopping when someone asks	☐	☐
including people instead of excluding	☐	☐
listening	☐	☐
deciding to try to talk things out	☐	☐
asking for help	☐	☐

2. What is your guess about what they do well?

3. Are there any other things they mentioned or that you noticed?

✳ ACTIVITY ✳

WILL THE CASTLE BE BUILT?

ORIENTATION

"Today we're going to watch a Lego castle being built. Notice what you think about the way the builders work together." *Note:* This is an excellent activity to use as an introduction to the Cooperation Construction Unit (p. 62) and to Family Groups in general (Chapter 2).

PREPARATION

Pick four people who are not class members to stage the role play. Use parent volunteers if you can. If parents are unavailable, choose older students. Meet with these four in advance for five minutes to explain the secret role each will play while they are working on the Lego castle. Describe the roles using animals as symbols of qualities. One person is the shark and dominates the situation. One person is a turtle and avoids contributing or making decisions. Another person is a monkey and distracts the group from making progress. The fourth person is an owl who takes wise leadership but is undermined. *Option:* Provide funny hats to set up a lighthearted spirit.

PROCEDURE

1. *Castle Building, Take One:* Students watch as the parents or older students work with the Legos. Don't inform the class what role each person is taking. As shark, turtle and monkey carry on, despite the owl's efforts, the castle never gets built.

2. *Discussion*

   ◆ One at a time, focus on each of the four roles. Ask students: "How did you see this person?" Help them give feedback to the parents about the way they behaved.

   ◆ Tell students the four animal names and ask them to guess which each person played.

   ◆ Now ask students to tell volunteers what they could do differently. Give specific advice to each person; for example, "Give your idea for the walls but listen to other people's ideas next time and see if that works."

GRADES: 1st–5th

FOCUS: Students identify unhelpful and helpful behavior after watching a role play

MATERIALS: Legos or other building materials such as marshmallows, dry spaghetti and toothpicks

PLAN: Arrange for parent volunteers or older students to do role play

3. *Castle Building: Take Two:* Now all parents take the qualities of helpful, communicative collaborators. The castle gets built.

STUDENT CASTLES

Divide the class into small groups so that each team will have an adult observer. Give each group marshmallows, dry spaghetti and toothpicks or other building materials. The observer takes notes on how the group does on listening, making suggestions, looking for agreement, and staying focused. Specific actions are noted.

CLOSURE

Walk around and look at each castle. The observer reads a list of the specific things the group did that helped them cooperate on the building.

SOURCE

Sue Liedl, conflict management director at St. Philip's School in Bemidji, Minnesota, invented this activity and has created many other ways to teach important concepts.

For more information about the model program that Sue Liedl has created, contact her at St. Philip's School, 720 Beltrami Ave, Bemidji, MN 56601.

❋ MUSIC ACTIVITY ❋
FEELINGS AND CONFLICTS
Discussing Song Lyrics

BACKGROUND

"Children need a non-threatening way to talk about feelings and basic values. Music is an ideal vehicle for working indirectly on personal and family issues. It appeals to children's love of fantasy and also can speak to real-life skills. Songs can zoom in on important themes in childhood." — *Debbie Rubenzahl*

Two guidance counselors inspired this activity. They made extensive use of song lyrics to help children discuss important social issues. Andrea Stone in Montvale, New Jersey created a recording and book of fourteen key songs she brought to classrooms before becoming a school principal. Debbie Rubenzahl, family counselor at North Parish School in Greenfield, Massachusetts, had begun work on a book about using songs as an entranceway for sharing feelings before her death.

PROCEDURE

First, play a song to introduce a topic and ask students to listen to the words. Then, pose a discussion question, or ask, "What stays with you from the song?" At the end of the discussion, play the song again.

"THERE'S ALWAYS SOMETHING YOU CAN DO" (p. 21)

1. Say, "Tell about a time you felt angry or upset and what you did." Ask pairs to discuss the question first.

2. Next, class members write their responses on paper.

3. Meet as a whole class. Pass a "talking stone" for the speaker to hold. This custom is based on Native American traditions. By having the speaker designated, interruptions are discouraged. An interesting rock, shell, or special object will work.

Debbie commented, "I use this song to address a basic problem for children. When they hold their feelings in, the feelings often come out indirectly through acting out behavior or holding in behavior. Children remember the melody and bring the song home."

AGES: 2nd–6th

FOCUS: Listen to a recording to initiate discussion

MATERIALS: Selected songs

"TALK IT OUT" (p. 98)

1. Arrange students in groups of three. Use an icebreaker to encourage communication skills: ask students to complete the sentence, "If my shoes could talk, they'd tell you that I _____."

b. *Brainstorm:* "What are some reasons why a person would like never to talk out a conflict?" This allows students to express fears: for example, that someone will make fun of them, that the problem will get worse.

c. Explain that the song was written in a cajun style and performed by a zydeco band called "The Barnstormers." Play a recording of the song or learn it from the transcription. Ask students to think about why the songwriter chose a fast style of music for the lyrics.

d. Discuss in small groups first. "Why do you think the friends didn't want to talk out the problem? Why did they change their mind? What situations in your own life did the song remind you of?"

e. Explain that the songwriter said, "I wanted the music to show the anxiety people feel when they are dealing with conflicts. I felt the accordian, electric guitar, and trap drums would convey the fast heartbeat we get when we're upset, and then the excitement of breaking through fear to talk out the problem."

f. In two facing lines, act out the song with partners.

Resources: Andrea Stone's *Sharing Thoughts* includes "Courage" by Bob Blue, "Two Good Legs" by Patricia Shih, "Tell the World" by Joanne Hammil and "Under One Sky" by Ruth Pelham, and is available from the Discovery Center. "Talk It Out" is on the recording *Magical Earth* (Resources, p. 169).

TALK IT OUT

© 1993 words and music by Sarah Pirtle, Discovery Center Music, BMI

I'm so an-gry I can't see straight. I'm mad as a bull break-in down a gate.

You and I are in this fight, got-ta find a way to set things right.

Chorus: Talk it out, I don't wan-na do it, talk it out. Do I haf-ta go through it?

Talk it out, there is no doubt, got-ta jump back, come back, talk it out.

Verse 2

I walked up to talk to you,
But you turned your head.
What can I do? I try to talk and you run away,
Gotta jump back, hear me out today.

Chorus

Talk it out. You don't wanna do it.
Talk it out. You have to go through it.
Talk it out. There is no doubt.
Gotta jump back, come back, talk it out.

Talk it out. I'm gonna burst.
Talk it out. Do I have to talk first?

Talk it out. There is no doubt.
Gotta jump back, come back, talk it out.

Verse 3

I didn't give up, I said "Come on,
This fight's been going on too long."
"I know," you said, and you nearly cried.
Jump back, come back, we both tried.

Chorus

Talk it out. Talk to me.
Talk it out. Now I see.
Talk it out. You're my friend.
Jump back, come back, friends again.

❋ ACTIVITY ❋

WRITING CONFLICT RESOLUTION SONGS

PROCEDURE

1. Think about recent social problems and concerns in your class and use these as a basis for songwriting.

2. Ask an interesting question to begin the writing.

3. Encourage students to talk about the topic and from this create a "seed" for the song: a chorus, a first verse, or sentence starters for a song pattern.

4. Talk about what kind of tune would fit the content and mood of the song. Should it be slow or fast? Think of an existing tune and try your words with it.

5. Make up more words using the pattern set by the tune.

THE DO-OVER SONG

Example: A third-grade class in Bellows Falls, Vermont wanted to focus upon friends arguing and not knowing how to make up. Together we came up with this question: What if we had "do-overs" in friendships the way we had "do-overs" in kickball and other games?

Here's what they wrote:

I've been really mad at you
I've been mad for a long, long, time.
But I can remember
when you were a friend of mine.

The group wanted a slow tune. They found that the tune for "Go Tell Aunt Rhody" fit the mood and the first words they created made a first verse. They added this second verse:

Does it matter anymore
what made us so mad?
When our fight goes on and on
It makes me really sad.

Chorus:

Let's have a do over, Let's make a do over.
I want a do over. Be my friend again.

Option: Write more verses to the "Do Over" song using the tune "Go Tell Aunt Rhody."

AGES: K–6th

FOCUS: Address the problems most important to the class through writing

MATERIALS: Chart paper, writing paper, pencils

PROBLEM SOLVING IN COOPERATIVE GROUPS

1. *Creating a Boat: Write a Song to Set Group Rules.* Ask a group of 3–4 students to create a boat together, a situation where students need to make decisions. First, each person picks the role they want, even if it means more than one captain. Plan ways to interact:

   ◆ Make a steering wheel that the captain steers.

   ◆ Be a sail that the captain adjusts by pulling the line.

   ◆ Form a rotating motor or a rudder to move.

2. Next, each group gets a turn showing their boat. Then discuss and evaluate the process by songwriting.

   ◆ *Tune:* "Hello Everybody, Yes Indeed" by Charity Bailey.

   ◆ *Question:* "What are the steps to follow when you're trying to make a decision fairly in a small group?"

   ◆ *Pattern:* When you make a decision in a group, in a group, in a group, When you make a decision in a group, don't leave anyone out.

   ◆ *Verses:* from Karen Schweitzer's first and grade class in Williamsburg, Massachusetts. Zip these words into the pattern, repeating words to form the verse.

   Each person gets to choose their part.
   Make sure there's room for everyone.
   Put ideas together. Use a part from each person.
   Don't forget to check if you want to make a change.

Karen comments, "This game is important for conflict resolution because every core issue that individuals have comes out, like 'will my voice be heard?' Here they are listened to and receive help with their issue." Play the game again of creating a boat shape. Let children pick new roles. Use the song as a reminder of the group agreements to follow.

NEW IDEAS FOR SONGS

ANGER SONG

◆ *Tune:* "She'll Be Coming Round the Mountain."

◆ *Questions:* "What does anger feel like to you? What is a wise thing you can do when you're angry to help yourself listen to what's upsetting for you?"

◆ *Pattern:*
 When I feel angry I _____ (2x)
 I'm as mad as a volcano/and I feel like a tornado
 But I guess I'll try _____.

BEING FAIR AT RECESS

◆ *Tune:* "He's Got the Whole World in His Hands"

◆ *Chorus:*
 We've got a place to belong in our school. (3x)
 We won't leave anyone out.

◆ *Questions:* "What game do lots of children like to play at recess? What things do you need to do and think about so that each person is treated fairly?"

◆ *Pattern:*
 If we play _____ [name of a game]
 everyone can play.
 [For the next lines list two things you can do to include people in the game.]
 That's a fair way to play _____[name of game].

◆ Example from M.J. Long's second-grade class in Williamsburg, Massachusetts:
 If we play basketball, everyone can play.
 We'll teach all of the kids the rules.
 Each team gets the same amount of players.
 That's a fair way to play basketball.

CONSTRUCTIVE COMMUNICATION

◆ *Tune:* "I've Been Working on the Railroad"

◆ *Question:* What actions can you take when you want to solve a conflict?

◆ *Pattern:*
 I've been working on this conflict all the livelong day.
 And I really want to solve it, can you think of a way?

I could _____ I could _____
I could _____ I guess I'll ____.
Chorus:
 Don't let the conflict go, don't let the conflict grow,
 Don't let the conflict blow your sta-a-ack.(Repeat.)

PEOPLE GROW AND CHANGE

◆ *Tune:* "When the Saints Go Marching In."

◆ *Chorus:*
 People can change, people can change.
 Oh, yes I know, people can change.
 And I want to be in that number.
 I know people can change.

◆ *Verse questions:* What are ways you've changed physically? What are ways you've changed your opinions, behaviors, or habits?

◆ *Verse pattern:* Don't use rhymes — keep emphasis on the content.
 We all change, oh, yes it's true.
 And I'll tell one way to you.
 I used to ____, but now ____.

SENDING A MESSAGE

◆ *Tune:* Pick the tune of a popular song, for example, "What the World Needs Now," music by Burt Bacharach.

◆ *Question:* Who is a person you want to communicate with? Who would you like to send a message to? (For example, parent, lost friend, family member, the world.)

◆ *Pattern:* Create a pattern to fit the tune. Use sentence starters such as these:
 If I could talk to ____, I'd say ____.
 I wish you knew ____.
 I want you to understand ____.
 Sometimes I feel ____.
 Verse written by 7th grader:
 If I could really talk to my parents.
 I'd say I wish that you'd try to understand me more.
 Sometimes I feel like a tiny pebble
 Waiting on a beach.

For Cooperative Songwriting: Take the pattern of one song and create a worksheet that provides blanks where students can write in new words.

HOW TO MAKE YOUR CONFLICT RESOLUTION PLAN

WE FORM our internal map of constructive communication both with our minds and with our hearts. It is not a process of memorization so much as a process of experience. Through experiences with caring adults and friends, a student has the opportunity to realize:

- *When I start to scream, the tension increases.*
- *When I call names, the situation gets worse.*

They build memories of what helps:

- *When I tell what I'm feeling, it's easier for people to listen to me then if I'm screaming at them or calling them names.*
- *When I look at the person and really intend for us to solve this, we find a way.*

Classroom lessons supplemented with experiments in real life help create a bank of concrete experiences that the student can draw upon as the need arises.

This chapter presents lessons where students can practice basic skills like sharing, using "I messages," and brainstorming solutions. A general framework for understanding constructive communication is useful.

WAYS TO PRESENT A FRAMEWORK

Select the words that work best for you and your class:

1. A contrast of worse and better:

- What makes the problem worse?
- What makes the problem better?

Example of how to use this: A child is needling a friend. The friend is getting upset. You ask the child: Is what you are doing making your situation worse or better?

2. A continuum of open and closed:

- What opens communication?
- What closes communication?

Example of how to use this: In a role play, the actors show a problem between students at recess. You ask the ob-servers, "What could the characters say and do now to open communication between them?"

3. Paying attention to sending social messages:

- When we talk, we send a message. Sometimes people send nonverbal messages with their faces and with their body language.

Example of how to use this: A child is teasing another. The second child doesn't want to be teased and is conveying this by a worried facial expression and by body language of shrinking back. Ask the person who is teasing: what message is this child sending you? Can you show that you get the message?

4. Choosing what makes a conflict smaller, not larger:

Sue Liedl, a conflict management coordinator in Bemidji Minnesota, draws two contrasting thermometers on two charts and provides these summaries:

- A conflict gets bigger when you:
  1. Say "you."
  2. Don't listen.
  3. Work for win/lose.
  The mercury in this thermometer is rising high.

- A conflict gets smaller when you:
  1. Say "I feel"
  2. Listen.
  3. Work for win/win.
  The mercury in this thermometer is getting lower.

Example of how to use this: Post these summaries on a wall chart and refer to them during the day when a problem arises: "It looks like the mercury in the thermometer is going up on that problem. Take a look at the wall chart to see what can help it go down again."

Conflict resolution programs all over the country have devised different ways of describing negotiation methods, but they share common elements. Although each situation is unique, here is a general sequence that applies to most problem-solving methods:

We agree to meet and take turns talking. We hear each other, and by listening to feelings, concerns, and needs, we become better able to think clearly as to what the conflict is about. Sometimes by listening to each other, we gain new insights or find more facets to the problem. Then, as we identify what the problem is, we focus on ways of solving it. We consider different options and weigh what works for all concerned, until we can select a solution beneficial for all, a "win/win solution."

Every conflict resolution trainer has developed her or his key phrases to describe this process, drawing upon models available all over the country. Why are there so many variations? This is because each one of us has to get "inside" the subject matter and make our own meaning of it based on our own experiences, just has children have to live the material to fully understand it.

ENCOURAGE STUDENTS TO NEGOTIATE

1. Provide a Basic Format.

Sue Liedl simplifies the procedure like this:

◆ *What do you feel?*

◆ *What is your side of the story?*

◆ *What do you want next time?*

Children use this pattern: *I feel _____ when _____ and next time _____.* Sue has made use of the structure of an "I statement" and has added the phrase "next time" to give a clear focus for a new plan.

Craft the words you want in your basic format using phrases that fit the language of your students. Post the steps on a chart, and add illustrations or photographs of students in your class negotiating together.

2. Create a Setting That Encourages Negotiation.

You can designate a Peace Place or Peace Table, or make that concept portable. As a classroom teacher, William Kriedler kept a rug or bathmat rolled up. Children would unroll it and sit on it to talk out a problem. Special talk-it-out pillows can serve the same function.

3. Provide Concrete Materials for Talking Together.

Have a method available to facilitate taking turns talking: talking stones, of talk-it-out animals to hold. I suggest two stuffed bears for early childhood classrooms so that both the talker and listener have something to hold.

4. Provide Concrete Materials That Help Students Carry Out Their Plan.

If students decide to each take a turn with something they both want, they will need a way to measure how long each turn will take. Provide a timer for students to hold. When the sand runs out of a sand timer, or when five minutes are up on a clock timer, they will know when they switch. Provide a special penny to flip.

ADULT-FACILITATED NEGOTIATION

It is often difficult for peers to talk out a problem without assistance from mediators or adults unless they have already participated in many adult- or peer mediator-led negotiations. Think about when you can be available to help negotiate problems. *Options:* (a) students sign up to meet with you during certain times of the day, or (b) you are available on the spot for brief negotiations. *(Resource:* See Barbara Porro's book, *Talk It Out: Conflict Resolution in the Elementary Classroom,* Association for Supervision and Curriculum Development, 1996.)

Make a chart in your own words to describe the negotiation process you want your students to use. As you select words, you'll find that you understand the process better.

Here is a detailed description for you to simplify. Picture each of these stages, create logical steps, and decide how you want to formulate the steps into appropriate words:

Stages of Talking Together

◆ Students meet face-to-face and agree to talk constructively. Sometimes they agree at the start to take turns, and not to use put-downs, hitting, yelling or blaming.

◆ Students take turns telling what they experience. They air their feelings so they can think more clearly. They speak for themselves using "I messages" to communicate their feelings, needs, and concerns. Sometimes they paraphrase each other to make it clear that they hear each viewpoint.

◆ They focus on the problem and what they want to have happen next. They notice if there are several parts of the problem that need to be solved. They devise solutions that will provide what they need. They react to each other's ideas and evaluate: are they doable? Do they address the needs of all involved?

◆ They agree to a plan and talk over how to carry it out. They make sure that the first step is clear. Sometimes they write down the plan.

◆ They do the plan together.

ACTIVITY

Conflict Book

Photographs and captions

GRADES: PreK–6th

FOCUS: Take posed photographs of conflict resolution and ask students to help write a story

MATERIALS: Camera, paper

PROCEDURE

1. This activity helps introduce the specific methods you have selected to help facilitate negotiation. Meet as a whole class and introduce or review the stages of talking out a problem in the wording you are choosing to use:

a. Decide to talk it out.
b. Meet together face to face.
c. Take turns talking.
d. Ask: What will help?
e. Think of ways to solve the problem.
f. Choose a plan you both like.
g. Carry out the plan.

Stage a role play with another adult, or coach two children through a role play to show that it looks like in action.

2. Ask for two volunteers to pose for photos of a story that shows students in a conflict deciding to use this negotiation procedure. Select a storyline for the book of a common classroom problem your students have encountered.

3. Now, take a sequence of photos to show each step and to model the use of the talk-it-out methods in the classroom.

Example: In an early childhood classroom when children need to talk out a problem, they go to a covered basket containing two identical bears. Each child holds one of the bears to help calm down. For a storyline for the book, choose an object in the room that two children could pretend to want, such as a toy truck. Bring that object to the circle and take a photo of it. Next, have the two children freeze in a posture that shows they both want it—they are both tugging on it. Ask them to pose with pretend angry expressions on their face. Show this argument over a truck negotiated using the talk-it-out bears. The photos illustrate:

1. One child puts up their hand and says, "Wait. Stop."

2. Both children go to find the basket of bears.

3. They sit together on chairs facing each other.

d. One person talks while the other listens.

e. The other person talks while the first person listens.

f. They make an expression that signals they are thinking, "How can we solve this?" — they scratch their heads, or put one finger to their cheek.

g. Thumbs up: They both put their thumbs up to show they've found a plan they both like.

h. For closure, they shake hands.

4. Take two or three photographs illustrating how the solution could be carried out. For instance, let's say the parties have decided to take turns. One person will hold a timer while the other one uses the truck, and then they switch. Add other parts to the story: perhaps they now decide to use the truck together.

5. Frequently, many children will want to pose for the photographs. Bring three rolls of film. Disband the group meeting and take photos of other children while the rest of the class is engaged in free-choice activities.

6. When the photos are developed, paste them in sequence into a book, leaving room for captions. Engage the whole class in deciding how to caption each photograph. This helps them think through the negotiation process.

SOURCE

I created this activity and brought it to Mohawk Nursery School in Shelburne Falls, Massachusetts, directed by Lois Bascom. A wall chart describing the stages of talking out a conflict and a book were made from the photos. Sometimes one child would bring another to the wall chart and say, "This is what we should do." Lois lets each child take the book home for a night. This helps parents learn the methods in use in the classroom.

❋ ACTIVITY ❋

ALWAYS SOMETHING YOU CAN DO

Puppet Role Play

GRADES: K–6th
FOCUS: Use puppets to deal with common classroom problems
MATERIALS: Hand puppets

ORIENTATION

Tell students: "We'll be using puppets to act out common problems that you have. They'll help us explore ways to handle these situations."

PREPARATION

Find as many puppets to use as possible so that every child has one. Make simple puppets by decorating small paper bags or by gluing or sewing eyes on old socks. *Variation:* If you don't have enough puppets for every student, place a pile in the center for common use.

AGREEMENTS

Make a clear agreement that the puppets aren't for hitting and fighting. If a child punches with a puppet, give a reminder, "We've agreed that these puppets are for solving problems and not making problems worse." Ask, "Can you stop yourself or do you need help stopping?" If the child continues to punch, say, "I see that you do need help stopping. Please take the puppet off for a moment and give it a rest."

WARM-UP

Sending a Message: Set up a very simple role play that requires a brief response. *Younger students:* One puppet will be in a silly mood and will reach out to tickle the other. The second puppet doesn't want to be tickled. Brainstorm what recommended words or actions will send the message: body language like raising a hand to say stop, or words such as, "I don't like that," "Stop," or "I don't want to be tickled." *Older students:* Choose a challenging situation, like one puppet saying, "Give me some of your snack," but the other puppet not wanting to. How can each stay firm without retreating or becoming aggressive? Brainstorm responses. Here are three ways to facilitate this role play:

1. The teacher takes one puppet and goes up to each student,

one at a time, doing the problematic behavior — tickling, or asking for food — while the student responds constructively.

2. The class watches one pair of students at a time act out the problem.

3. Students stand in two "hassle" lines, facing their partners. One line does the problematic behavior while the partners in the opposite line practice responding by sending a constructive message. The role plays take place simultaneously (Hassle lines, p. 106).

PROCEDURE

1. Pick a problem that is important to the class. *Example:* Two friends at recess discover each wants to do different things.

2. Ask pairs of students to make the problem specific. Decide what each of the characters they represent wants to do at recess. If they aren't wearing puppets, ask them to plan which puppet from the common pile they will put on. *Example:* "I'm the turtle and I want to slide down the slide. I'm the bird and I want to swing."

3. As a class, brainstorm all the different types of solutions. Record each possibility on the board or on newsprint. If a person gives a general suggestion, like "share" or "switch," ask them to be specific — how would that work? Nine ways to solve the problem are listed here:

a. "At one recess we'll do what person #1 wants and the

next recess what person #2 wants."

b. "We'll spend some time doing what each of us wants to do; we'll ask the recess teacher when half of recess is over and switch then."

c. "We'll spend some time doing what each of us wants to do: we'll start with what person #1 wants, and switch when person #2 asks."

d. "We'll figure out a number of times to do each activity and that will tell us when to switch. For instance, we'll slide three times and then swing ten times."

e. "We'll choose a third activity to do together."

f. "We'll both join another group and play what they are playing."

g. "One person will agree to do what the other wants to do."

h. "We won't play together today but we'll agree we're still friends, and we'll eat lunch together."

i. "We won't play together today but we will tomorrow."

4. After hearing the brainstorm, each pair discusses how their puppet characters will resolve the problem. Ask them to pick one specific method from the list of choices. Next, practice acting out (a) what the problem is, (b) how they talk about it, and (c) what plan they make. If pairs don't have puppets, they hold their hands like puppets and rehearse.

5. Watch each puppet play. Listeners identify which solution is being demonstrated. The following are sample problems for skits:

◆ *Mistaken accusation.* "You have my pencil."—two pencils look alike.

◆ *Name calling.* Select an epithet that is problematic but not off-color, like "you're a baby," or "you're stupid."

◆ *Friends and loyalty.* You are sitting at a table at lunch and someone from another table throws a hot dog bun at your best friend.

◆ *Dealing with annoying behavior.* You are starting a math quiz when the person behind you grabs your pencil.

◆ *Family.* Your brother offers to feed your pet fish while you are away. When you come home the fish is dead.

6. Add music if you like. See page 21 for the lyrics and transcription of the song, "There's Always Something You Can Do."

CLOSING

Sing "Kumbaya." Make up verses with the different emotions:
> "Someone's angry my friend Kumbaya (3X)
> oh dear friend, Kumbaya."
> "Someone's crying my friend Kumbaya (3X)
> oh dear friend, Kumbaya."

Create hand motions or use American Sign Language.

EXTENSIONS

◆ *The Problem Puppets — What Will Help:* Designate two special puppets and call them the Problem Puppets. Bill Kreidler shares this custom, which he learned from teacher Kathy Allen in Lincoln, Massachusetts. Present a specfic problem using the puppets. For instance, let's say you are using a monkey and a raccoon puppet. "Monkey is trying to learn to use words instead of hitting or pushing. Monkey was running in from the playground and look what happened." "Show monkey being pushed by raccoon." "How does monkey feel? What could monkey do?" Play out the suggestions made by the class.

◆ *Puppets Practice Skills.* Focus on a specific tool or method and ask pairs to use that tool with a problem. For instance:

◆Use an "I message."

◆Respond by listening. Say to the person who is upset, "Tell me more."

◆Restate their words so that they know you understand, and then tell your own feelings and thoughts.

◆Make a request.

◆Use friendly talk to help yourself make good choices.

Example: Review the main concept you have selected, "When I'm upset, I can stop and think." Provide a scenario: "You are getting in line. Someone has just pushed you. Show with your face how you might feel. Now, stop and think. What could you do? What would be a good choice. Let's show with puppets what it looks like when somebody stops to think what to do."

◆ *Puppet Shows for Younger Classes:* Bring your puppet plays to a younger classroom to teach specific skills. At St. Philip's School in Bemidji, Minnesota, a third-grade class worked with parent volunteer Janet Rith to create puppet shows for the first grade. These showed animal puppets interacting with an animal who is bullying the others.

SHARKS, TURTLES, AND KANGAROOS

Conflict Resolution Unit

BACKGROUND

When you approach a conflict do you attack like a shark? Retreat like a turtle? Or jump in with a readiness to engage? We have the capacity to act in all these different ways. In a sense each of us has a shark, a turtle and a kangaroo inside ourselves and many more approaches as well. If we habitually act like a shark or a turtle, we are stuck, and a first step is to become aware of different choices. Through role plays we can become more familiar with our habits and with our options.

In the 1980s Gail Sadalla and the Community Board Program in San Francisco showed other conflict resolution trainers the potential of using animals to symbolize different styles of handling conflict. (See Resources, p. 169)

ANIMAL METAPHORS

Sue Liedl, from Bemidji, Minnesota, uses animal puppets in conflict role plays. Following the five animals suggested by Community Board, she brings five puppets to classrooms: a shark who confronts, a turtle who avoids, a monkey who distracts, a teddy bear who compromises and goes along, and an owl who problem-solves. Children hold one of the puppets and invent the words that animal might say.

Another approach is to discuss the different stances like aggression or withdrawal and ask students to decide of all the animals that exist which they would select to symbolize that attitude. Which one will designate combative communication? Which one will represent hiding and avoiding? Which will stand for engaged problem-solving? It's important to bring cultural awareness in because various animals have different meanings from culture to culture. For instance, to an Iroquois child, a turtle would not represent avoidance, but rather strength and persistence.

Once in my graduate "Cooperation and Conflict Resolution" course with elementary schools teachers, the participants selected the Tyrannasaurus Rex for aggressive confrontation and a porcupine for armored defensiveness. "What animal do you want to use to represent problem-

solving?" I asked. A Brattleboro, Vermont teacher, Margaret Dale Barrand, suggested the kangaroo. She observed that kangaroos are vigorous, eager, confident and have pouches ready with extra supplies. When a shark or T Rex, is roaring angry, the kangaroo responds: "Hey! Will you talk to me about this?" The kangaroo jumps in eagerly, "We'll find a way to solve this together."

I have brought the image I learned from Margaret Dale Barrand to many classrooms and teacher trainings since. The emblem has stuck. There is something captivating about the vigor. At the start the kangaroo may not know the exact words it wants to say, but it jumps in with a positive attitude and finds those words. In this "Shark, Turtle, and Kangaroo Role Play" activity, students try on the same situation from the three different positions symbolized by the animals. This helps them gain insight as to which of the approaches feels most familiar. If the attitude of a kangaroo is new, they are challenged to contact this approach and try on new behavior. For example, one teacher in a training caught herself becoming indirect when she tried to be a kangaroo. She said, "I wanted to flatter the person so they would listen to me. I told them I liked what they were doing when I didn't really like it because I was afraid." As we repeated the role play she experimented with being direct.

Students like to watch what happens when a kangaroo stands up to a shark. Will the kangaroo get through? Experimenting in role plays, we watch how over and over the kangaroo's persistent respectful way of speaking calls forward the kangaroo within the other person as well. Students report that when they are doing the role play from the shark position, they shift as they face a kangaroo. The kangaroo's positive attitude is infectious. In each person there is that kangaroo capacity, that ability to problem-solve and engage together. If we expect the other person to be a shark and stay a shark, we block their kangaroo side from leaping up. If we treat the other person respectfully and speak concretely about what what we need, making requests instead of demands, we may engage their caring side.

Once the kangaroo image is clear, ask students to identify people they know who are kangaroos. Discuss famous peacemakers: Martin Luther King, Gandhi, Jane Addams and other Nobel Peace Prize winners. Look at community heroes like the Guardian Angels in urban neighborhoods and subways. Highlight people they know who are role models like neighbors, teachers, grandparents, scout leaders, and camp counselors.

I'll find a way to talk this out.
I'll jump in like a kangaroo.
I'll talk from my heart and turn this about.
There's always something I can do.

❋ A C T I V I T Y ❋

HASSLE LINES
Shark, Turtle and Kangaroo Role Play

O V E R V I E W

Hassle lines refers to two facing lines where students do a role play with the person opposite them. This method was developed by leaders of nonviolence training. When all students are in a simultaneous role play, it reduces embarrassment. Standing in two facing lines also gives the teacher a chance to monitor how the interactions are going. Before you begin, establish a Zero Noise Signal (p. 60) such as a bell that will call for silence.

P R O C E D U R E

Introduce the format first as a creative dramatics activity. Ask students to shake hands with their partners in a friendly way. This clarifies who is working together, and it gives a quick check on self-control. Intervene if students squeeze hands hard. Establish that students in one line will be people working at a restaurant. Each student's partner in the facing line is coming to the restaurant to order his or her favorite sandwich.

1. *Scene A: Ordering Food.* Patrons order a sandwich they really enjoy. The waitperson takes the order, fixes the sandwich, and then serves it. The patron eats it. When the sequence is complete, sound the Zero Noise Signal and discuss how the scene went. Once the basic method of simultaneous role play is familiar, add an element of conflict.

2. *Scene B: Overload on the Job.* Switch roles. Add more elements. The people in the first line are the patrons now. Each plays the part of someone with a big appetite. He or she is the last customer of the day and the waitperson is very tired. The customer keeps ordering more and more food. When the waitperson becomes exhausted, ask the group to show the people talking with each other about this problem in a fair way. Again, use the zero-noise signal to end this sequence. Keep it going as long as it is productive.

Ask for volunteers to demonstrate what they did, and distinguish between fair and unfair ways for the two characters to communicate.

Use the restaurant example to specify the differences between three styles of behavior. Discuss and ask volunteers to demonstrate how the waitperson would act:

◆ as a shark — say angrily, "Stop bugging me!"

◆ as a turtle — say nothing but sigh heavily.

◆ as a kangaroo — describes feelings and how they experience the situation, "I want to help you get the food you want, but I'm very tired. You're my last customer." Then make a request like, "Could you make this your last order?"

How would the customer act:

◆ as a shark? Say, "Hurry up. You're so slow. I want my order now."

◆ as a turtle? Feel hungry but not order more food.

◆ as a kangaroo? Describe feelings and needs, and request, don't demand. "I notice that it's near closing time. I'm really hungry. Could I order more food?"

Once the differences are clear, use the hassle line format to try out the three stances. One person in each pair will repeat the same situation three times. Each time they will do it from a different approach: as a shark, as a turtle, and then as a kangaroo. Go now to a role play that involves a student conflict.

3. *Keeping Clothes Clean.* Scenario: Two students are sharing paints. They paint across the table from each other during an art lesson.

  ◆ *Line 1, Person A.* You are dressed in your best clothes. You have been asked to keep them clean all day because you'll be going somewhere special after school (for example, getting a photo taken, going to a relative's house).

  ◆ *Line 2, Person B.* Art is your favorite activity. With great exhuberance you fling the paint on the paper and it starts to splash. Give Person B a specific line to begin the scene. This will be repeated three times. They say each time: "I love painting!" and then actively splash with their brush.

1. Person A, as a shark, communicates concern that his or her clothes will get splattered by Person B. When the talking is too loud, end the scene with the zero-noise signal, and ask students what that was like.

2. Say, *"We will wind the camera back and begin the same situation."* This time Person A is a turtle. Person B initiates the scene with their opening line. End the scene after a few moments, and discuss.

3. Review the characteristics of a kangaroo — finding a fair way to talk, using caring language, speaking with "I feel" instead of blaming "you" language, making requests instead of demands. Again, rewind the camera and begin the scene as if the other two versions had not happened. Watch the action and look for students who are particularly successful. Ask them to demonstrate afterward what they said.

Draw out the students in the role of Person B: What is it like to face a shark? a turtle? a kangaroo?

4. *Scene D: Friends Disagree.* Switch roles. Designate the other person as the one who tries the position of shark, turtle, and kangaroo.

Scenario: Two friends are planning what they want to do together on Saturday and discover they have very different interests.

◆ *Line 1:* The fixed character initiates the action by saying, "Look, the only thing I want to do is _____." This actor can decide what that is.

◆ *Line 2:* This actor selects a different preference, expressing it first as a shark, then as a turtle, and finally as a kangaroo.

Give time before the role play for each pair of actors to create a context. Does one of them have a hurt foot and doesn't want to play active sports? Have they often done a particular activity together? This final scene is selected to simulate a real experience they might encounter.

Again process each phase of the role play and ask for volunteers to show examples of kangaroo speech.

EXTENSION

The function of a role play is not to produce immediate behavior changes but to present alternatives which students can practice. Through experimentation with new behavior, it becomes possible to transfer it to real life. Other role play methods:

◆ *Stop in the Middle:* A small group acts out a problem for the class. They stop and seek suggestions from the au-

dience for how they could resolve it. The actors choose which of the proposals they want to try. One way to set this up is to divide the whole class into small groups designing a problem to be solved. Make it clear that actors can't touch or shove each other. Physical encounters have to be portrayed without actual contact.

◆ *Role Reversal:* Provide a scenario with two characters, for example, one student likes to play-fight and fool around. A friend is concerned that if the two of them fool around, they will get into a real fight.

Try the roles for a moment, but specify not to touch the other actor. Now reverse roles. Afterward, talk about what each role felt like.

◆ *Adults Model Constructive Behavior:* Take a real incident you have observed and portray it with another adult to help students gain perspective.

�֍ ACTIVITY �֍

CHOOSE YOUR OWN PEACEMAKER ANIMAL

PROCEDURE

1. *Discuss animal behavior:* All animals have methods of protecting themselves. All animals have ways to communicate. They don't attack for the sake of attack. Animals use attacking behavior when they are hunting for food or to warn others to move away from their home or their babies. Ask students to name an animal and then clarify how it sets boundaries and communicates.

2. Next, list the qualities and specific behavior of peacemakers. How do peacemakers act? What do peacemakers do? How do they feel inside?

3. Ask each student to think what animal would help them remind them of their own ability to be a peacemaker. What animal will help you make the choices that a peacemaker makes? Let the selection be very individual; a student might choose a tiger to emphasize strength, or a dolphin to represent friendliness and flexibility, or a hawk for vision and perspective.

4. Anchor the choice through drawing or journalling. Then provide time for students to share their animals and their reasons if they choose.

✳ ACTIVITY ✳
TWO KINDS OF POWER

SOURCE

This activity was created by Maggie Carlson from Bemidji, Minnesota, with additions by Candy Roberts, also from Bemidji, who offers another way to present it.

ORIENTATION

Tell students: "Today we look at two different kinds of power."

PROCEDURE

1. *The Hammer:* "Here is one kind of power." Take out a hammer hidden in a bag and process the students' reactions. Ask, "What kinds of words or actions have the power of a hammer?" *Examples:* "Make me!", "Go away!", "I hate you!", hitting, kicking, pushing.

2. *The Light:* If we wanted to change ice, we could crack it with a hammer, but how could we change it without the use of this kind of force? Discuss the power of heat and light. What words or actions have the power of light? *Examples:* "Let's talk about this," "That's not okay with me," "How can we change this?", talking, listening, asking, stating how you feel.

Discuss: Who on television uses the power of a hammer? Who is a person you know that uses the power of light? Related activity: "The Web of Human Unity" (p. 159) distinguishes power-over from power-with.

Variation: Candy Roberts starts this activity simply by setting up a lamp and shining it on ice. She leaves this without explanation. Then she brings out the hammer. Usually the students back away, and she helps them explore their negative reaction. All this is done before talking about power. Next, Candy hits the ice with a hammer. Now, students are directed to the melting ice, as she asks, "What happened to the ice under the lamp?" Finally, she poses the question, "If someone was trying to change you, which way would you want them to use — like the light or like the hammer?"

3. *Role Play:* Tell the group, "Let's have a chance to compare the two kinds of power. I'm going to pretend that I'm a person who uses my fists everytime I want something. I'm out

GRADES: 3rd–6th
FOCUS: Comprehend personal power that is different than aggressive force
MATERIALS: hammer hidden in a bag

at recess, and I want to be team captain of the recess game, but I've already been captain for two weeks. How can you talk to me about being fair? I'm going to ask you to try to help me change."

"Try first using power like a hammer." Bring up volunteers to work with you or ask the whole class to work on the problem simultaneously. "What do you notice when you hammer at me?"

"Now help me change using the power of the light." Encourage the group to work with you from the direction of the second kind of power. "How did I react differently when you approached me with the power of light?"

EXTENSIONS

Read or tell the Norwegian folk tale, "The Sun and the Wind," which recounts a struggle between the sun and the wind to see which is the more powerful. They both try to get a traveler to take off his coat. The wind uses forceful blowing but it doesn't work. The sun succeeds by shining. Act out the story with your class.

Sing the song, "This Little Light of Mine," a traditional African American gospel song.

Chorus:

This little light of mine, I'm gonna to let it shine. (3x)
Let it shine, let it shine, let it shine.
1. Everywhere I go, I'm gonna let it shine.
2. All around this world, I'm gonna let it shine.
3. All around this class, I'm gonna let it shine.

✳ ACTIVITY ✳

"YOU MADE ME"

ORIENTATION

Tell students: "Have you ever heard someone say to another person, 'You make me mad'? When we're upset, we want to do something about it, but blaming and fighting language shuts down conversation. Today we are going to work on using 'I feel' language instead."

PROCEDURE

1. *Question:* What Is a Trigger?

   a. Make a list of situations that aren't necessarily dangerous but some people find upsetting. *Examples:* seeing a spider, hearing thunder, seeing a scary movie, being startled by a friend as a joke, suddenly encountering a tall person.

   Explain what the word *trigger* means. When a person is triggered, something in the present reminds them of a situation in the past that may have been unpleasant, confusing or actually threatening. This sudden association is unconscious and may call up present-day feelings of fear, nervous laughter, or anger and a desire to defend oneself.

   b. Use the example of a clown to discuss the different ways the same event can trigger different people. Help the class meet in small groups. Ask the students to describe how they feel when they see a clown now and how they felt at other ages. "What does the sight of a clown falling down trigger for you? When you see a clown, do you usually laugh? Do you have no particular reaction? Can you remember a time when the sight of a clown triggered feelings? What were those feelings?" As you reconvene, compare different responses.

   c. Introduce students to the process of noticing when they feel triggered for anger or fear. What body signals let them know they are upset? People have different reactions to feeling triggered, and our work is to respond constructively and help ourselves. Here are helpful quesrions that you can teach a child to use for reflection: Am I in danger right now? Am I in a safe place? Is there anything I need to do to feel safer? Is there anything I need to say?

GRADES: 4th and up

FOCUS: Help children switch from blaming language to owning their feelings and expressing their requests.

MATERIALS: Props for skit: spider, math test paper and sweatshirt. Two copies of the script.

Note: When a child has been mistreated, a variety of circumstances — such as loud voices, sudden actions, tall people, finding classroom furniture rearranged — can be triggering. Notice the triggers for students in your class and provide extra attention to help them feel safe.

2. *"You Made Me" Skit* . Explain that the skit will show three ways a person was triggered and the efforts he or she makes to communicate constructively. Show the scripts to two students and give them a chance to study the words. Make sure they understand that the words in parentheses are silent stage directions. Give Person 1 three props: (a) a bag hiding a paper spider, rubber toy spider or spider puppet, (b) a math test with "Excellent" or "100%" written on it, and (c) a sweatshirt to carry or wear.

3. *Discussion.* Review the skit and ask the class to identify the three things that were triggering for Person 2. Discuss how Person 2 could use "I Statements." Frame the language to communicate constructively.

I Statement (see p. 112):

I feel _____
when _____
because _____
and what I'd like is _____.

Use this format to frame messages about the spider, about the math test, and about the identical sweatshirt.

Note: Feel free to photocopy this script.

"You Made Me" Script

SETTING: School playground waiting for school to start.

PERSON 1: Hi, I found something really neat on the way to school. Would you like to see it?

PERSON 2: Sure.

PERSON 1: Here it is *(takes out the spider)*.

PERSON 2: *(screams)* Get it away. Spiders make me scared. They give me the creeps.

PERSON 1: I didn't know that.

PERSON 2: Put it away!

PERSON 1: Okay. If you don't want to see it, I won't take it out again *(puts the spider back in the bag)*.

PERSON 2: Don't even bring it to class today. I saw a really scary movie about giant spider when I was five and I've never forgotten it.

PERSON 1: I can understand that. I was thinking of letting it go before school starts.

PERSON 2: Good. Anyway, I wanted to ask you about the math test yesterday. How did you do? Can I see your paper?

PERSON 1: Yeah, I got all the answers right. *(shows the math test paper)*

PERSON 2: You did? I got four wrong. That paper really makes me sick. You always get the answers right.

PERSON 1: *(shrugs)* My brother showed me how to do it and now I like math.

PERSON 2: What's that? *(points to the sweatshirt)*

PERSON 1: A sweatshirt I got last night. *(shows it)*

PERSON 2: I've got the same kind. I wore it yesterday. You make me so mad. You've got the same one as me.

PERSON 1: Wait a second. This is just a piece of cloth. What about it makes you mad? *(holds up paper)* This is just a piece of paper. Why does my doing well in math make you mad?

PERSON 2: I don't know.

PERSON 1: Well, what about this math test?

PERSON 2: *(sighs)* That test was hard. I'm afraid I'll never learn how to do it.

PERSON 1: What would help?

PERSON 2: Would you show me how to do the math sometime like your brother showed you?

PERSON 1: Sure. I can show you right now before class starts. What about this sweatshirt?

PERSON 2: I feel upset when someone has the same clothes as me. Don't wear it at school.

PERSON 1: Let me think about that. *(pauses)* No, I just got this from my grandmother and I wanted to wear it today. I'm still going to wear it.

PERSON 2: No fair! That means you're not my friend!

PERSON 1: No, I'm still your friend. Some things that you ask I'll choose to do, and some I won't choose to do.

PERSON 2: That makes me mad!

PERSON 1: I'm not making you mad. Friends don't have to do everything their friends tell them. I have to think for myself.

PERSON 2: I see what you mean.

PERSON 1: I'd still like to help you with math.

PERSON 2: Right now?

PERSON 1: Sure, after I let this spider go.

✳ ACTIVITY ✳
HEART STATEMENTS
Role Plays

ORIENTATION

Tell students: "This week we'll study what it feels like to handle problems by expressing what you feel and what you need."

PROCEDURE

1. *Clarifying the Skill:* Tell students: "When you want to respond to what is happening, you can reach for the word, 'I.' You can tell others what is going on for you."

Some people call this "using I statements" or doing an "I to I." Marshall Rosenberg from Texas calls it "using the language of the heart." Inspired by his work, here we will call these "Heart Statements."

Explain the framework of a Heart Statement:

I feel ___ ("name the feeling")

when ___ ("describe what is going on")

because ___ ("express how this affects you")

and what I'd like is ___ ("make a request, describe what action you would like")

2. *Comparing the Two Outlooks:* Help students experience the physical contrast between the two outlooks: a blaming or defensive approach and a heart-centered approach. Make agreements first not to touch anyone else during this silent role play.

◆ First, tell students: "Let's begin with blaming and defensiveness. Hunch your shoulders. Look around like you are prepared for someone to attack you with their words. Put your pointing finger out. You're ready to defend yourself. Look around like you are finding an attacker — 'You did it,' 'You made me angry,' 'Your fault.'"

◆ "Now try on a different outlook. Sit relaxed. Look around and notice different reactions. 'I see this,' and now turn another direction 'And I see that.' Let the sights of the people around you come toward you without any need to be afraid or defend yourself. Again, turn in one direction and then another: 'This situation feels okay,' and then 'I feel upset about this situation and I can

GRADES: 3rd and up

FOCUS: Practice using "I" language

MATERIALS: Paper and pencil for each group

PLANNING: Plan small groups of 3 to 4

handle it.' Each time breathe in a relaxed confident way. Turn back in the first direction, 'I have no particular reactions to this situation,' and in contrast, 'I feel triggered by what is happening. I can speak up. I'll make a request.'"

◆ "Talk with each other. How did each outlook feel? How would you describe your body posture and your breathing each time? Which felt safer?" If students have done the activity, "Our Whale Hearts," (p. 117) refer to it. The second confident stance has the same feeling as the whale heart.

3. *Creating skits:* By presenting a skit, each group will explore their understanding (a) of being triggered or bugged, and (b) of responding using Heart Statements. **Note:** This kind of collaboration takes a great deal of skill. Here is a plan for how you can assist each group step by step. Expect that the process will take two to four practice sessions. Give each small group a chance to do one step before moving to the next phase.

a. *Step One: Planning the skit.* In small groups, ask the students to brainstorm situations, behaviors, or things that bug them. Then ask them to describe the situations without using anyone's name: "Which would be the easiest to portray in a skit? Which would give an opportunity to show people using Heart Statements instead of blaming? Which situation gives enough roles so that each person in the group will have a part?" Ask them not to call out which part they want yet, but wait until later in the process to discuss it. Decide what situation to work with. Have them talk about how they could show the problem situation. Identify which characters are the main characters who are responding to a difficult situation.

b. *Step Two: Taking Parts and Getting into Character.* Each small group works to identify enough parts for the number of people in the group. Include a narrator who will tell the audience where this scene is taking place and any other information that they need to know.

Next, go around the circle, allowing each person to say which part he or she would like, even if another person has said that role. Now, after hearing all the preferences, find a fair way to decide which part each person will take.

Try out the basic conflict. Ask: "How should your scene begin? Start working with the scene and exploring the dialogue that you might use."

Help students get into their characters. Work with them in small groups or as a whole class. Ask: "How does your character walk when he/she is happy? How does your character look when she/he is angry? How does this person express anger? What parts of resolving conflicts are they good at?"

c. *Step Three: Planning on paper or out loud*

1. Identify words the characters would use if they responded to the problem using blaming or other forms of unconstructive language.

2. Identify what words the characters could use responding with a Heart Statement. Fill in the pattern on the sheet of paper or go through the sequence out loud:

> *I feel* _____
> *when* _____
> *because* _____
> *and what I'd like is* _____.

d. *Step Four: Blocking out the Action.* Ask the students to decide how they will show the characters struggling with the problem. Do they use unconstructive behavior at first? Is one character skilled at "I Statements" (Heart language) or do they all together find a way to resolve it? Start by getting back into your characters and try the scene with the Heart Statements in mind.

e. *Step Five: Teacher Feedback.* Review each Heart Statement and meet with any group that needs help revising.

Small groups present their skits to the class first as a work in progress. This allows the teacher to assist each one. Provide help and give each group its next direction to work on — for example, "Could you make it clear that the problem begins with a misunderstanding?"

Or, "Could you work more on the request that your main character is making?"

f. *Step Six: Final Presentations.* To determine if the skits are ready, ask each group:

◆ Does the narrator know how to introduce the skit?

◆ Do you know how the scene begins?

◆ Is there a clear Heart Statement in the skit?

◆ Do you know how the skit ends?

◆ Provide sufficient time for each group to present their work.

C L O S U R E

After each skit is presented, pause to give the actors feedback. Each actor picks one person to make a specific affirmative comment about what they did in the skit.

Ask one person in the audience to identify the complete Heart Statement depicted in the scene.

S O U R C E

Dr. Thomas Gordon, author of many books, including *TET: Teacher Effectiveness Training*, is known for widely disseminating "I Statements" and active listening. He was influenced by the work of Carl Rogers. You can learn about books and trainings by Marshall Rosenberg by contacting The Center for Nonviolent Communication, P.O. Box 2662, Sherman, Texas, 75091 at 903-893-3886. The center has a web site at http://www.cnvc.org.

Additional Note About Heart Language: Students may have parents or other significant people in their life who frequently direct blaming language toward them (for example, "You kids make me crazy"). Help provide perspective: "You might hear adults say words like 'you make me so mad.' 'You statements' are a common habit many people have. But it's a habit that can change. The change I'm teaching you is new for lots of people. After you work on this skill, you may find yourself noticing even more what people say. We can't change other people, and it's not our job to correct them. Each person is in charge of their own learning and growing."

❋ ART ACTIVITY ❋

CONFLICT CARTOONS

PROCEDURE

Prepare paper in four squares and write a heading on top of each square: *1. Argument; 2. Stop and Think; 3. Talk it out; 4. Decide.*

Brainstorm a list of typical conflicts that students encounter at school. Each person selects one situation and draws it, providing four stages of the event. Show students how to use cartoon balloons to add words and thought bubbles for thoughts. For example, a fourth grade student named Shayna showed an argument starting from someone accidentally stepping on a girl's foot. In the second box, both stop and think. In the third section, she discovers it was an accident. In the final box, they each apologize. The first person says "sorry" for the name-calling. They end by saying, "See you tomorrow" to each other.

GRADES: 1st to 8th

FOCUS: Use a cartoon format to help students think about the stages of resolving conflicts.

MATERIALS: paper, markers

SOURCE

Ruth Suyenaga, art teacher in Gardner, Massachusetts, created this activity to accompany a residency on writing songs about conflict resolution. This is a variation of the activity "Comic Strips" in *The Friendly Classroom for a Small Planet, p. 65.*

❋ ART ACTIVITY ❋

PEOPLE CAN CHANGE

PROCEDURE

1. Ask students to brainstorm the changes they have observed in people around them. K to 2nd-grade students can talk about physical changes, ability to do new skills, and their change from hitting to talking out problems. 3rd- to 6th-grade students can also list "Behavior and attitude changes in America in the last 150 years" such as voting rights, civil rights, conflict resolution, and respect for diversity. Talk about the time it takes to make changes.

2. Ask students to brainstorm changes they have experienced: e.g., adjusting to divorce, recovering from an injury, learning how to speak a new language, moving, becoming a mediator.

3. Ask each person to pick the biggest personal change and think about how they could show that change in a drawing. For instance, a fourth-grade girl wanted to illustrate what it was like when her parents got divorced and her father remarried. She drew what her dinner table looked like before and after, and showed that she had to change the chair she

GRADES: K to 8th

FOCUS: Affirm students' ability to change and grow using an art activity.

MATERIALS: Paper, markers.

sat in to make room for her new step-mother.

4. After all students have made their drawings, provide the option to share work with the whole class.

EXTENSIONS

◆ Draw a change that has happened since you were born— a change in your neighborhood, city or town, our country, or the world.

◆ Illustrate a change you'd like to see in the world by drawing what the future would look like if this change were in effect. See "Picturing the Future," (p. 46)

◆ Put ideas in the "People Grow and Change" song (p.

✴ ACTIVITY ✴

FRIENDLY VOICES

OVERVIEW

What is inner speech? According to Chris Brewer, co-author with Don Campbell of *Rhythms of Learning* (Zephyr Press, 1991), inner speech is how we hear ourselves think. In order to develop impulse control, children need to develop inner speech, the ability to hear their own voice inside. This is a skill we are born with, one that is intact by age nine or ten. At six and younger, children experience their thoughts more by saying them than by hearing them inside.

I have taken this concept and added to it the idea of contradicting unhelpful inner voices and setting an affirmative direction. For children who have already internalized negative self concepts, this work can be challenging, but it is one method of assisting them.

ORIENTATION

Tell students: "Do you know what it's like to hear a tiny voice inside, your own voice speaking to you your thoughts? Today we're going to practice listening to that inner voice."

OPENER

Food Words. Say the name of a food many children enjoy, beginning with a word of few syllables: e.g., Progress from "cheese" to "pizza" to "apple pie." Ask for silence in the room. Say one word at a time and ask children to raise their hand if they can hear the word with their inner voice. Progress to more complex words and phrases like "cheese burrito with chicken."

PREPARATION

Now provide longer inner voice sentences which relate to the news of the day or immediate sensations, sentences like, "The wind was cold today," "I can smell lunch cooking in the cafeteria," or "I'm part of a third grade class." Ask students to contribute ideas and hear their words in inner speech.

MAIN ACTIVITY

Tell students: "We are going to practice hearing a friendly voice inside our minds." Provide an affirmative statement and ask children to take a moment to hear it in their inner voice: for example, "I do my best," "In our class everyone is im-

portant," "I have my way of being smart," or "People in this class are glad I'm here."

Ask students to suggest other phrases a friendly voice would say, and work with their affirmations.

CLOSING

Tell students: "See if you can hear your inner voice at another time today. At the end of the day I will ask who stopped to listen to their inner voice."

EXTENSIONS

Friendly Voice Drawings. Ask each student to select words for their friendly voice and decorate a sheet of paper with these words using their favorite colors. Add any pictures of animals or parts of nature that also feel helpful. Post the drawings or ask children to keep them at their desk as reminders of the voice of encouragement inside themselves.

Poems or Stories; Friendly Voice Role Models. Make a list of people children know who examplify for them a person who speaks in a friendly voice. Ask, "Who gives you encouragement?" e.g., grandfather, mother, guidance counselor. Have them expand the list. Children can add characters in literature, famous people in history, people from television programs to the possibilities. Say, "when you feel discouraged, imagine what one of these people would say to you, or invent an imaginary person and give them a name like 'My Neighbor-with-the Bread' or 'My Guardian Angel.'" Create a poem or a drawing about that real or imagined person with the encouraging friendly voice speaking to you.

Recess Reminder. Before recess, provide a reminder in a very friendly tone which conveys confidence. Ask children to take a moment to hear that reminder in their inner voice: e.g.,

"I can find words to say what I need" or "I'll look for someone who needs a person to play with and ask if they want to play."

Drawings of Our Conscience at Work. Discuss: what does the word "conscience" mean? How does our conscience work? Make a drawing of a child facing a moral decision; e.g., a child gets up from lunch and a classmate is looking at his or her snack and wanting to take a bite while its owner is gone. Show how to make "thought bubbles" in a cartoon. Ask them to use "thought bubbles" to convey what words their inner voice might be saying as (a) they are noticing what they are wishing, and (b)they are evaluating what to do.

VARIATION

OVERTURNING THE CRUSHERS

Grades: 3rd–12th

Orientation: Tell students: "We can use our inner voice to hear friendly encouraging voices or mean discouraging voices. We can learn how to focus on the friendly words and steer our inner voice in an encouraging direction."

1. Brainstorm mean words a person might hear. Begin each sentence with "You...." *Example:* "You are stupid." Label these as "crushers" and clarify them as untrue statements.

2. Choose one phrase that has the most "charge" for the class. Now work together to think of its opposite. Draw an arrow and show the mean words changing to encouraging words. Begin the affirmative statement this time with "I" in-

stead of "you." Write as many contradictions as you like.

Example: "You do everything wrong." Change the words not to "I do everything right," but a phrase such as, "I do my best in every way" or "I keep growing."

3. Use this pattern to show the overturning of the crusher and ask the group to recite it together:

If you hear a crusher in your head saying,
you _____,
This is a lie. That's not true about you.
Here's what's true: I _____.

Example:
If you hear a crusher in your head saying,
you are no good.
This is a lie. That's not true about you.
Here's what's true: I am good. Part of being human is making mistakes. When I make a mistake, I'm still good. I'm learning and growing.

Option: Students select individual crushers and write the opposite. Take time to help each person find an affirmative statement.

Source: Professor Lee Bell at SUNY New Paltz and Valerie Young devised the "Overturning the Crusher" activity based on the work of Jerry Weinstein in his course, "Education of Self" at the University of Massachusetts. Lee and Valerie used this activity in their empowerment workshops for women called, "Imposters, Frauds, and Fakes." I adapted it in 1991 for elementary school classrooms.

❈ ACTIVITY ❈

OUR WHALE HEARTS

OVERVIEW

This physical position supports peacemaking skills because the body is in alignment and a fundamental safety is accessed.

ORIENTATION

Tell students: "If you've ever heard whales breathing out on the ocean, their breath comes like a pop. There's one sound — ha! — and then a very long pause as they take more air into their enormous lungs. We're going to find our whale hearts and breath like whales."

PROCEDURE

Find Your Whale Heart. Say to students: "Try to sense your own heart. Close your eyes and feel your heart beat. Now imagine that you have an enormous heart like a whale. Your heart is so big that it stretches from one shoulder to the other. It doesn't push you forward; it just is very big and very safe.

"Now let's begin to breathe like whales. Put your hand on your heart. These are your pectoral muscles. We will keep them still. Put your other hand on your belly. This is the part that is going to move. We breathe from the strength of our diaphragm muscles. The air comes in and seems to fill your belly and then we make a sound as the air comes out like the sound of whales breathing out on the ocean — Ha!" (Pause to slowly fill up with more air. Set a slow unhurried pace for the breathing).

"Check the position of your head. Imagine there's an opening at the top where the sun shines down on you. Allow your head to receive all that sunshine. This is a very safe way to stand and move."

CLOSURE

Have the class stand or sit in a circle. Say to the class: "Put your palms out and imagine there's a stream of water in a circular donut shape that runs counterclockwise around the circle refreshing each person. Stretch your hands to the left and receive it. Bring your hands across and over to the right like you are delivering refreshing water. Stay together in rhythm." Option: Add a closing song like "Row, Row, Row Your Boat" or "Across the Wide Ocean" by Sarah Pirtle on the recording *Linking Up.* Notes: During the day, refer to the posture of the whale heart to help children physically contact their inner peacemaker.

GRADES: K–4th

FOCUS: Learn how to place yourself in a centered posture that promotes peacemaking

EXTENSION

Moving Like Whales. Establish the boundaries of where the group can move: for example, stay on the rug or stay inside the area of the chairs.

Say: "We are calm and powerful whales. We're going to walk around, giving ourselves plenty of space because we are so large. The killing of whales has stopped and we feel completely safe. As we breathe out, use one hand at the top of your head to flick the spray of your breath up to the sky." Establish a pattern for walking. All breathe out together with a sudden — ha! — and a flick of hands, then slow walk for 1, 2, 3, 4 counts on inhale. Breathe out, then walk for 4 counts. Move in the space designated.

Caring Like Whales. Tell students: "Now I'm going to invent a signal that the whales use when they need help. Continue to walk slowly but we won't breathe out loud together. I will tap one person as we are walking to tell them that they will be the whale who needs help. They will sit down and make a soft high call. You sit down as if you dove under the water for safety. When you notice the message, swim over to them and create a star around them. Lie down on your stomach, stretching your flippers toward them. The trick is to leave enough space so that everyone can fit. Let's practice this first. Find out how much space we need. When everyone is around them, without pushing, they are safe."

Scientific correlation: Humpback whale pods do make a circle formation with all heads in the center.

SOURCE

This image comes from the work of Justina Golden, the Profound Sound Voice Studio, P.O. Box 60295, Florence, MA 01062. E-mail: divafolk@aol.com

✺ ACTIVITY ✺

PEACEMAKER COUNCIL
Visualization and Reflection

OVERVIEW

Tell students: "With our eyes closed we will make a journey in our imagination to talk to a wise teacher. Each of us will sense or see this in our own way like a dream."

PREPARATION

1. Select an archetype of nonviolent wisdom figures that will have meaning for your students — such as the Clan Mothers from Native American cultures — or use a general term like the Wise Council of Peacemakers. For some students the character of Yoda in *Star Wars* might convey these qualities.

2. Summarize for students what will happen. Clarify that our imaginations work in different ways and that they won't necessarily see shapes. Some people may receive a mood or impression. Tell them the sequence to expect. They will go to the council. They will ask for help or advice. This request can be about a specific problem or it can be a general request for assistance. A teacher will come forward. This might be any kind of living creature. (Don't name examples or this will influence their inner search.) Their teacher will be with them. Perhaps they will take them someplace. The teacher might *not* give them a direct answer, though he or she also might. When they are ready, they will return to the council.

3. A journey of the imagination like this takes concentration. Other activities also involving visualization can help prepare for this more extensive experience: Communicating Memories (p. 31), Story Drawings (p. 63), and The History in Our Hands (p. 70). Talk about the quiet that will need to be maintained in the room. Also, let them know that at various stages you will ask them to wave a finger, still with their eyes closed, if they have completed that part. Their goal is not to "pop out of the dream." Explain that it helps to keep eyes closed throughout and to continue to stay with their inner landscape.

4. Have paper for writing or drawing ready. Say that immediately after this journey, silence will be continued as they record impressions.

GRADES: 3rd and up

FOCUS: Tap inner resources.

MATERIALS: Paper for journal writing or drawing.

PROCEDURE

As you go slowly through these stages use the finger signal to help you make your best guess as to how to pace it. For instance, after the first step, say, "When you are at the place of the Council, wave your finger."

1. "You are entering the place where the Council meets. They welcome you to join them now."

2. "They ask how they can help you and you say you're looking for a teacher to help you in your next stage of growth. You tell them anything you want about the kind of help you would like, or keep silent and let them use their skill to learn what will assist you the most at this point of your life."

3. "Now the teacher comes to you who will help you now. They may be any kind of living creature."

4. "Your teacher might ask you to stay right there or they might take you to some place that will be of help, to some kind of experience. Follow this experience."

5. "When it feels complete, go back to the Council room."

6. "Keeping your eyes closed, receive something from the Council or your teacher."

REFLECTION

Immediately ask students to maintain silence and write or draw anything they remember. Select a method for sharing this experience.

EXTENSION

Use this method to articulate abstract concepts and to seek help as a group for specific skills. Make more journeys to the Council.

STAYING INSIDE YOUR OWN WISDOM

Here is a Peace Warrior skill that takes a lot of strength. Often times if a person talks to us or treats us in a particular way, we match what they are doing and return the same energy to them. If they call us names, we call names back. If they threaten us, we threaten them back. If they say they don't like us, we say we don't like them. But Peace Warriors work a different way. They choose the energy they want to use in the world and keep that energy no matter what happens. They don't let others push them off balance. This takes a lot of training. We might call this skill, *"Staying Firm and Not Matching Energy."* We will go back to the Council today and search for teachers who can help us learn how to do this.

ACTIVITY

CHANGEBRINGERS

GRADES: 3rd and up

FOCUS: Show that positive social changes are the result of the concerted actions of many people.

ORIENTATION

Tell students: "When we study famous people it is easy to forget that the efforts of many unseen or lesser known people are necessary as well for positive changes to be made."

PROCEDURE

1. Ask, "Who was the first African-American person in the South to refuse to move to the back of a public bus?" Most students will name Rosa Parks. A fifteen-year-old girl in Montgomery, Alabama was the first and she inspired Rosa Parks. (See *Freedom's Children: Young Civil Rights Activists Tell Their Own Stories* by Ellen Levine, G. Putnam's sons, 1993). Clarify that change comes from many people working for a common cause over a period of time as well as from key actions by brave people. It was at the Highlander Center in Tennessee (Resources, p. 169) that Rosa Parks learned about nonviolence and gained a vision that change was possible. For another example of the groundwork for change, we can look at the methods of nonviolent social change that Nelson Mandela uses as leader of South Africa. These methods were conceived of seventeen years earlier when people deliberately planned what they would do when freedom came. For instance, he has instituted Amnesty Hearings that help the victims of crimes during apartheid bring these events to light. This idea was planned by the group envisioning positive change
2. What is a conscience? How do we hear it? Think of a time you could hear a voice of conscience. What did your inner voice say? For example, a white fifth grader went to an ice skating rink with her friend who is black. The white owner of the rink treated her friend unfairly and her conscience told her that the behavior was "wrong," and urged her to speak up. We are born with a conscience. What inner standards do you carry?
3. Events are caused not just by us as individuals, but by our times, our communities, our "holding environments" to use a term of Robert Kegan in *The Evolving Self* (Harvard University Press, 1982). Talk about the way friends and families help us.
4. Do a role play of an intervention that changes the course of history. *Example:* You are on the Board of a chemical company that is considering releasing a drug after tests show it could cause cancer. Others want to put the drug on the market because of the money the company has already spent developing it. You convince them not to release it. What do you say?
5. Option: Learn the song, *Last Night I Had the Strangest Dream* by Ed McCurdy. from *Children's Songs for a Friendly Planet* (CCRC, 1986). The song says, "I dreamt the world had all agreed to put an end to war."

❈ ART ACTIVITY ❈
YES AND NO DRAWINGS

SOURCE

Polly Anderson, art teacher at Buckland-Shelburne School in Shelburne Falls, Massachusetts, developed this activity for fifth graders in Trudy Teutsch's class after they had developed skits about making decisions.

PROCEDURE

1. Ask students to think about a decision they have made.

2. Distribute paper and pencils and ask them to use words and lines to show how it felt to make that decision. Clarify this is a first draft where they can experiment.

3. Meet in a circle asking each person to present their pencil drawings and describe the decision-making process they are representing. This allows students a chance to see other methods of drawing and reflect upon their first draft.

4. Provide white paper and black ink, paint, or markers. Black pen and ink is the recommended medium because it allows lots of different types of lines with varying thicknesses to be created. Ask students to embellish upon their first draft and create a final drawing, incorporating any new ideas they have.

Example: Michelle Chatfield exhibited an exuberant debate of words at different angles filling the paper — yes, no,

GRADES: 4th–6th

FOCUS: Use a drawing to reflect upon a decision

MATERIALS: Paper, pencil, black markers, ink or paint

maybe, I should, and I shouldn't — displayed with exclamation points.

5. Reflect upon the drawing and write an essay or poem. Example: Karen Burnap's drawing contained a large radiating black area at the top. She commented, "This is a cloud hanging over my thoughts."

EXTENSION

Complement a social studies unit on famous people by asking students to make a Yes and No Drawing about one decision this person faced. This relates to the activity Conflicts of Community Builders, p. 42–43, where a moment of choice is dramatized.

Yes is persistent and begins to dissolve No.

Making Decisions
by Wade Bassett

❊ CREATIVE MOVEMENT ❊
YES AND NO DANCES

ORIENTATION

Tell students: "Today we'll explore saying yes and no with our whole body."

OPENER

How do we use our kinesthetic intelligence? Here's how Anne Lief Barlin helps students get in touch with this ability: put your arm behind your back without letting it touch the chair or anything else and sense what it feels like. Focus on your arm and on yourself experiencing your arm. Bring your arm back and discuss what you were aware of. Secondly, open and shut your hand two different ways: sharply and quickly with bound tension, then slowly and smoothly with flowing energy. Ask students to move in these same ways as you, by modeling instead of describing the contrasting energy in words. Next, invite them to supply adjectives to describe the difference in how the two ways felt.

PREPARATION

FREEZE IN A SHAPE

1. Ask the whole group to stand up and find a place where they can swing their arms without bumping — their own kinesphere of space, or "space bubble." Every time you clap, or play the tambourine or drum, students make a new stretching shape and hold it for a moment. This is Freezing in a Shape.

2. Explore as many different ways as you can say "yes" with your whole body each time you hear the beat. Add the word each time: yes, yes, yes.

3. Freeze in shapes that express "no." Change the shape each time you hear the beat: no, no, no.

CALL AND RESPONSE WITH A PARTNER

1. Help the group divide into pairs. If possible, move into two lines with partners facing each other. "Before we do yes and no together, let's practice matching any shape your partner is making." Indicate those students in each pair who will lead off. If you are in lines, point to the students in one line

GRADES: 3rd–6th

FOCUS: Expand awareness of the expression of yes and no

MATERIALS: Optional drum or tambourine

to be the first leaders.

2. As you sound the beat, one person in each pair freezes in a shape and a partner matches it. Now, switch and let the other person in the pair take the leadership role.

3. "We'll match our partners again but this time they will be expressing three no and then three yes." Lead the group in chanting as they move: no/no, no/no, no/no, yes/yes, yes/yes, yes/yes.

4. This time, watch your partner and do the opposite. If he moves high, you go low. If she expands, you contract. Give both people a chance to lead.

5. Now we'll do the opposite of our partner: no/yes, no/yes, no/yes, switch yes/no, yes/no, yes/no. Again switch leadership.

MAIN ACTIVITY

YES AND NO DANCES

1. "Now, I'm going to mix up the yes and the no. Sometimes you'll be the same and sometimes you'll be the opposite. Listen to how the sequence will go this time: no/no, yes/no, yes/no, yes/yes." Follow the interests of the group if they want to suggest other sequences to try.

2. Instead of calling "yes" and "no" out loud, this time we will feel the power of doing the movements in silence. In fact, you can choose either to do the same or the opposite.

3. Pairs or groups of four meet by themselves to create a Yes and No Dance using any sequence that they want. If they like, they can tell a story in their dance. Give them a choice of saying "yes" and "no" out loud or doing the dance in silence.

After planning time and rehearsal, ask groups to show their dances to the class.

SOURCE

This is based on the "Call and Response Activity" of Anne Lief Barlin in her book then adapted and extended by Anne and me. You can order the book Teaching Your Wings to Fly by Anne Lief Barlin and accompanying audiocassette from Learning Through Movement, 2728 N. County Rd., 25 E Bellvue, Colorado 80512. (970) 482-6908. Email: doug@lily.aerc.colostate.edu.

✵ ART ACTIVITY ✵

OPPOSITES MEET

ORIGIN

Polly Anderson, art teacher at Buckland-Shelburne Elementary School in Shelburne Falls, Massachusetts, created this activity for fifth and sixth graders in Wanita Sioui Laffond's class after hearing a story in which two opposite characters meet.

PROCEDURE

1. Ask students to choose two opposite words.

Examples: quiet and loud, soft and hard, violent and peaceful

2. To plan, write down these words and decide what colors you will use to express them. Decide what type of art materials express each word.

Example: Fifth grader Beth Redeker wrote:

Happy	*Sad*
Light blue and pink	Dark blue with purple
Chalk, colored pencil	Markers and colored pencils

Discuss the biases associated with colors and help students think about how to go beyond them. For instance, in working with the words *violent* and *peaceful* a stereotyped interpretation would be to use the color black for the violent shape and the color white for the peaceful shape. Challenge students to experiment with different ways to use colors. Try depicting violent with pink and express peaceful with black and brown.

3. In pencil, students do a rough drawing of their shapes. Tell them, "Get your ideas across by the way you draw your lines."

4. Students talk about their plans and evaluate them with their teacher.

GRADES: 5th–12th

FOCUS: Drawing opposite figures inspires reflective writing

MATERIALS: Paper, colored pencils, paint. chalk

Example: Beth discussed her rough copy and decided that the happy shape looked sad because it drooped. Polly Anderson asked Beth how she could use different types of lines to make the happy shape look frolicking, as if it were trying to get the stern sad shape to play.

5. Students carry out the finished drawing with paint, chalk, and/or colored pencil.

6. Instruct students: "Write an essay about the drawing. Make up a title for your essay. Note that by drawing, students will see new themes in their work as the interactions between the shapes bring them to life."

Examples from 5th and 6th graders:

◆ "Reaching Out," by Cathy Mayer

If more people tried reaching out, this world wouldn't be like it is now. We need to open our eyes and our hearts to the people and animals that need help. Everyone is different, I know, but we can't just stand there wondering whether we should greet them or walk away. If we share with one another during times when we have something to share, it will all come back to us eventually. The world has to learn this.

◆ "Rejection," by Jenni Burkham

Have you ever been rejected when you greet another person just because you were different? We know that feeling really hurts. So next time you hear a friend, or even yourself, giving someone else a hard time because they are different or

even just because they aren't popular, try and think how it feels when someone treats you like that."

◆ G. Patrick Welsh drew a violent dog meeting a peaceful dog. The violent one bares his teeth, but the peaceful one leans toward him with a compassionate look on his face.

"The Violent One and the Peaceful One,"
By G. Patrick Welsh

We think that when the violent one and the peaceful one meet they may become friends. The violent one has more evident power but the peaceful one can calm him down by his soft voice and the way he accepts the violent one's pain.

We humans need more peaceful ones. We can get these by helping each other to accept each other's faults. We also can be friends and be nice to each other and help each other to mature.

7. Share work with the class.

Soft Meets Hard
by Amy Morey

PROBLEM SOLVING METHODS

METHODS

Conflict Resolution Unit

RIVER LISTENING

BACKGROUND

I invented the term "River Listening" in 1981 as a way to create a context for conflict resolution. I've found that students enjoy the mythic atmosphere it creates. The metaphors help subtle dynamics become clearer. I like to use a conch shell for a talking object. After people have had a turn speaking, as facilitator I hold the shell to my ear as if it has collected all their words. I pretend I am listening to the shell as I summarize what has been said.

OPENER

Introduce the process of River Listening. Select a special rock or shell that is the "talking stone." Whoever is speaking holds this object.

Say: "Imagine we are part of a village culture, and in our village whenever there is a problem we go to the River Listener who helps us listen to each other. Here's how a River Listening works. Those involved in solving the problem sit together in a circle. That means the River Listening could include the whole class, or a smaller group of ten students, or five students, or two people — whoever is part of the situation. We imagine that we are like a river travelling to the same place together. The parts of the river need to learn about each other. Try to picture this river. Some of the water passes over rocks, while other parts travel by logs. Different paths of water join together. Even though there are different sections of the river, there is at the same time one whole body of water that is connected. We are like a river because each of us has our own important voice, and yet we are also part of one united group. What each of us does can affect everyone else in the class.

We will pass a special rock or shell and let each person

GRADES: K–6th

FOCUS: This framework promotes consensus and listening

MATERIALS: A special rock or shell

WHERE TO USE: School, camp, or family

hold it and tell what they see, and what they feel about the situation that has brought them to the River Listening. This is like hearing where each part of the water in the river has travelled. We have our own way of looking at things and all viewpoints are heard at a River Listening. When the problem is understood, we listen again to all the different voices to find a way to solve it that everyone can agree to. We call this, finding the place where the river has one voice."

PROCEDURE

1. *How to Lead:* In taking on the role of River Listener, one takes on a position of neutrality and impartiality, yet also compassion and fairness. The River Listener restates, clarifies, asks questions and provides safety. In the first phase of the process, the River Listener helps each person take a turn to speak and describe their concerns or viewpoints. This involves being aware of the need to share time and not let the river get stuck too long in one place. It is important to pause and summarize what has been said at felicitous moments so that a collective picture of the problem is forming. The imagery of a river helps children see the problem from a distance.

The metaphor helps identify the contributing factors:

"I hear one strand of the river saying we need to

look at ____ while another strand of the river is saying that ____ . We'll take time to think together about both of these parts of the situation."

The metaphor helps provide calm reassurance:

"The river feels very churned up right now. Let's find our why. As we listen to each other, we can find a way for the river to travel smoothly again."

2. During the second phase, the River Listener is assisting the group to contribute solutions and reach for consensus on one of the plans that is proposed. For example: "I hear the river tell us we need to take into account this factor, and this factor, and this factor. How can we put all these concerns together?" Collect suggestions.

3. Next, ascertain where there is agreement and help the group move toward a decision. Help the group understand the ways in which seeking consensus is different from voting. When there is not yet agreement, the river keeps looking for another path, another way that all the voices can be heard and united.

FACILITATING CONSENSUS

As the participants start to formulate a plan that addresses all the facets of the problem, it may happen that one or two people do not agree with the idea that is emerging. The River Listener summarizes what stage the group is in without moving from a position of neutrality. Here are options for how to proceed:

◆ **Look For Agreement:** Tell students: "I hear that all the voices in this river are in agreement with this part of the plan, ____, but some voices are saying that the second part of the plan, ____, doesn't solve the problem of ____. Let's look just at that problem for a moment."

◆ **Clarify How Strongly People Oppose:** In group decision-making, when a person is not in agreement it is helpful to find out how strongly they hold their concern. Do they want to oppose and block the suggestion? Or, are they not in agreement but will stand aside and let the proposal go ahead. Tell students: "I sense a strong force in the river to go in this direction but I notice that two parts of the river are not in agreement. Every member of the river is important. Let me ask whether you want to put up a rock in the river and say — absolutely not — or whether you disagree but feel it is okay let the river go ahead in this direction."

◆ **Bring Out the Insights of Participants:** Ask students: "Can you tell us more about what it is about the plan that does-

n't work for you? What are you concerned could happen if we follow it?"

A lone voice can have important pieces of information that others are not perceiving. The seeking of consensus makes room for minority voices to contribute insights and help amend proposals.

◆ **Seek Amendments:** Ask students: "How else could this be solved? Are there some changes that could be made in the plan that would help it work for everyone here?"

CLOSURE

At the end of the River Listening, summarize where the group has come. Either describe the plan that has been made or verbalize the standoff or stalement that exists and invite the group to go further with the process another time. Use a gesture that signifies that the River Listening is over for the day — passing a hand shake around the circle or placing the special rock or shell in the center.

EXAMPLE

At Journey Camp, a summer peace camp at Woolman Hill in Deerfield, Massachusetts, campers in second to sixth grade call for a River Listening whenever they need help with conflicts. For instance, two different friendship groups were having trouble sharing the same area at lunchtime. I listened as each person had a chance to air their concerns — both those who were in the thick of the problem and those who were observers — and then we looked for a point of agreement: the place where the "river" has one voice.

What helped the situation was to look beneath the dynamics of two groups and focus on common problems they were facing. The circle focused first on a problem of sharing food. When some people had a special lunch treat, they would advertise it loudly and then use it as a way to exclude some of the others. The tension that had built up around the exclusion became diffused when they formulated a general policy together: they decided that if you had a special snack you could either keep it for yourself or offer it to all people in the area. Another problem the circle addressed involved one child purposefully teasing others and saying she wanted to annoy them. When people asked her to stop, she had responded, "I don't have to." The context of one river, of being members of one community, introduced a different framework. As they created this agreement — if someone asks another person to stop teasing, they need to stop — this brought her closer into the community.

Three children present decided they wanted to help lead other River Listenings, using training they had as school mediators.

❊ PROBLEM SOLVING METHOD ❊

FISHBOWL

ORIENTATION

Tell students: "I know that many people have a concern about [name the current problem, such as disagreement over the rules of a game at recess]. We're going to use a method called 'The Fishbowl' that will help all of us listen to each other. Five people will talk and listen to each other in the center, while the rest of us watch and listen."

INTRODUCTION

The name *Fishbowl* comes from the sense of talking as if you are unaware of the listeners in the outer ring. It also got its name because there will be a big circle on the outside like the round bowl and a small group of students in the center who the rest of us are watching as if they are the fish. The people in the center are the ones who sit on the pillows (or chairs)."

MAIN ACTIVITY

Prepare a space for those in the center and those on the outside. If you are working on a rug, place a ring of five pillows in the center, while the listeners form another circle behind them on the rug. Or, arrange a large circle of chairs on the outside and a small circle of chairs or pillows on the inside.

As the small group in the center discusses together, this allows them to have a more responsive conversation than if everyone in the class were participating at once. The speakers (a) do not address remarks to the outside ring, but look only at the members in the center, and (b) listen and respond to each other, rather than making rehearsed comments about fixed positions.

1. What is the problem? The teacher asks who would like to go into the center and describe what the problem is. Or if it is already clear, the teacher summarizes what problem is being addressed by this meeting.

2. What can we do to solve it? Five students who have ideas go into the center and take turns talking. The teacher and/or a student takes notes on various solutions raised by participants in the discussion.

GRADES: 1st–6th

FOCUS: This format encourages listening when you are working with a problem concerning the whole class

MATERIALS: 5 chairs or pillows (6 if using an open fishbowl)

What Makes a Fishbowl Work:

◆ Everyone on the outside is totally silent.

◆ People in the center are not only speakers, but active listeners. They look at each other and work to understand other's viewpoints.

◆ When a teacher selects children to go into the center, these people do not need to have something ready to say. It is as important to pick people who will participate by skillfully listening.

◆ It's necessary to have a Timekeeper who calls time at the limit you've set. For instance, "We'll let this group talk for seven minutes and then switch so that new people can come into the center for another round."

◆ Feel free to call an end to the discussion when you feel it is becoming unproductive.

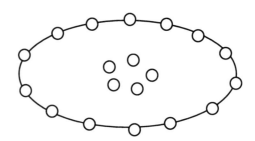

A FISHBOWL LOOKS LIKE THIS

— Members of the class are listening quietly.

— The speakers and active listeners are seated in the center.

— 5 chairs or pillows are in the center.

OPTIONS

A Closed or Open Fishbowl: In a closed fishbowl there are exactly the same number of seats as there are participants, and no one from the outer circle joins. This is a good first step while the class is becoming familiar with the method.

In an open fishbowl, there is one empty seat so that new people from the outside ring of observers may enter the discussion as appropriate. The ground rules are that when a new person comes in, someone from the center must leave. This way there is always an empty pillow available. However, for this to run smoothly, it is important that new people wait for each configuration to gell and converse before jumping in to join. If there is a flood of new participants, the conversation will be less productive. Also, speakers should not sit down, say their thoughts, and then leave. They need to focus as much on listening as speaking. Place six pillows to create groups of five talking together.

ANECDOTES

◆ This method has been used by teachers of first graders and up. A first-grade class got into an argument when they received their Unicef boxes; they tried to grab the boxes from each other and needed to process what had happened. Their teacher, Carol Corwin, used a fishbowl to give the group a chance to discuss what occurred and make recommendations.

◆ A middle-school class had a free hour which they could make use of however they wished. They talked with each other using the fishbowl format to decide what they would do with that hour.

CLOSURE

Using the Suggestions: After the fishbowl, post a list of the solutions raised. Your choices are to:

◆ Identify a consensus you heard in the fishbowl and ask if there is agreement.

◆ Vote on the list.

◆ Work on selecting one choice from the list by continuing the fishbowl.

◆ Break into small groups where each comes to agreement on one suggestion and then reports back to the class.

Optional Closing: "**One Word Poem**." Come back into one circle. Ask each person to say one word or phrase expressing their thoughts. These might be words like *hungry, friends, listening, popcorn, still angry, not finished, happy.* You don't need to connect your word to the word that comes before. This experience is a brief way to acknowledge how each class member is feeling.

SOURCE

Teachers and trainers learned this method from the National Training Lab (NTL) and brought it to nonviolence training. Probably it was developed by indigenous societies.

EXTENSION

Fishbowls don't have to be confined to problem solving. Use fishbowls to share information, or give short reports. Encourage students in the fishbowl to respond to the information and interact with questions.

�֎ PROBLEM SOLVING METHOD �֎

SPOKES

OPENER

Writing in the Air: This challenging movement helps a group to focus attention. You will ask students, "Write each of the letters of your first and last name in the air using the opposite hand from the one you usually write with."

ORIENTATION

Tell students: "We are going to work with a conflict many people here are concerned about. First we'll come up with as many solutions as we can in the large group, and then we'll break into small groups to discuss them. A spokesperson from each group, called the Spoke, will report."

PREPARATION

Brainstorm: This is a well-known method of creative problem-solving. Start with a clear question relating to the concern, like "What are all the ways you can think of for selecting teams at recess?"

The class makes as long as list as possible within the time limit you set. Record everything. Make clear this isn't a time for debating or evaluating the ideas but expanding the possibilities. Afterward, discuss any item that is unclear e.g., instead of calling on the child who offered the suggestion, ask if anyone else could explain the item to test for understanding.

MAIN ACTIVITY

1. Divide into small groups of 3–5. Each group needs to try to reach agreement on a solution, using the ideas that came up in the brainstorm. You can combine suggestions, but you need to come up with one proposal. Give the group a time limit between 7–15 minutes.

b. Each group selects one member, the Spoke, to be their

GRADES: 4th and up
FOCUS: Make a decision by building consensus instead of by voting
PLAN: Arrange the room so that small groups have enough space to meet

spokesperson. This person practices summarizing the proposal and gets feedback as to whether they are presenting it accurately.

3. The Spokes sit in the center of the room together, configured as they were in the Fishbowl. Everyone else listens in the outer ring. The teacher can join the center circle as discussion facilitator. Each Spoke presents the group's proposal. Some further clarification and discussion occurs.

4. Unless all groups have reached the same decision, return to small groups and look for a way to combine the concerns.

5. Spokes return to the center to try to create a class consensus.

CLOSING

The whole class sits in the circle. Each person says one thing they appreciated in the problem-solving together, naming the way a person helped the group. Or, lead a One Word Poem (p. 127).

SOURCE

These methods are used in community groups and nonviolent affinity groups to build consensus. The National Training Lab (NTL) helped people be aware of this technique.

CHAPTER 6
Bias Awareness Activities

BUILDING BRIDGES
Thinking About Bias

WHEN WE as teachers reflect upon the messages we got about bias growing up, it helps us understand ourselves and our students, and it helps us examine the insidious ways that bias will be perpetuated unless we actively step in.

I REMEMBER...

In my elementary school in suburban New Jersey in the 1950s, the adults rarely talked directly about the bias that existed, but I was acutely aware of it in different forms. I was aware of signals that people described certain neighborhoods as better than others. Our school district was talked about as not as "good" as others in town. This felt confusing because I liked my neighborhood and I thought with our smaller houses closer to each other we talked to each other more. One day a man came to our door with a petition to prevent a public housing complex from being built two blocks away, and my father was the only person on the street who refused to sign. He explained that our neighbors were afraid to have black people move nearby, and he said that our family didn't feel that way. I felt very upset. I'd assumed that this positive feeling of unity in our neighborhood was meant to extend to everyone.

The bias I remember even more vividly was the pecking order of popularity in the classroom. Anyone who was overweight or too skinny or talked too much or talked too little — who was "too" of anything — moved further down on the pecking order. Shouldn't we be friends with everyone as they said in our church? Yet some days I felt driven by a hunger for safety, and all I wanted was to fit in. There seemed no way to be truly safe. I ached and felt confused when children in my class were mistreated by other children and no adult stepped in. If the teachers knew that the first-grade boys were chasing the girls to pull up their skirts, why didn't they stop it? If the teachers knew that Italian children were called dirty, why didn't they intervene?

At the end of seventh grade I went away to a camp in the Berkshires of Massachusetts and had a very different experience. At Rowe Camp, for the first time I lived in an atmosphere that felt safe not only for me, but for everyone there. Shy children were encouraged to talk, and discussion groups were run so that each person had an equal turn. The counselor who wouldn't kill any insects wasn't laughed at; there was curiousity about her Buddhist beliefs. People were actively involved in the Civil Rights movement. It was there I learned that by making social agreements, you could set up a different atmosphere. I learned that safety came not from trying to fit in, but by creating a community where each person could be himself or herself. I wanted to help make classrooms that felt like this camp and not like the school I knew. This process of reflecting back on the layers of messages I received growing up has helped in the lifelong process of facing and deconstructing racism, classism, and other forms of bias.

OUR GOALS AS TEACHERS

The aim of this chapter is to create a supportive classroom where differences are valued and bias is interrupted. These activities help children make their own social discoveries—to develop their own understanding of the problem of bias and to awaken their own passion for justice. Jim Carnes, author of *Us and Them: A History of Intolerance in American*, says we are part of a democracy in progress. Bullying, name-calling with the intent to harm or intimidate, and expressions of bias are undemocratic forces in the classroom. They turn a win/win classroom climate into win/lose. Children need to learn how to interrupt bias and unfairness themselves.

◆ Children need to be able to perceive injustice and unfairness.

◆ They need to be able to say, "This unfairness is not okay."

◆ They need to have the tools to intervene and help stop the undemocratic actions from occurring.

A discovery approach toward bias awareness involves bringing in questions and raising topics, listening to what responses are evoked, and helping children draw their own conclusions. For instance, school counselor Jana Standish shares an activity that asks students to make assumptions about a classroom visitor they have never met before.

The activities in this chapter build upon a cooperative atmosphere that has been developed by previous work. Priscilla Prutzman of CCRC reports that she doesn't begin the year with activities about bias; rather, she allows community building work to prepare enough safety to address prejudice.

As you begin this unit, make it safe for children to reveal what they notice about bias, what they wonder about, and what they have experienced. The activity "Prejudice Exists" gives room for students to speak what has happened to them. At that moment we have to rely on our heart to lead us in how to respond — to listen deeply, not superficially; to help this be a time of healing, a rising up of a community to stand with the speaker so that they feel how we wanted it to be different. It is hard in the listing of steps of an activity to express how to treat these important moments, yet they are the most crucial.

The key is to follow the lead of the students and help them express what may have been unspoken but what needs to be shared. Let the realities of prejudice and oppression be acknowledged so that children can have better tools to deal with these undemocratic parts of our world. This means that students who are white need help moving beyond the distorted mirror of unconscious superiority that comes from being handed the "knapsack of privileges," as Peggy McIntosh, associate director for the Center for Research on Women at Wellesley College, so brilliantly names it in her article, "White Privilege: Unpacking the Invisible Knapsack." It also means that students who are targeted — for race/ethnicity, gender, class, physical difference, religion, for all the ways society has given approval to vent hatred — need support, encouragement of their leadership, and a reality check that unfairness is indeed occurring.

The Students' Creative Response to Conflict program (SCRC) in Cincinatti, Ohio lists these goals in the area of bias awareness and appreciation of differences:

◆ Increased awareness of how others differ from self

◆ Ability to recognize commonalities between self and others

◆ Demonstrated understanding of how all people (all life) is interdependent

◆ Recognition that we all have biases

◆ Decreased amount of "put-downs" based on differences

◆ Demonstrated pride in one's own individuality while respecting differences in others.

Here are seven assumptions that undergird this work:

1. **People aren't born biased. Bias is learned behavior and can be unlearned.** We were born curious about each other's differences.

2. **When one person is targeted, no one truly feels safe.** All forms of targeting undermine classroom safety, whether the bias is based on skin color, cultural background, religion, learning style, physical size, or personality traits. Bias is a corrosive force.

3. **It is important to defend the safety of all.** When a teacher hears bias and doesn't intervene, it sends a strong message to the children that some forms of unfairness are condoned.

4. **A person's identity doesn't cause bias.** It's what we do with the differences, not the differences themselves, that is the problem.

5. **Children need our assistance to learn how to develop friendships and maintain a secure feeling of self-worth without excluding others.** For instance, in a third-grade classroom in Minnesota each evening a girl called up her closest friends to discuss what earrings and clothing they would wear the next day so that they would look alike. An atmosphere of exclusion developed, and the social safety of the others in that room was undermined. The activity "Open and Closed Circles" (p. 144) describes how teachers dealt with this situation.

6. **Children need assistance in learning how to be allies for each other.** Bullying flourishes when bystanders don't intervene.

7. **When we teach unity, we help children find a strong foundation for transforming bias.** *The realization that we are all part of one human family fosters an understanding of the unity that undergirds our diversity and an understanding of the responsibility we all have to help end the oppressions that would separate us.* Our aim is to help children actively construct a classroom community that works for everyone. When these students are in turn adults, our hope is that they will then know what steps to follow to make any community they are part of safer and more equitable, and they will join in to build a world that works for everyone.

Bias Reduction and Mediation

by Catherine Woolner

The Mediation and Training Collaborative, Greenfield, Massachusetts

The Mediation and Training Collaborative began in 1987 as a comprehensive community dispute resolution service. Originally called Franklin Mediation Service, this group has worked with over 1200 students and teachers, mostly in Massachusetts, to teach conflict resolution and mediation skills in the schools.

AT THE Mediation and Training Collaborative in rural Greenfield, Massachusetts, it became more and more apparent that many of the conflicts that were coming to student mediators were bias-based.

The incident that brought the students into mediation might have been name-calling, pushing, stealing, or any of the usual precipitating events. But the underlying issues were bias or prejudice, expressed as racism, classism, sexism, homophobia, and ethnocentrism (as in neighborhoods, culture, religion, etc.). We began to examine the larger picture, which reveals oppression as one of the roots of conflict and violence. If mediation only helps disputants to arrive at a solution that meets their needs, while not really addressing those more complex and controversial issues, both for the disputants and for the mediators, are we not only missing an important opportunity, but also missing the boat?

Given that all disputants and all mediators bring learned biases and internalized oppressions with them to the negotiating table, we must recognize and reflect that in our mediation trainings. All mediators and disputants bring the baggage of racism, classism, homophobia, etc., to the conflict resolution process. Without this knowledge, mediators will be prepared to help disputants sort out wants from needs, positions from interests, and get to the underlying issues.

School mediation philosophy suggests that it is not enough merely to train students and have a program. Rather, it is important to reinforce the concepts of talking instead of fighting, working toward a win/win solution, and meeting the underlying needs of the parties throughout the culture of the school. The curriculum, the language, the conflicts that do not go to mediation, even staff meetings, can all be opportunities for supporting the principles of creative conflict resolution.

In the same way, if a school is working toward bias awareness and prejudice reduction, it is not enough merely to include these issues in the mediation training. The curriculum, language, leadership, books and other materials, staff awareness, etc., should all be consistent with the overall goals of the mediation/anti-bias training and program.

We began to ask ourselves, "How can we ensure that mediation itself does not perpetuate stereotyping, bias, and oppression?" If we assume that the mediation model commonly used is appropriate for all students, are we reinforcing dominant (white) culture while ignoring all the mediators and disputants not represented? For example, we teach that agreements usually are written, especially at the middle and high school levels. Does this fit with cultures who do not trust or even use written agreements? What does a written agreement mean, for example, to Native American students, given the history of broken treaties? Another culture-bound assumption is that eye-contact is an indication of attention or respect. At the most basic level, one has to recognize that there are cultural differences regarding the value of conflict in approaches to conflict resolution and in styles of communication. All of this must be factored into successful mediation and mediation training.

Just as we hope to inspire those children who are touched by mediation as disputants and as mediators, to use the win/win needs-based negotiation model in other settings, we also hope that the anti-bias work done by the trainees and woven into their mediations will ripple out for them and their disputants. Racism, sexism, homophobia, classism, and ethnocentrism are serious and dangerous problems affecting the lives of students today. It is not enough to prepare them with skills to solve problems without resorting to force. It is not enough to inspire the next generation of peacemakers. We also need to be nurturing the next generation of those who stand for justice as well.

Each of us has personal experiences with bias. All of us can remember a time when someone was prejudiced against us, if only as children being told we were too young to understand or manage something we truly could have handled. Each of us can remember how it felt and what we would have liked to have happened differently. In mediation, one of the questions often asked of student disputants is, "What could you do differently in the future if this conflict arises again?" In order for that question to be answered in a meaningful way, disputants in a bias-based dispute need to understand the pain from the other person's perspective. The mediators need to be able to facilitate that process. As trainers, we need to have done our homework and be able to help the mediators with theirs.

✳ ACTIVITY ✳
PLEASE TOUCH TABLE
Special Family Objects

PURPOSE

Bias awareness needs to be built on a foundation of self-awareness. The goal of this activity is to help each student affirm and express his or her cultural identity.

ORIENTATION

Say to students: "Let's plan together about bringing in things from home that are special to our families."

PREPARATION

1. Explain that next week the class will have a Please Touch table with something from each person's family on the table.

2. Create a letter to parents, translating it into languages spoken at home as necessary. Read the letter to the class and answer any questions about it. Think in advance about any family for whom this might be difficult and make appropriate arrangements. Sample:

Dear parents,

We are studying families and culture now. We are asking each student to bring an object from home which they like that connects them to their family — it might be a spoon, a weaving, a piece of carved wood, a doll, clothing, a bowl, a picture, a necklace, a handkerchief, a game — anything. Please choose something that is okay for other children to touch. We will place it on a "Please Touch"

GRADES: K–6th

FOCUS: Share special family objects as a basis for sharing family culture

MATERIALS: Select a table for the display and bring in two cloths

PREPARATION: Send letters to families

table. We will take care that nothing gets hurt, but it's best not to send fragile items.

I will help all the children to say something about their special objects. Please explain any history about it so that they will be able to tell us. For example, it might be something that belonged to their grandparents or an object you got on a trip.

We are giving families a week's notice so that you have a chance to plan and talk about this. You are very welcome to call me at _____ [list phone number and times to reach you] with any questions or concerns. Please send this object on _____ [give date]. Thank you.

3. Designate a location in the room for displaying these objects. Place a pretty cloth on the table to signify respect. Make an agreement together to be careful of the objects. Use a second cloth to cover the objects; this indicates when the table is closed and off limits for visiting.

4. Choose one day as the time to place objects on the table, checking off the names of all those whose items are there, but plan to talk about the objects the next day so that those who forgot have a chance to bring something in. Send reminders or call home to help. If parents tell you details about their family's object, write down notes.

5. Bring in extra objects yourself to fill out the table with many types of things. If a child doesn't have something from home, help them select one of the items you brought and prepare to talk about it.

PROCEDURE

Sit in a circle near the Please Touch table. Explain that everybody will have a chance to touch everything. Remind children about taking care of the objects and also taking care of feelings: "If someone said, 'what's so great about that?' that would really hurt, wouldn't it? Each object is great and important to someone here and we want them to know that we understand."

Ask one child at a time to go to the table, pick up her object, and sit with it on her lap as she talks about it. Help draw her out as she explains what it is, what she likes about it, and anything about its history. Affirm every object.

CLOSING

Choose a plan that fits your group for exploring and touching the objects:

◆ **Plan A:** Each person keeps his object, and when everyone is finished talking, they are all passed around.

◆ **Plan B:** As each person finishes talking, the object is passed around.

Talk together about when the Please Touch table will be open later today and later in the week. Remind the group that if the objects are covered with a cloth, the table is closed.

EXTENSIONS

◆ Draw and write about your object.

◆ Draw and write about a different object from the table.

◆ Each person picks an object that they didn't bring, and tells what they remember about it, who brought it, and why it is important to that person.

◆ Think about how various objects are connected and draw or write a poem about how they interrelate.

❋ ACTIVITY ❋

NAME CELEBRATION

OVERVIEW

As students share information about their names, they express what is unique about themselves and receive an affirmative response from classmates. This activity also provides a way to talk about the problem of people making fun of other's names. Safety agreements (see procedure) need to be set up beforehand.

ORIENTATION

Tell students: "Today we're going to learn more about the meaning behind the names of people in the class."

PROCEDURE

1. *Setting Agreements:* Tell students: "Before we begin, let's spell out what we will do during this activity to make sure that everyone is treated with respect." (Give examples: "It would feel hurtful to hear someone laugh when we talk. If you hear something unexpected or surprising, ask a question.")

2. *Sharing Name Information:* "Think about all the parts of your name: your first name, your middle name if you have one, and your last name. Think also about any nicknames you might have. Do some people in your family call you a different name than you are called at school? We're going to go around the circle and hear one or two things from each person about their name.

　　Often our names tell us something about our families. Here are questions to reflect upon: "Who thought of your name? Why was your name given to you? Were you named after someone else in your family? Can you tell us the country or ethnicity of your name? Do you know the meaning of your name?" *Reminder:* In this, as in any activity, provide the option to pass. *Examples:* "Although everyone here at school calls me Kyle, my real Korean name is Haesook, which means 'Ocean of Virtue.'" and "My parents named me Orion for the constellation Orion that they saw one night before I was born."

3. *Courtesy Agreements:* Work on pronouncing each person's name correctly. Talk about calling people what they want to be called. During this discussion, be sensitive to the fact

GRADES: 2nd to 6th and up

FOCUS: Each person shares information about part of their name

that this may give an opportunity for a person to ask to be called something different from what has previously occurred at school. For example, José-Luis enters kindergarten, and his teacher decides to call him Joe. This may be the day he has support to reclaim the name José-Luis.

EXTENSIONS

◆ *Respecting Names:* Ask students to discuss: "Has anyone ever made fun of your name? Have you ever heard someone make fun of somebody else's name?" Share stories without putting anyone on the spot. Remind students that saying "I'm just teasing," doesn't mean the teasing doesn't hurt. Talk about what it feels like to intend not to hurt others.

◆ *Practice Interrupting Unfairness:* "What could you say to someone if you hear them making fun of somebody else's name?"
Example: "Let's imagine that a new student is going to join our class next week, and you hear somebody say, "Did you hear the name of the new student? It's _____. What a wierd name!" What would you say in response?"

◆ *Discuss:* Some people feel uncomfortable when they come across something unfamiliar such as a name they haven't heard before. When we encounter what's unfamiliar, we can learn about what is new instead of making fun.

✳ ACTIVITY ✳

MUSICAL WALLS AND BRIDGES

ORIENTATION

Draw a picture of a wall (a tall thin rectangle) and a bridge (an arc or rainbow shape), and introduce the activity to students: "Today we'll be exploring what it means to have a wall between people and what it means to build a bridge." Ask students to demonstrate with their hands what walls and what bridges look like.

OPENER

As the teacher, relate a personal story from your life or the life of someone you know that relates to the theme of bias and prejudice. Recite as a poem or sing the chorus to my "Walls and Bridges" song on the next page.

PROCEDURE

MUSICAL CONVERSATION

1. Decide whether the whole class or only half the class at at time will do the activity. Assemble enough rhythm instruments for all members of the class or enough for half the class to use at a time.

2. Introduce a visual Zero Noise Signal (p. 60) that means stop playing, such as forming an X with your hands. Place instruments in the center and allow participants to select instruments and experiment with them until you give the signal for silence.

3. Ask students to play instruments simultaneously in such a way that they are representing a wall. For instance, they may be conveying, "I'm only thinking about myself." After the sound builds, give the signal to stop. Discuss how it felt to be in the midst of a wall.

4. Next ask students to convey a bridge in the way they play together. Allow them to experiment with how to express this. Stop the group and ask if they got across what they wanted to, and whether they would like to try again.

5. Structure ways of doing musical "bridges." For example, one person starts a rhythm pattern while everyone else closes their eyes. Keeping eyes shut, others use their own instruments to connect to the rhythm. Pick another rhythm leader and repeat. Next ask students

GRADES: 3rd–6th

FOCUS: Experience the contrast of walls and bridges between people

MATERIALS: Rhythm instruments, and "Walls and Bridges" lyrics or recording

to listen and improvise all together. You can use a theme such as "Ocean," or "Rain."

SONG DISCUSSION

1. Before sharing the song, plan in advance who will meet together as partners afterward. Explain that I based this song on two true stories. Play a recording of the song "Walls and Bridges," arrange for it to be sung from the transcription, or read it as a poem. Then ask partners to discuss what stays with them from the song and what it reminds them of. Next, ask the whole group to share any experiences they or others they know have had with "walls," that is with exclusion and prejudice, or with "bridges."

2. Ask students to explain how the Musical Conversation experience and the story of the song are connected. Present this quote: "People are lonely because they build walls instead of bridges."

3. Help the group memorize the chorus as poem or song. Stand together in two facing lines with the same partners opposite each other. Repeat the words of the chorus as each pair acts it out. End with everyone forming bridges.

Resource: The "Walls and Bridges" song is on the recording *Magical Earth* (Resources, p. 169).

EXTENSION

Make posters and invent captions relating to ending walls of bias and building bridges of understanding. Place the completed posters around the school.

WALLS AND BRIDGES

© 1993 words and music by Sarah Pirtle, Discovery Center Music, BMI

Jackie moved to this school Art class is where we met We both liked to draw peo-ple's fac-es I drew her, she drew Mal-colm X Every one knew we'd be best friends. They heard us laughing in the hall. But when I in-vi-ted Jack-ie home, we bumped in-to a wall, we bumped in-to a wall.

Chorus Why do we make walls? These walls di-vide us. Why do we make walls? These walls just hide us Why do we make a fist, When we could reach out our hands? I wan-na make a start, build-ing a bridge from heart to heart, build-ing a bridge from heart to heart.

Verse 2

When Jackie came to my house
My mom stood at the door.
She had a look on her face
I'd never seen before.
All night she kept on scowling,
Later on we had a fight.
She said, "Don't bring Jackie back again
Cuz she's black and you're white,
Cuz she's black and you're white."

Verse 3

I went to Jackie's house
Her mom was working on a song.
We stood around the piano bench
She asked me to sing along.
Week by week we came to visit
One day we cooked a casserole.
I took them over to our house —
My mom's face froze.
Jackie's Mom stretched out her hand
Jackie's Mom broke on through.
She said "Our daughters are best friends,
I'd like to know you, too,
I'd like to know you, too."

Verse 4

How do you make a bridge?
It's built of many days.
Starts with a single step
Even when you're afraid.
Starts when you're speaking up,
Starts when you're tall.
Build a strong bridge, my friend
No one can make you build a wall,
No one can make you build a wall.

✹ ACTIVITY ✹
NAMING DIFFERENCES

ORIENTATION

Tell students: "Today we're going to recognize and affirm ways that people in America are different from each other."

OVERVIEW

This activity helps contradict the message that certain identities are the norm and that "it's not okay to be different." The bias exhibited against many different groups is often not seen by people who aren't members of that group. We are working to create classrooms where each student's identity, physical qualities, abilities and family structure is affirmed.

PROCEDURE

This activity has two parts:

◆ Listing many types of differences.

◆ Detailing specific kinds of differences.

1. *Name Various Types of Differences:* In what ways are people different from each other? Can we think of more than five? List the aspects that students name. Examples: Different types of housing, different economic classes, gender, languages spoken, food preferences, religious or spiritual practices, race/ethnicity, age, physical size, learning styles, types of work, physical differences, types of families, lifestyles. Discuss the fact that some kinds of differences are visible, such as whether a person wears glasses. Other kinds of differences, like which of the multiple intelligences they are strongest in, we don't see until we are working with people or get to know them better. *Affirm all differences that children mention and follow their lead about which differences they notice.* Note: Students in our classes have important people in their lives who are gay or lesbian; family members, babysitters, friends of their parents. Yet put-downs relating to sexual orientation are rampant. Provide inclusive messages that fit for your students.

2. *Name Specific Differences:* Pick two or three types of differences that will have the most meaning for your class, and elaborate. Ask students to tell you within that category what

GRADES: 3rd and up

FOCUS: Create a comfortable atmosphere for articulating differences

types of differences are possible. For example, students are smart in different ways. What are all the ways that children can express their intelligence? Reflect about which differences would be most helpful for your class to name.

Example: Name different kinds of families with children, taking care to list the family constellation of every child in the class.

Sample partial list:

◆ Mom and child or children.

◆ Dad and child or children.

◆ Child switches between two different homes living sometimes with mother, sometimes with father.

◆ Blended family: parent, stepparent, children and stepchildren

◆ Foster family

◆ Adoptive family

◆ Mother, father, one child

◆ Two moms or two dads with children

◆ Extended family: The family unit is joined by grandparents, uncles, aunts or cousins.

Concept: There are many types of family constellations. Each person's family is important to them. Phrases such as "love makes a family" and "every family is a good family" help to convey this.

Race/ethnicity: Name different ethnic heritages present in this classroom.

Sample partial list:

◆ Puerto Rican	◆ Haitian
◆ French-Canadian	◆ African-American
◆ Irish-American	◆ Thai
◆ Ojibway	◆ European-American

3. *Discussion:* Currently our society sends the false message that European-Americans are superior to people of color; that is, people who are Latino/Hispanic, Asian, Native American, Pacific Islanders, and African-American. The targeting that people of color receive is not only a matter of individual encounters that express prejudice but a systematic pattern stemming from cultural standards, expectations, and economic and other social institutions, including the media. Racism is often summarized as "power plus prejudice." In our classrooms, in order to counteract these messages, we need to actively teach the equality of all people and specify that this means no racial or ethnic group is superior to or "more normal" than another.

The goal is to deconstruct the dominant position as the norm. Let's look at how this operates in terms of the identity of being European-American. *European-American* designates a Caucasian person living in America who is of European, Scandinavian, Slavic, or Mediterranean descent. For instance, a person whose ancestors are from Germany, France, or Italy would be called European-American. A person, on the other hand, whose parents are both Swedish-American, could also be called *Swedish American.*

Sonia Nieto, in *Affirming Diversity: The Sociopolitical Context of Multicultural Education* (Longman, 1996, p. 16), writes: "Many European-Americans are a mixture of several European ethnic groups. They may not at all identify with a European heritage. Nevertheless, they are European-Americans because their habits, values, and behaviors are grounded in European mores and values, although they were later adapted and modified to fit a different culture within the United States. Because whites in U.S. society tend to think of themselves as the "norm," they often view other groups as "ethnic". . . whites [are encouraged to] define themselves in ethnic terms."

Bicultural means that a person's ancestors are from more than one basic ethnic group. For example: Rene is bicultural; his parents are French and Filipino.

Explain that people are in charge of defining their own heritage. *Example:* Jory, whose mother is Scotch-Irish, Native American, and whose father is African-American, chooses to identify as African-American.

Make this an occasion to correct misinformation and misperceptions. *Example:* Li Min is Chinese and not Oriental.

4. *Using Songs or Poems to Affirm Diversity:* If possible, use a song or poem pattern as a framework for this discussion. Here are two unity songs and the frameworks they provide for creating new verses. Using these patterns, the ethnicity of all children present can be named and sung, and other differences that are important for the class to explore can be affirmed.

◆ "Under One Sky" by Ruth Pelham on her recording, *Under One Sky.* (Contact Ruth Pelham Music, P.O. Box 6024, Albany, NY 12206.)
We're _____, and we're _____. (2x)
We're _____, and we're _____. (2x)
Chorus: We're all a family under one sky,
We're a family under one sky. (2x)
Example:
We're African-American, we're Mohawk
We're Mexican-American, and we're Chinese.
We're European-American, we're Irish-American,
We're Filipino and Vietnamese.

◆ "Sing About Us" by Sarah Pirtle on her recording, *Linking Up* (Resources, p. 169).
My friends are _____
My friends are _____
My friends are _____
You don't have to be just like me to be my friend.
Example:
My friends live in different families:
Some are families with one child.
Some have sisters or brothers, too.
You don't have to have a family like me to be my friend.

You can vary the content of the verses and sing about different eye colors using the same patterns: "Under One Sky": *We have brown eyes,/ we have blue eyes,/ we have green eyes,/ or gray eyes, too.* "Sing About Us": *Some friends have brown eyes or black eyes. Some friends have blue eyes or green eyes. Some friends have gray or hazel eyes, too. You don't have to look the way I look to be my friend.*

5. *Closing:* End the lesson by reminding students of our fundamental unity. Use a song to send this message.

◆ "The Colors of Earth" by Sarah Pirtle, on *Linking Up, The Wind is Telling Secrets,* and *Sharing Thoughts.* The song begins, "We are made of the colors of earth. Each color is different. Each color is true. We are made of the colors of earth, and I love the colors that made you."

◆ "Love Makes A Family" by Two of a Kind. Contact: Jenny and David Heitler–Klevans, 130 W. Nippon St., Philadelphia PA, 19119–2427.

✺ ACTIVITY ✺

PREJUDICE EXISTS

Talking about Bias

ORIENTATION

Tell students: "It's important to know the ways in which the world isn't working the way it could. Today, we will look at bias and prejudice and think about what it does."

QUOTE OF THE DAY

Write on the board:

It's not the differences themselves,
It's what we do with the differences.

Discuss: "What do you think this means?"

PROCEDURE

IDENTIFY BIAS ABOUT DIFFERENCES

1. Share this quote: "Life is not a level playing field."

2. Draw a seesaw on the board.

3. Take a specific category from the ones discussed in the activity, "Naming Differences" and identify how bias works in that category. Here are two categories that work well.

Gender

a. If you are a person who wants to be a leader in a business, in government, or in a university, how does your gender matter? Who has a better chance of being a leader, a man or a woman? Refer to the see-saw diagram.

b. In terms of the see-saw, who is up? Males, although men are 49% of the population. Who is down? Women.

Age differences

a. If you want your ideas taken seriously by other people, how does your age matter? At what ages are people's ideas favored?

b. In terms of the see-saw, who is up? People between the ages of 21 and 65. Who is down? People who are too young or too old.

VOCABULARY ABOUT BIAS

Instead of continuing to use the words "up" and "down," here are vocabulary words commonly used to describe bias.

GRADES: 4th and up

FOCUS: Look at the reality and the consequences of bias

Targeted: Person treated unfairly or discriminated against on the basis of identity, or being part of a targeted group which receives unfair treatment just on the basis of who they are.

Dominant group: Group with the economic, political, and other resources; the favored group.

Discrimination: The practice of giving different treatment to a person based on race, sex, religion, ethnicity, age, learning ability, physical ability and/or sexual preference.

Racism: Prejudice plus Power

CONSEQUENCES OF BIAS

Help students understand that prejudice can have serious consequences. Read each example and ask the discussion question.

◆ In a neighborhood in Texas, a particular group of white teenagers stand on a street corner and harass every Mexican teenager they see on the street with name-calling. What happens to a person as a result of the fear of harassment if they walk down the street?

◆ In a school classroom, a particular teacher calls upon boys twice as frequently as upon girls, and acts like they believe that boys are smarter than girls. What happens to a person as a result of not being recognized as having something important to say?

◆ On a school bus, a child who walks with a limp because one leg is slightly longer than the other, is mocked every day by two other children. What could happen to a person as a result of being mistreated every day?

Return to the quote:

It is not the differences themselves,
it is what we do with the differences.

Notice that the identity of being Mexican, or being female, or having a physical disability did not "cause" the targeting to happen. Explain and clarify that bias, prejudice, oppression, mistreatment are not about differences. They are about power relationships of taking power over others.

PERSONAL SHARING

Ask: "When have you been the target of discrimination? How did you feel? What did you do? What do you wish you had done? What kind of support would have been helpful in this situation?" Give each person who chooses to speak ample time to be heard and understood.

EXTENSION

EXAMINING THE PATTERNS OF BIAS

◆ Take as many aspects of differences as you can and create a chart. Delineate who is "up" and who is "down" in respect to each difference. Notice that an overwhelming number of people are targeted for some aspect of difference. A minority of people are in the dominant group for every category: male, currently able-bodied, Christian, European American, heterosexual, between the ages of 21 and 65, owning class, not too tall or too short. This provides a perspective on the problem of sharing a small planet using win/lose social constructions.

◆ Draw a spectrum of the ways that the bias can be expressed. On one side of the spectrum list jokes, moving into verbal harassment, moving into exclusionary practices (for example, "You can't live here"), moving into threats of violence (for example, cross-burning) and on the other side list violent expressions.

SOCIAL STUDIES

American history has numerous examples of one group targeted by a dominant group. Ask students to list the examples they know. How have groups of people been targeted in American history?

Resource: *Us and Them: A History of Intolerance in America* by Jim Carnes (Oxford University Press, 1996). This book is available to schools at no cost from the Southern Poverty Law Center. This quote from the back cover provides an important summary:

"This is the story of some Americans who were hated by others simply for who they were, what they looked like or what they believed. Their experiences remind us that our democracy is still a work in progress."

Examples:

◆ In 1660s in Massachusetts Mary Dyer was hung for her religious beliefs. As a Quaker she was targeted by the dominant group of Puritans.

◆ After the Indian Removal Act was passed in 1830, the Choctaws, the Creeks, the Seminoles, and the Cherokees were removed from their homes by the U.S. military and their land was given to white settlers. The forced 800-mile journey of the Cherokees is called the "Trail of Tears."

◆ Japanese Americans were taken from their homes during World War II and imprisoned in concentration camps in contradiction of their identity at U.S. citizens.

SOURCE

Trainings led by Joan Lester and Carole Johnson, founders of Equity Institute, and Andrea Ayvazian, founder of Communitas, inspired these activities. Contact the Equity Consulting Group, Carole Johnson, 1016 Middlefield Road, Berkeley, California 94708, or Communitas, Inc., Andrea Ayvazian, 245 Main St., Northampton, MA 01060.

❋ ACTIVITY ❋

I REMEMBER

ORIENTATION

Tell students: "Each of us carries some kind of bias. When we know ourselves better, we can notice and change the bias. We can learn and grow, instead of letting bias control us."

PROCEDURE

1. Review what *bias* means.

- ◆ It involves having distrust or dislikes toward a group of people, or false beliefs about their abilities, or having favorites toward other groups.

- ◆ It is based on incomplete information or misinformation that gets generalized to a whole group of people.

2. Ask children to listen to these stories and talk about the bias they hear.

- ◆ "Connie goes to a Head Start program. One of the children in her class, a boy named Ellis, was born without fingers on one hand. Connie sees Ellis laughing and playing in the sand with his friends but she feels afraid and always stays away from him."

- ◆ "Mark is four years old. He likes building blocks at the home day care he attends. Whenever Yolanda comes over to join him, he says 'Go away. Girls can't play blocks. Blocks are for boys.'"

3. Gain perspective by asking questions.

- ◆ "When children are babies, do they have bias?"
- ◆ "Did Connie and Mark invent bias out of thin air?"
- ◆ "What experiences might they have had to introduce them to prejudice?"
- ◆ "How young do you think bias begins?"

Emphasize that Connie and Mark are not being bad. They are showing pre-prejudice they've acquired, and they need assistance from adults to help correct their misinformation. Define what information Connie and Mark need. Children want to understand differences and they look for cues from the people around them about these differences. If someone they know is uncomfortable with differences, they can sense this even without words.

Provide the information that at two or three years old children can develop pre-prejudice. Explain that each one of us

GRADES: 5th and up

FOCUS: Personal reflection yields insights into how bias develops

MATERIALS: None

carries some kind of bias. We get it from hearing jokes, from noticing the opinions or hearing comments from people in our families, and people we meet, and we get it from the media — from television, movies and books.. We're not bad for having bias and prejudice. But we are responsible to face it and think about it, and make new choices in how we act toward other people.

Since we learned prejudice, we can also unlearn it.

REFLECTION QUESTIONS

I remember... "Let's think back to the earliest memories we can find. Can you remember noticing any types of differences? This is a normal part of human development. What did you observe? Do you remember what your thoughts were? Were you interested or curious? Were you afraid? Did you ask adults about the difference? If not, why? If you did talk to an adult, what did they say?"

I remember... "Now that you know what bias is, can you identify any biases in the messages around you growing up? For example, did you get a message 'to stick with your own kind,' to stick with people like yourself or that certain friendships or certain types of people were not okay? Were these messages of safety or messages of bias?"

I remember... "Has a friend or a relative ever made a statement or joke about a group of people that you disagree with?"

SOURCES

These questions synthesize the inspiring work of Andrea Ayvazian, Louise Derman-Sparks, Carole Johnson, Joan Lester, and Patricia Ramsey. For more information on children 2–5 years old, see the book *Anti-Bias Curriculum* (Resources, p. 169) by Louise Derman-Sparks et al.

❋ ACTIVITY ❋

RECOGNIZING STEREOTYPES

SCHEDULING

These activities cluster well together. You can use short versions of several in a single lesson plan, or use them separately on different days.

ORIENTATION

Tell students: "We're going to examine the human process of generalizing and making assumptions about people and look at what can happen when stereotypes lead to prejudice."

PROCEDURE

1. *Quote of the Day.* Write on the board:

We aren't guilty for the misinformation we've picked up, but we are responsible for not passing it on.

2. *Social Identity:* Tell students: "We each have a social identity. Some aspects are visible, and other aspects aren't readily seen. What are some parts of our social identity?" Write the headings in three columns:

◆ What we can see

◆ Sometimes we can see

◆ What we usually can't see

Examples of what students might say:
◆ Age
◆ Ethnicity/race,
◆ Family composition
◆ Gender
◆ Sexual orientation
◆ Economic class
◆ Learning abilities
◆ Physical abilities
◆ Housing
◆ Religion/spirituality affiliation

Discussion: You can limit this activity to ten minutes to introduce a point, or stay with the discussion if it is bringing up ideas and feelings important to the group. Discuss how a person might choose to wear a religious symbol or wear clothing that provides more information about social identity. Gangs create hidden but specific ways to tag their membership for those who can understand the symbols.

GRADES: 4th–12th

FOCUS: Examine stereotypes we've heard

MATERIALS: None

KIDS TODAY

Sometimes we make assumptions about people and then act on biases we may carry about people who have a certain social identity. Let's look at age. Here is how Cheryl Fox, training coordinator of the Mediation and Training Collaborative in Greenfield, Massachusetts, leads this discussion. She has been using this activity since 1991 with great success:

1. Ask students if they have ever heard their parents or other adults say, "Kids today are..."

2. When the students reply, "Yes!," ask them to name the attributes that follow those words, and write the words on the blackboard or on newsprint. The descriptions are almost always negative: lazy, irrresponsible, wild. After they are done calling out words, read the list and ask them—how does it feel to hear those descriptions? If adults think this about you, does that affect your behavior? Let them know that this attitude constitutes stereotyping and that stereotyping leads to prejudice.

3. Ask the students if they have ever experienced prejudice based on that fact that they are young. Lead a brief discussion on how it feels to be the object of prejudicial treatment.

4. Conclude this exercise by referring back to the brainstormed list, asking, "Is this the way kids today really are?" Brainstorm a new list based on their descriptions of what kids are like. This is also a good time for adults to add affirmations of young people.

DEFINING STEREOTYPING OURSELVES

Engage students in helping to define the word *stereotype*. Focus on allowing them to think about it and use their own words rather than asking them to guess the "right" definition. Here are some reference points which you may find useful:

◆ A stereotype is an unfair generalization based on assumptions about a group.

◆ Stereotypes convey misinformation about the members of a group with a common social identity.

◆ A stereotype is an oversimplified and unvarying idea about the characteristics of members of a group. (This definition is from Stacey L. York's book, *Roots and Wings*, Redleaf Press, 1991).

STEREOTYPE BOXES

Joan Lester and Carole Johnson, founders of Equity Institute, devised this method of using four squares for exploring stereotypes:

1. On the board make a large rectangle and sub-divide it into four boxes.

2. After you add heading, write all the stereotypes that the stu-

dents can think of in that box.

a. Supply one heading for the first box — people over 65. This gives a chance to focus on stereotypes about age at the other end of the age spectrum.

b. Ask the group to supply the other three headings. This way they can work on categories that have the most meaning for them.

Example: A group of Catholic teenagers in the Midwest selected these categories.

◆ People over 65
◆ Teenage Parents
◆ Mexican Americans
◆ Catholic Teenagers

3. After you have written the stereotypes for a group, then pause and ask a student to think of and describe a person they know who is in that group. Do these stereotypes apply accurately to them?

For example, these stereotypes may be written for "People Over 65": *Don't go out of the house much, poor health, don't have a lot of interests.* Then students are asked to identify people they know who are over 65. *Example*: "My grandmother does folk dancing and goes to a folk dancing camp each summer." Look for people you know who contradict the stereotype.

SCHOOL VALUES AND HOME VALUES

How do the values at school and at home interface? Here is an essay I devised for elementary schools to use in discussions with parents and staff.

It is the job of the school to create a context that explicitly affirms each student. School is a place where we learn to negotiate our differences. Yet each family makes their own values, and when children come together at school, they bring different family values.

There are two school values that may be in contradiction to messages, beliefs, and values taught at home or at work in our neighborhoods. The first involves use of physical force. Parents may teach hitting to defend oneself, or they may use hitting for discipline, which may be culturally condoned. The school teaches a different approach. The school affirms using words to negotiate conflicts and negotiate differences. Secondly, if parental values say that it is okay to hate or shun some people due to race/ethnicity, sexual orientation, or disability, the school cannot support these belief systems. The school says that we can be different without hating or hurting each other.

A school supports differences in these ways:

1. We learn that our self esteem derives from embracing our own unique identity, not by comparing ourselves to others in a manner which diminishes. (e.g. I can feel good about my own height without disparaging people who are taller or shorter than myself, or I can feel good about my ethnic identity without acting as if those of my same identity are the most valuable).

2. We acknowledge that in our country people are still treated unfairly based only on their identity. At school we endeavor to create a truly democratic community.

3. We acknowledge that some people have "more " — such as more dexterity at sports, or more money. We don't let these realities make us forget that everyone is valuable.

4. We learn about our unity. We hold two truths: that we are different and that we can be friends. We actively make sure each child feels included and supported in our school.

Bias Awareness Activities

❋ ACTIVITY ❋
MAKE ASSUMPTIONS
A visit with a community member

GRADES: 5th–12th

FOCUS: Interviewing a guest provides an opportunity to look at the process of stereotyping

MATERIALS: paper

ORIENTATION

Tell students: "I have invited a guest to our classroom, and before we get to know them, we'll share our assumptions about the person."

SOURCE

School counselor Jana Standish at Colrain Central School in Massachusetts watched Cheryl Fox of The Mediation and Training Collaborative (p. 133) begin a teacher training by asking the group, "Make assumptions about me." Jana elaborated on this idea and now uses this activity every spring with her sixth-grade students.

PLANNING

Select a visitor from the local community who you think is not already known to the students. *Example:* During the three years Jana Standish has led this activity, she invited these three people:

◆ A man who sells his oil paintings nationally.

◆ A woman who is the Town Clerk.

◆ A man who is an antique dealer and is in a wheelchair.

Prepare your guest by explaining the sequence below. Invite them to bring anything they may want to take out during the interview to share their work, hobbies, or other experiences.

PROCEDURE

1. Hand out paper to all students at the outset. When your visitor enters the classroom, ask students to write down two things that they think about this person.

2. Next, ask the group to make assumptions. Say: "What are your guesses about this person and his or her life?" If anyone happens to know her or him, this student needs to listen and not talk at this point in the visit. Use questions as needed, to help focus. *Examples:*

◆ "What work do you think they do?"

◆ "Do you think this person has any children?"

◆ "Do you think this person has any pets?"

With these and other questions, tease out any stereotypes based on the person's appearance, gender, or physical abilities. Write the student's assumptions on the blackboard so that you can refer to them later.

INTERVIEW AND DIALOGUE

Once the assumptions have been spoken, check with your guest about the accuracy of the statements. Encourage dialogue with the students. Ask him or her to share anything they would like to about their life, their interests, and any special trips or experiences. For instance, when Hale Johnson brought in his oil paintings, students were so interested that they extended his visit for two hours.

REFLECTION

1. Write two things you think about the person now. Compare these with your first list. What made that difference?

2. Where do we get our assumptions from? Where do we get the biases we hold? From the media? from our families? Talk about the "isms"— sexism, ableism, homophobia, racism. Note that we all have biases and when we get to know somebody our assumptions change.

3. What do you think your biases are? *Example:* A student reported, "I hate men who wear ties. I think they are lazy people." When he was asked, "Where do you think you got that?" he said, "That's how my dad feels."

4. Discuss the consequences of having stereotypes. For instance, if someone is old, do you go up to them and get acquainted?

❈ ACTIVITY ❈
SPEAKING UP

ORIENTATION

Tell students: "Today we will learn how students can stand together to help address bias and change unfair behavior."

PROCEDURE

1. Tell a true story you know or present one of the true stories here. Ask students to think about how someone could have intervened.

Example: "It's just a joke."

> *Aaron is standing in a group of his fifth grade friends. One boy starts to make mean jokes about Jewish people. Everyone else laughs at the joke. Aaron is Jewish. He laughs, too, because he doesn't want the group to turn against him. Suddenly one person says, "I'm not so sure about that joke."*
>
> *"It's okay," says another. "Aaron's laughing and he's Jewish."*

- ◆ "How does Aaron really feel? What could you say if you were in that circle?"

- ◆ "Why is it hard for the person who is targeted to show that it matters?"

Explain that a biased joke or biased behavior doesn't just hurt the person who is the target — in this case, Aaron. It's generally offensive. Bias hurts everyone because we are all connected.

2. To speak up, you can simply say "that's not okay with me." Or you can use Heart Language (p. 112). Here is a general format for speaking up with Heart Language. Explain that students can paraphrase with the words they want to use:

- ◆ I'm uncomfortable with _____
  or, It's not okay with me when _____
  [Name the specific behavior — for example, what you just said, what you just did, the look you just gave, the decision you just made.]

- ◆ because _____

Pinpoint what felt disrespectful or not inclusive or simply say, "because it doesn't feel fair,"

- ◆ and I'd like _____.

Ask students: "What do want to have happen next? Is there a specific action you want to suggest?"

Example: *That joke isn't okay with me because it puts down Jewish people, and I'd like you to not tell that joke again.*

3. Here is a situation involving sexual harassment, which means unwanted and unwelcomed sexual behavior:

> *Sharon and Risa are walking down the hall together to the school cafeteria. A boy in their class named Jeremy hurries by and grabs Sharon's "butt." She tells him, "Stop," but smiles because she is fearful of protesting too strongly. Jeremy laughs and runs ahead.* Discuss how Risa or a teacher could support Sharon and intervene. See the Gender Peacemaking Unit, p. 154, for information about the Mentors in Violence Prevention Program.

4. Discuss: "Who stops unfair things from happening? Are there unfair things that you have seen happen and no one has stopped them? Would anyone like to mention an incident and have people in the class discuss what it would have been like to intervene?"

GOING FURTHER

Talk through these guidelines:

- ◆ Take action. Don't stand by when unfairness happens.

- ◆ Don't assume just because others are going along, that they think it's okay. They may be waiting for someone else to act.

- ◆ Act from what you feel is right.

- ◆ Whether or not a person targeted by the joke or the action is in the room, speak up about what is unfair.

- Don't wait for a targeted person to act first.

- Speak up firmly but without using unfair behavior such as bullying or putting down the other person.

- Your actions matter not just to the person targeted: you are doing this for yourself and for everyone.

RESOURCES

- *It's Our World, Too: Stories of Young People Making a Difference (And How They're Doing It)* by Phillip Hoose (Little, Brown and Company, Boston, 1993) has detailed stories with photographs of young people who took a stand for something they believed in. It includes the story of Neto Villareal, a high school football player, and Andy Percifield, a Student Council leader, who helped their whole school stop the racist behavior of fans at school football games.

- *Bullyproof: A Teacher's Guide on Teasing and Bullying for Use with Fourth and Fifth Grade Students* by Nan Stein, Lisa Sjostrom and Emily Gaberman (National Education Association, 1996) Eleven sequential lessons help students learn strategies to prevent and respond to teasing and bullying.

EXTENSION

Social Safety: Apply the concepts of win/lose and win/win to the issue of speaking up. Explain that if people are allowed to put others down and no one intervenes it creates the feeling of "win/lose" within that group.

1. Articulate win/lose. List behaviors that students feel are unfair, such as talking behind someone's back.

2. Articulate win/win. Describe a "safe classroom."

3. What are the promises or agreements that the classroom could make to create that feeling of equal safety and a win/win classroom community?

Example: At a Congregational Youth Group in Northampton, Massachusetts, everyone decided to make a promise to say only positive things about all members of the group and that this applied whether people were present or absent that day. This created a strong feeling of solidarity.

✳ ACTIVITY ✳

WHO LIKES THIS ACTIVITY?

SOURCE

Priscilla Prutzman, director of the Children's Creative Response to Conflict program.

ORIENTATION

Tell students: "Today we'll look at the activities we like to play."

PROCEDURE

1. Ask students to list all the different activitities they can think of for children their age. *Examples*: kick ball, tag, Legos, reading, soccer, drawing, football, hockey.

2. Go through the list and read the name of each activity. Ask, "Who likes this one?" Priscilla Prutzman finds that for many activities an equal number of girls and boys will raise their hands to say they like them.

3. Ask: "What do you notice about this list?" Often stu-

GRADES: 1st–6th

FOCUS: Examining favorite games contradicts assumptions about gender preferences

MATERIALS: Chart paper and marker for listmaking

dents observe that some games are called "girls' games" or "boys' games." Examine these assumptions. *Example*: Hockey may be seen as a "boys' sport" but girls like it as well, and today there are women's hockey teams. Explain that we can choose what we like to do — not because we are a girl or boy, but according to our own preferences.

4. Extend the discussion to cover any important issues in your class that relate to equity and fairness. Is equipment being shared fairly at recess? Does everyone have access to the playing fields, or does one group always have use of the best play space?

❈ ACTIVITY ❈

WORD WATCH

OVERVIEW

You can use this activity to explore bias exhibited in language and to respond to a problem or complaint about words that have hurt someone's feelings. Children have different awareness of word meaning at different ages.

ORIENTATION

Tell students: "We are going to think of words, phrases and expressions that have violence, racism, sexism, or put-down of people with disabilities in them, and then substitute a different way to express the same thought."

PROCEDURE

1. Begin with associations with violence. Brainstorm phrases that aren't directly about violence but use violence to convey the thought. Reframe each phrase.

Examples: "stab in the back" can be reframed as "betray"

2. Ask for phrases that contain subtle put-downs. As you list each item, stop to clarify

a. what the expression means

b. what a substitute phrase would be

c. where the bias is

Examples:

◆ *blacklisted* means, "to be put on a list of suspected persons to be punished or to be refused a job" and the bias is that "black" is used in a negative way. Another way to say it would be "to be ostracized."

◆ *blackball* means, "to vote against or to exclude socially" and again, the bias is that "black" is used as a put-down. This word also means to ostracize.

◆ *manpower* means "the work force or the human resources" and the bias is that it refers to both women and men in the group but eclipses the presense of women.

Resource: *The Dictionary of Bias-Free Usage: A Guide to Nondiscriminatory Language* by Rosalie Maggio (Phoenix: Oryx Press, 1991).

Some words may appear to be sexist, but have a different origin. The word *history,* for example, comes from the Greek word *historia,* whose root means "to know, to in-

GRADES: 2nd and up

FOCUS: Examine words and phrases for bias

MATERIALS: Chart paper and marker for listmaking

quire, to learn." Yet in common usage the prefix *his* takes on emphasis. Some people like to add the term "herstory" to be explicitly inclusive.

3. Be sure to ferret out expressions like "Are you blind?" or "Are you deaf?", which put down physical disabilities as expressions of disdain. Talk about preferred terms relating to disabilities. Explain that to say, "Lena is crippled and confined to a wheelchair" has derogatory connotations. Instead, we say "Lena is a wheelchair user." Our language can help us focus on the person instead of seeing a disability as the most important thing about her or him.

4. Some expressions obscure the multiplicity of the world, and make one group the norm.

a. Explain that until the 1980s, products like bandages or crayons labeled "flesh-colored" were sold, implying that white skin is the standard skin color.

b. In reference to social studies, the term *discovery* — as in "Columbus discovered America" — disregards the people whose homeland has been entered and implies that an area isn't important until it has been learned about by Europeans.

c. The word *race* was socially created and used to rationalize slavery. By inventing the idea of separate "races" rather than one human race, and thereby calling some ethnic groups "inferior," the practice of mistreatment has been sanctioned.

SOURCE

Priscilla Prutzman has been leading word exploration since 1985 and has found that students are fascinated with uncovering this hidden source of bias. Ideas from Susan Hoy Crawford and Joan Lester are incorporated.

Bias Awareness Activities

ACTIVITY

Open and Closed Circles

Exclusion

ORIGIN

At St. Philip's School in Bemidji, Minnesota, students in the third and fifth grades were playing a game they called "Smear the Queer." At recess, leaders of a clique selected one person to target that day. Then the group hit that person with balls or tackled them. Here is the activity that teacher Sue Liedl devised to intervene. She led this as a workshop for two classes (forty students) in a large room with open space, not the familiar classrooms — once for fifth grade, and once for third. After this workshop, this targeting stopped.

ORIENTATION

Tell students: "Think about groups you belong to that have clear rules: sports teams, scouts, gymnastics, or dance groups. These groups are set up and run by adults. At your age you are starting to experiment with making your own groups and your own rules. Today we will look at one way of creating group rules and see if it is working for everyone."

OPENER

Share with students this analogy: when a person is driving toward a city sometimes they can see a cloud of pollution hanging over the city ahead. But as they get into the city, the cloud seems to disappear. They can't see the pollution anymore once they are inside the city. We are going to look at a situation today from outside of it, like looking at the pollution of a city from a distance.

Next, students stand up with space between them. They stand in their own "space bubbles" and practice having a sense of their own space. This introduces the theme of not invading another's personal space.

MAIN ACTIVITY

Represent four types of friendship circles using animal symbols. Put either a stuffed animal or puppet of an owl, turtle, teddy bear, and dinosaur (or just the names of the animals) in each of four circles. These animals symbolize different approaches:

- Dinosaurs: *I like to make rules my way* (leaders of exclusion).
- Teddy bears: *I follow other people's rules* (followers).
- Owls: *I decide for myself what's right. I like being with others or by myself* (quiet leaders).
- Turtles: *I hope things will just get better* (bystanders).

Say, "We're going to show four different ways to create friendship groups." Students are randomly placed in one of the four circles. If you like, look for where the children who are spearheading the exclusion are standing and group this quadrant as the dinosaurs.

Next, use props to show what it feels like to be in each type of circle.

- *Dinosaurs:* Use strong orange tape (the kind used to mark trees) or twine to cocoon the dinosaurs. No one can get in or out of that group.
- *Turtles:* Put the two blankets over the turtles. When they are under blankets, they can't see or respond to what is going on.
- *Teddy Bears:* Tape their legs together. They can't go anywhere alone. They have to be together.
- *Owls:* No props added. People can join or lead this group as they choose.

Now talk about what are the consequences of these styles of friendship groups.

- Persons who want to get a drink at the water fountain can't get there as teddy bears because they are all taped together.
- Persons who want to bring their lunch tray over to the dinosaurs can't get in because the circle is taped shut.

GRADES: 3rd and up
FOCUS: Students study how cliques operate
MATERIALS: Four stuffed animals, two blankets, tape or twine

Ask students for other examples.

Discuss that these groups aren't based on popularity, but are based on need for security. *Option*: Explain the meaning of each position by making cardboard thermometers illustrating that animal's need for security. The dinosaurs have the highest need for sense of belonging and the highest need for security, so the red "mercury" colored on their thermometer goes the highest of the four. The owls will have the lowest.

CLOSURE

Release all students from the circles and sit together in one big circle.

EXTENSION

It is very important for adults to intervene whenever hurtful language is used. In this instance it would be important to follow up with students about the name of this game, "smear the queer." If homophobic epithets go unchecked, if any one group of people is allowed to be targeted, then no one is truly safe. Find words to express your concern, like. "You're using the word *fag* as a put-down and I feel concerned about that." One fourth grader told his teacher, "A fag is somebody we're not supposed to like." Explain that in a democracy everyone must be safe and free to be who they are, no one is allowed to be mistreated, and no one deserves hatred.

❋ ACTIVITY ❋
INTERRUPTING TARGETING

SUMMARY

When children in the class are targeted, we can intervene with a three-pronged approach:

◆ New agreements

◆ New perspectives

◆ New activities.

We will use the theme of targeting, excluding, and scapegoating to be an example of how you can create a new direction for your class based on a problem or need you perceive.

These same questions can be used for any problem you encounter.

GATHER INFORMATION

What is the problem that concerns you?

Fifth-grade students are dividing into cliques.

What specifically is happening in the class?

One girl is telephoning her friends each evening to tell them what clothes to wear, how to style their hair, and what earrings to put on. They come to school looking alike, and immediately other girls feel left out and her clique is visible. This group stares at other girls at lunchtime and whispers. Girls have been in tears over this. Upon further reflection,

it's not accurate to say there are cliques. Actually, there is one small group that is excluding others, and the children feel helpless to change this.

What would you say to yourself if you decided to ignore or dismiss the problem?

"This always happens with girls this age. Nothing can be done. They just have to figure it out for themselves."

Now, decide not to ignore it. Examine the deeper roots of the behavior in the adult world. Extrapolate as broadly as possible. Brainstorm all the imbalances in the adult culture that this behavior reflects. What social forces help to drive this kind of behavior?

Women are judged by their physical appearance and not the content of their character. In the media, appearance is paramount. Young girls are socialized to start preparing to compete for boys very early in imitation of "catching husbands." There is a belief, one that borders on a social reality, that for a woman to be safe and secure she needs to be married for economic, social, and physical protection. Girls are taught to handle the tension they feel by jealousy or attacking each other. A social pattern of excluding, targeting, and scapegoating rather than respecting and nurturing all members of the human community has been passed down the generations for centuries. The personal power of girls and women is not fully welcomed in society.

How can you keep this broad perspective in mind, yet think about where the children are at this moment and speak to them in a child-oriented way? Beginning where they are, what is their next step? What are they now ready to understand in a new way?

I could tell them that there is a human problem that we are trying to change and that is the problem of leaving people out. When one person is hurt in our classroom community, the whole group feels less safe. I've noticed that people are feeling less safe and less included, and we're going to work together to bring back the feeling of safety.

How can you ensure that the children who are "carrying" the hurtful behavior will feel safe as you help them change?

I can start off by looking into them and seeing the part of them that wants to participate in fairness and speak to that part. I could talk to them privately about their ability to be leaders and their responsibility as leaders.

I would explain why planning with a small group to look alike is hurtful to others. I would look for other arenas and activities during the day when I could ask these individuals to take positive leadership.

How can you ensure that the children who have been targeted by the hurtful behavior will feel safe, seen, respected, and valued?

I could talk to them privately and assure them that there is nothing they have done to cause or deserve being left out, and let them know that I'll help with this situation. I could work with them on "standing in their light" and believing in themselves no matter what others do.

Let's revisit this quote from the CCRC book: "The goal is to encourage teachers and others who work with children to move beyond the treatment of isolated crisis situations by developing a positive dynamic." What would a positive dynamic look like with respect to this problem?

Girls would be able to take turns interacting in school with every class member. Each girl would be assured that she has friends. Students would maintain an ethic that no one is to talk about another behind her back. All students would have their leadership abilities encouraged.

Are there classroom agreements you could formulate which would carry this as a code of behavior?

"Let's make an agreement that we will talk positively about all members of our class whether or not they are present. Let's bring problems to class meetings."

What activities would students need to participate in to have concrete practice of this skill?

They would need cooperative activities where many students have a chance to take leadership. During these groups, I will make sure that patterns of exclusion don't take hold. I will need to overtly encourage the personal power of the girls to come forward and show that each can be supportive of each other's strengths. Playing sports like basketball together is one effective way to develop unity.

Three directions to remember:

1. Adults need to take responsibility. We may not know the best way to step in, but we do need to intervene instead of ignoring the problem. The problem exists because of the imbalance in adult culture and not because "children are like this."

2. Use child-centered language and activities. Work at the level where children are — offer their next step. Think about your broader analysis as an adult, but don't impose adult activities inappropriately. Work from a balanced place inside yourself.

3. Maintain safety for all group members. Make sure that your actions say, "All people here are to be respected: we aren't punishing, we aren't labeling people bad." This means, for example, that the ones who are doing the targeting and the ones who have been targeted both are treated respectfully.

This same approach applies to children who habitually hit or call names. It applies to behaviors where disabled children are ostracized, girls are harrassed in school hallways or children of color are treated unfairly. These behaviors reflect the adult society. When people hit, exclude, or make racist remarks, these are antisocial behaviors, but they are occurring because these people are acting out of their injury. Hitting, excluding, and oppressing are ways for people to place themselves in a dominant position, but these are evidences of wounds — deep social wounds that have gone untreated. Our generation is trying to change social patterns that have existed for centuries. We don't have all the answers, but if we can formulate our intentions soundly, then together we will create the new directions.

✳ MUSIC ACTIVITY ✳
SINGING SPANISH

ORIENTATION

Tell students: "Learning more languages is an important way to build bridges. The language spoken most frequently next to English in the United States is Spanish."

PROCEDURE

Ask which students speak more than one language and applaud them. Make sure that students are affirmed rather than targeted for being multilingual.

If you are not a Spanish speaker, encourage students who know a song in Spanish such as "De Colores" or "Cheki, Morena," to teach the class, or use this sequence of simple songs. One is traditional and three were composed to have bilingual songs that develop cooperation.

1. *Greeting song: Hola, ¿Qué Tal?*
        words and music by Sarah Pirtle

Hola, ¿qué tal? Hola, ¿qué tal?
Hola _____ , Hola _____
Hola _____ , Hola _____
¡Hola todos aquí! ¡Sí!
Hello, my friends. Hello, my friends.
Hi to _____ , Hi to _____
Hi to _____ , Hi to _____
Hi to everyone here! Yes!

Sing the names of everyone in the class by inserting their names in the blank spaces.

2. *Welcoming Song: Buenos Días al Cielo,*
        words and music by Sarah Pirtle

Buenos días al cielo, sí.
Buenos días a la tierra, sí.
Buenos días a todos aquí.
A tí, a tí, y a mí.
Good morning to the sky, sky, sky.
Good morning to the ground, ground, ground.
Good morning to all the people in the circle.
Let's take a look around.

Sing with hand movements pointing to the sky, and the earth, then waving to everyone in the group.

3. *Counting song: Chocolate:* This traditional Mexican song

GRADES: K–6th
FOCUS: Use simple bilingual songs to encourage learning both Spanish and English
MATERIALS: *Linking Up* recording

talks about stirring up a chocolate drink using the *molinillo*, a special wooden spoon that is twirled in both hands. *Bate* means to stir. As you sing, rub your hands like you're twirling the *molinillo*.

Uno, dos, tres, CHO, Uno, dos, tres, CO
Uno, dos, tres. LA, Uno dos, tres, TE.
Chocolate, chocolate, bate bate chocolate.

4. *Movement Song:* "Step by Step / Paso a Paso"
        words and music by Sarah Pirtle

Step by step, paso a paso, Paso a paso, así, así
Muevan las manos, muevan las manos.
Move your hands, move your hands.

During "Step by Step, Paso a Paso," walk around the room or walk with your fingers on the desk. On the second part of the song move the part of your body that is described. New verses:
Muevan los dedos, move your fingers.
Muevan la cabeza, move your head.
Muevan la cintura, move your hips.
Muevan la lengua, move your tongue.

Note: All four songs can be heard on the Linking Up recording sung by Sarah Pirtle and Roberto Díaz. (Resources, p. 169)

5. *Learning More Songs:* Encourage students and parents to bring in songs of their heritage. Songs are a window into our cultures.

Resource: José-Luis Orozco's five cassette set, *Lírica Infantil, Hispanic Children's Folklore,* available from Arcoiris Children's Music, P.O. Box 7428, Berkeley, CA 94707.

GENDER PEACEMAKING

Bias Awareness Unit

OVERVIEW

In your classroom are girls and boys friends with each other? One of the goals of the activity units in Chapter 4 is to help girls and boys have positive experiences working together in small cooperative groups in order to encourage friendships. Feelings of unity between boys and girls provide an important foundation for this unit.

Sexism is held in place by prescribed patterned behavior. Sexism teaches that girls should act in certain patterns (such as focusing on looking attractive to boys according to socially defined ways) and boys should act in certain other patterns (such as not being receptive to the requests made by girls and women but rather being tough and unyielding); if they don't, they will face unpleasant or even dangerous consequences like ostracism or exclusion. When we see that these patterns are not truths but socially created agreements, we gain the tools for changing them. In our classrooms we can teach that both males and females contribute and come together to solve this problem. In so doing we help children enter a conversation that will be crucial for them throughout their lives.

What is a useful way as teachers to break the silence on sexism and on gender violence? How can our support of girls go deeper than presenting exceptional famous women during Women's History Month? How can boys be supported to develop not only their physical abilities but their nurturing abilities? These are questions worth carrying as teachers. Here are some ways to make it safe to talk about what's unfair and what needs to change.

1. Introduce children to men as well as women who are working to change sexism.

2. Help students notice patterns of behavior and expectations which show gender bias by involving them in social research to get perspective on the problem.

Since most communities now have visible groups of women working against sexism and because it is the purpose of this book to provide resources not easily obtainable, the first activity will focus on organizations of anti-sexist men. To high-

GRADES: 5th and up

FOCUS: Create a safe atmosphere for exploring gender bias.

light the work of girls and women, these other resources are highly recommended:

◆ *New Moon Magazine for Girls* and *New Moon Network for Adults Who Care About Girls* can be reached at 1-800-381-4743. New Moon Publishing P.O. Box 3587, Duluth, MN 55803-3587. On the Web: www.newmoon.org. Also see their resource catalog.

◆ The Center for Research on Women, Wellesley College, 106 Central Street, Wellesley, MA 02181-8268.

✻ ACTIVITY ✻

NEWS ABOUT GENDER PEACEMAKING

BACKGROUND

There is an old story about a dragon on the edge of town. The dragon looms, threatening everyone, but people don't talk about it. They say, "We will be safer if we pretend it is not there." This silence is even more terrifying for the children because they see the dragon. If there is something dangerous that the grown-ups won't talk about, then it means the grown-ups don't know what to do and that is even more scary.

Our world has many such dragons that children see but we haven't done battle with yet. One is gender-related violence and aggression. According to the F.B.I., over 90 percent of interpersonal violence in the U.S. is committed by men, and yet according to anti-sexist activist Jackson Katz, public discussion about the roots of violence only rarely acknowledges gender as a significant factor.

The dragon in this analogy does not represent men. The dragon represents patterns of domination and sexism that perpetuate violence and silence minority voices. Overcoming this dragon involves supporting both women and men, girls and boys, and allowing the many voices of what it means to be male and female to be heard, not just the dominant images of tough he-man and subservient Barbie doll.

OVERVIEW

As children prepare to take part in the adult world, they may not know all the organizations that exist — or could be created — which relate to gender issues. The following four examples provide windows for young people to see more of the world they can take part in. The work of these men interrupts rigid stereotyping and communicates that being a man includes work against sexism and support of other men and boys. Just as racism cannot change unless white people help other white people change the power imbalance, so, too, sexism cannot change unless men help other men in a myriad of ways.

PROCEDURE

1. Before sharing these four examples, ask students to make a guess about the following:

   a. What do you think a Men's Resource Center offers for boys and men? Are there any right now in the United States?

   b. Picture an organization of African-American men supporting African-American boys. What do you think it does?

   c. If a man was a student-athlete and minored in Women's Studies, what job might he do today that combines both concerns?

   d. What would an organization called "Men As Peacemakers" do?

2. Share these examples to help give students a broader picture of what men across the country are doing. *Future Job List:* Ask students to make a list of the jobs, both paid and volunteer, that they can picture as a result of knowing about this work. What can boys do in the future that relate to what they learn from these examples? *Examples:* directing a men's resource center, leading a fathering program, being a mentor to a

younger boy.

Be sure to also present information relating to women's centers, national women's organizations and women's support groups, to make a similar list of all the jobs girls can do in the future related to building gender equity and supporting other women.

◆ *Example One:* The Men's Resource Center in Amherst, Massachusetts offers support groups, youth education programs, batterer treatment, resources including a quarterly magazine, a speakers' bureau and many types of training and consultation. It was started in 1982 by Steven Botkin as one part of "a larger movement of men throughout the world who are re-examining rigid gender roles and challenging interpersonal and institutional patterns of domination, discrimination, and violence." Here is how the MRC describes its mission: "We support men and develop men's leadership in challenging all forms of oppression in our lives, our families, and our communities. Our programs support men in overcoming the damaging effects of rigid and stereotyped masculinity, and simultaneously confront men's patterns of personal and societal violence and abuse toward women, children, and other men." For more information, contact Men's Resource Center, 30 Boltwood Walk, Amherst, MA 01002. E-mail: mrc@valinet.com. Web site: mrcwma.org.

Share these snapshots:

   ◆ *Youth Education Programs:* Men present workshops in area schools on issues such as sexual harassment, creating healthy relationships, and masculinity and sexism.

   ◆ *Alternatives to Detention:* Men lead after-school programs for junior high school students on respect, violence prevention and healthy relationships.

   ◆ *Fathering Programs:* Groups help fathers in a number of ways, including assisting new fathers with parenting skills and helping divorcing fathers feel supported and give emotional support to their children.

   ◆ *Young Men Overcoming Violence Groups:* A ten-week group helps young men, ages 14 to 19, who have been violent or abusive.

   ◆ *Speakers' Bureau:* Formerly abusive men and formerly abused women give public talks to share their experiences with others to help prevent family violence.

◆ *Example Two: African-American Men Launch 100 Black Men, Inc. and Concerned Black Men, Inc.* 100 Black Men, Inc has 64 member chapters in 24 states and has affected more than 60,000 young people. Its programs focus on mentoring, education, anti-violence, and economic development. It's goal is to overcome the cultural and financial obstacles that have limited the achievements of African-American youth. For more information on this group, call 1-800-598-3411, or write: 141 Auburn Ave., Atlanta, GA 30303.

Concerned Black Men, Inc. started in 1975 and works "to publicly recognize and aid the constructive African-American youth." Concerned Black Men, Inc. has chapters now throughout the country to "encourage African-American youth to be proud of their heritage, maximize educational opportunities, and to be socially conscous and responsible." See Web site: http://www.libertynet.org/cbmno, or write Concerned Black Men, Inc., ATTN. Dan Henderson, National Chairman, 7200 North 21st St., Philadephia, PA 19138–2102

- *Example Three: The Mentors in Violence Prevention (MVP) Program.* The multiracial Mentors in Violence Prevention (MVP) Program was created by Jackson Katz in 1983 at Northeastern University's Center for the Study of Sport in Society. Its purpose is to encourage male (and female) student-athletes at all levels to speak out against sexism and all forms of gender violence. The idea is that athletes have status in many peer cultures, and their active participation and leadership in anti-sexist efforts can help to create a climate among boys and men whereby verbal, emotional, or physical abuse of girls and women will be seen as completely socially unacceptable. MVP focuses on men not as perpetrators or potential perpetrators, but as brothers, friends, teammates, and classmates who can interrupt and confront abusive peers. The main teaching tool is called the MVP Playbook, which consists of a series of scenarios involving actual and potential assaults by boys and men against girls and women. Contact: The Center for the Study of Sport in Society, Northeastern University, 360 Huntington Ave., Suite 161 CP, Boston, MA 02115. Telephone: (617) 373-4025.

  Katz believes that we need to create a culture of men who are intolerant of violence against women. Coaches, for instance, can learn how to step in and take action if a player on a team is known to be being violent toward women, just as Bobby Knight of Indiana University kicked his star player off the team for beating up his girlfriend. MVP teaches that violence hurts the victim and the violator, and that those who know violence is occurring can speak up and say it is unacceptable. Jackson Katz was a student-athlete at the University of Massachusetts where he minored in Women's Studies (see question 1C above). Katz now directs MVP Strategies, which provides gender violence prevention education and training to the U.S. military and other public and private institutions. Contact him at MVPStrat@aol.com.

- *Example Four: Men As Peacemakers.* This organization in Duluth, Minnesota links individual men with community organizations that need volunteer help mentoring children, comforting victims of violence and teaching nonviolence. The group states, "Men commit most of the violence in our community, but are a very small part of the solution. Men as Peacemakers is changing that by getting men off the sidelines and involved in making peace." They also sponsor an annual Men's March for Peace and were involved with the *Duluth News-Tribune* in featured news reports that led to a televised town meeting, video documentary, and companion Teacher's Guide.

Contact: Men as Peacemakers, 320 West 2nd St., Room 503, Duluth, MN 55802.

ACTIVITY
Gender Research

SOURCE

This activity was inspired by Susan Hoy Crawford's book, *Beyond Dolls and Guns: 101 Ways to Help Children Avoid Gender Bias* (Heinemann, Portsmouth, NH, 1996). This book is highly recommended for action ideas that will inspire other classroom activities. The research quotes are from her book; in some cases I have added the word "most" with her permission. The research activity for "Do Boys Listen to Girls?" is from Lynn Benander, an educator from Shelburne Falls, Massachusetts.

ORIENTATION

Tell students: "Today we're going to look at an area of unfairness that affects all of us here — bias based on gender, different treatment, and expectations that happen based on whether a person is female or male."

BUILD SAFETY

Explain to students that it's important at the outset that we understand this isn't about boys against girls or girls against boys. It's not about anyone being bad. It's about noticing and questioning patterns of behavior and expectations that have been passed along from generation to generation so that we can choose whether to continue these patterns that have shaped the world differently for girls and for boys, each in ways that are hard.

RESEARCH

1. Introduce the concept that people can become conscious of unfair behavior they weren't aware of and try to change it, by giving an example of unfair behavior of adults, not children. Explain what it means to do research — to test a hypothesis — and tell students that the research finding you are about to share was tested by videotaping classrooms and by using trained college-age observers in classrooms.

   Research finding: "Most teachers call on boys more often than girls. Most teachers allow boys to call out answers eight times more often than they allow girls to do so. Male students ask and answer more questions. They talk more and longer. They interrupt both female students and teachers."

   Clarify that this isn't a prediction, but a description. Talk about this as a social pattern that adults are trying to change so that both female and male students have an equal chance to be heard.

2. As a class, choose one of the four ideas below and do your own gender research. The first one — examining books and magazines — is the easiest. Or, divide the class into groups of three or four students, possibly having girls work with girls and boys work with boys. Ask each group to choose any of the four areas. Go through the items, explaining what the research says and suggesting what they could do to test the research. The hardest to observe is whether boys listen to girls. You can invent other ways to test the research instead of using the suggestion.

3. If you are working in small groups, ask each group to select one of the four choices and discuss any changes they will make in the research idea. Help them talk through their plan and make an observation sheet if needed. Assign the group one week to complete their

research. Provide class time for this work. Talk about etiquette for research — don't make fun of people's answers, keep answers confidential, and allow privacy. Afterward, ask each group to meet and discuss what their findings showed and prepare a report to the class.

4. Before sharing reports, reestablish a safe atmosphere for looking at bias. Remind students that this is not "boys against the girls." If bias isn't found, it doesn't mean that the boys have won. If bias is found, it doesn't mean that the girls have won. Sexism is a social problem that all genders are trying to solve together as partners. See the activity, "What the Spirals Say" (p. 50) which provides research on centuries of partnership between women and men before the beginning of the system of male dominance.

REFLECTION

If you need help getting the distance needed to observe behavior in a non-threatening manner, use creative writing or creative dramatics. Pretend you are visitors from another planet examining the different ways females and males on the Planet Earth are treated. Notice: What gender are the leaders of governments? The jobs held primarily by which gender are paid more? Is childrearing paid for in any culture?

Note: This work requires sensitivity. It is painful to awaken to the existence of sexism. We are providing support for girls and boys to "complicate" their thinking and hold two kinds of awareness at once. Girls can go through developmental stages to be able to hold these two perceptions: "Sexism exists and women and girls are treated differently for no other reason than our gender," and "I as a girl am valuable, good, and smart, and I will respect myself." We help boys go through developmental stages to be able to say, "The unfairness of sexism exists, and as a boy I will get messages that suggest I should continue the way girls and women are mistreated," but "I can be a man who relates to girls and women as friends and partners to be respected without my manhood threatened."

GENDER BIAS RESEARCH IDEAS

1. Do Books and Magazines Favor Stories of Males?

GENERAL FINDING: Most libraries carry more biographies of men, most newspaper carry more stories about men in leadership positions, and most cartoons feature male characters, unless they have made a deliberate decision to try to change.

RESEARCH IDEA: Pick three magazines or newspapers for a general audience (not aimed at girls or boys, women or men) and skim through them to determine if these findings apply. In addition, look for a magazine that has made an effort to include an equal number of features about males and females.

2. Do People Expect Boys to be Smarter than Girls?

RESEARCH FINDING:
"When adults are asked to picture an intelligent child, 57% of women and 71% of men picture a boy."

RESEARCH IDEA: Find out if this happens among young people. At recess, tell students you are doing a research project and want to ask them a question. Ask an equal number of boys and of girls. Speak to students one at a time privately by themselves, and ask them to picture an intelligent child. Ask them if they have the picture clearly in their mind. Then ask if they are picturing a girl or a boy. Tally their responses on the lines below. Thank them for their help. Do not make any comments about their response. Be willing to share your findings when the study is done. Option: Test this among various age groups. Ask adults the same questions.

OBSERVATION SHEET: Record your findings anonymously.

◆ The person we talked is a ☐ girl ☐ boy

They pictured a ☐ smart girl ☐ smart boy

   OR, ☐ they said they didn't have a particular gender in mind.

◆ What do you notice about your findings? Did children tend to picture girls or boys?

3. Do Boys Listen to Girls?

RESEARCH FINDING: "Between the ages of three-and-a-half and five-and-a-half, many boys stop responding to girls' requests, suggestions, and other attempts to influence them."

RESEARCH IDEA: Observe a class of any age group at recess or free play.

BRING AN OBSERVATION SHEET:

1. Look for a time a boy made a request of a boy: Mark the result:
   ☐ He did it. ☐ He ignored it. ☐ He disagreed. ☐ A fight began.

2. Look for a time a girl made a request of a boy: Mark the result:
   ☐ He did it. ☐ He ignored it. ☐ He disagreed. ☐ A fight began.

4. Do Parents Expect Genders to Behave Differently?

RESEARCH FINDING: "Many parents tell their children outright that girls and boys are different types of creatures, and that certain behaviors can be expected from one gender and not the other."

RESEARCH IDEA: Interview ten children, five girls and five boys. This interview does not have to be private and can be done as a group. Tell them that you are going to read them three statements, and ask them which one is most true for their family. Put checks by the statements that apply.

1. My family has given me the impression that both girls and boys can be expected to be good at getting along with people, to do well at schoolwork, and to do well in the sports they choose.

2. My family hasn't given any particular messages about girls and boys.

3. My family has told me that boys will probably be better at sports and girls will probably be better at getting along with people.

◆ Any additional comments?

✳ ACTIVITY ✳

THE WEB OF HUMAN UNITY

ORIENTATION

Tell students: "Scientists have learned that all human beings are interconnected. Today we will explore what unity means."

PROCEDURE

UNITY DISCUSSION

◆ **Unity.** Ask students: "Can you think of a time you were in a group and people were excited about what they had done together? Were you on a team? Did you do a play? Can you remember a party where people felt united and happy to be together?" Seek out stories of teams, family parties, neighborhood block parties, performances. "These are memories of feeling united."

◆ **One Human Species.** "One way to think of our class is that we are all on the same team. Are all human beings on the same team?" As students explore this question in their own ways, you can add biological information. There are not really different races of humans — this is a misnomer. People from different groups can share blood and can intermarry. We are one race, one species.

◆ **People are United like a Web of Nerve Cells.** For students who are abstract thinkers, explain that scientists now believe that all humans are interconnected very much like the drawing of a spider web. This perspective on human unity is part of general systems theory. Explain that in the past Western scientists such as Isaac Newton thought about humans as separate entities, having impact on each other the way one billiard ball hits another and causes it to move. In contrast, today systems thinkers see humans connected like nerve cells in one body.

SPIDER WEB DRAWING

Note: Grandmother Spider is important to many Native American traditions, and she has different meanings as the Creator or as the Mother of the people.

"Once upon a time there were lots of people in the world, but they were feeling lonely and forgotten and far away from each other."

1. On the board, draw a collection of small circles the size of

GRADES: K–6th

FOCUS: Use discussion, drawing and movement to explore the interconnection of class members

MATERIALS: Paper, markers

a button, leaving lots of space in between.

"Then Grandmother Spider came and she found a way to connect all of these people."
Ask for volunteers to help draw lines that connect all of the circles. "This is a spider web drawing. When everyone is connected, we say that they are united."

2. "Now, I'm going to draw the same number of circles as there are people in our class. How many people are members of our classroom community? In the discussion, include adult staff — main teacher, resource teachers, aides, assistants, regular parent volunteers. Draw enough circles so that each person is represented. "Would you help Grandmother Spider come along and connect all the circles?" Ask volunteers to draw connecting lines. "This represents that everyone in our class is united."

"Now we're going to each make a Grandmother Spider drawing connecting all the people in our class."

3. Give each student a piece of paper and provide markers to share. Ask them to arrange circles (the size of a button) all over the paper. Use the exact number as the number of people in the class including adult staff. Ask them not to label circles with specific names. If they like, they don't have to use a circle, but can select whatever shape they want — stars, triangles.

4. Next, they use lines to show that all these people are united. Allow each person to create his or her own way of representing this concept. Help provide additional art materials to meet their imaginations. Some may want to embellish the pictures with pipe cleaners, sticks, glitter, or feathers.

◆ *Variation: Unity Collage.* Ask each student to bring in as many small objects as there are people in the class — acorn caps, buttons, pennies, cut paper shapes, tiny shells, pebbles. Select small objects that can be glued or taped to paper. Arrange these objects on paper and add interconnecting lines.

5. *Share the completed drawings:* Extend the understanding of unity: what does it mean to be closely connected as these drawings show? Talk about the sense that all people in the class are connected as if they were in one web.

SPIDER WEB HAND SQUEEZE

In the game "Telegraph" in *The Friendly Classroom for a Small Planet,* (Resources, p. 169) students hold hands in a circle and take turns passing a squeeze. In this variation, first just try crossing hands and passing a squeeze. Once this basic pattern is clear, change your hand formation to imitate a spider web. Small groups are easiest. Stand shoulder to shoulder without holding hands at first. Now reach your arms out and take hold of hands reaching from any part of the circle. Keep reaching and looking around until all hands are connected. Allow necessary adjustments; if the last two hands left unconnected are far away, reposition until everyone is linked without too much strain. (Make sure one section of the circle isn't an independent loop.) Now pass a squeeze. It helps to have each person say "Yes," as they receive the squeeze.

Nerve Cells: Tell students: "If we were nerve cells in one body, we would be sending signals to each other. Human beings in a community are connected like nerve cells. We send signals to each other about what we notice and what we request. As we do the Spider Web Hand Squeeze, let's pretend to be nerve cells sending a message."

EXTENSIONS

◆ **Pictures of Patterns in Nature.** Gather nature books and magazines from the library, including *National Geographic,* and ask students to search for photographs that express unity — patterns in nature, webs, animals in groups.

◆ **Songs of human unity.**

—"This Land is Your Land" by Woody Guthrie

—"If I Had a Hammer" by Pete Seeger and Lee Hayes

—"Kumbaya" — traditional

—"Under One Sky" by Ruth Pelham on her recording *Under One Sky*

—"The Colors of Earth" by Sarah Pirtle

—"The More We Get Together" — traditional (for K–3)

—"Common Threads" by Pat Humphries on her recording *Same Rain* (grade 4 and up).

—"Grandmother Spider" — Native American, on *Linking Up* (Resources, p. 169)

◆ *Power Over and Power With.* Systems thinker Joanna Macy contrasts the old and the new views of the world by using drawings. First she draws billiard balls having power over each other and pushing each other around. Next, she draws nerve cells with long filaments reaching out to other nerve cells to share information. This is how she contrasts the old model of power — power over another person to dominate them — with the new model of empowerment, or power-with.

◆ *Reflection for Older Students.* After relating the concept of humans connected like nerve cells, ask students "What does a healthy human nerve cell act like? Is it guarded and closed or is it open to receive information? If students in our school act like nerve cells, what actions would they be doing when they see problems that concern them?" Write a journal entry on these reflections.

Related activity: The Decisions of Cell Membranes, p. 39.

BACKGROUND

Information for teachers: Systems thinker Joanna Macy comments on this new understanding of humans as interconnected: "What had appeared to be separate self-existent entities now are seen to be so interdependent that their boundaries can only be drawn arbitrarily. What had appeared to be 'other' can be equally construed as an extension of the same organism, like a fellow cell in a larger body... we as systems participate and co-create in the living web, giving and receiving the feedback necessary for its sustenance... The dominant image is that of a neuron or nerve cell in a neural net. By its openness to thousands of fellow-neurons, it gives rise to intelligence." (*Despair and Personal Power in the Nuclear Age*, New Society Publishers, 1983).

✳ ACTIVITY: Research Unit ✳
THIS BEAUTIFUL RIVER
People in History Who Fought Bias

ORIENTATION

Tell students: "Democracy is something many many people have worked for. Only some of them are famous names known to you right now. Today we're going to look at the long line of people throughout history who worked for fairness. Together they make a beautiful river. We're going to create a bulletin board display with many names in one river."

DISCUSSION

THE RIVER OF PEOPLE BUILDING DEMOCRACY

Help students:

1. Understand that democracy is something citizens have built over the years.

2. Gain perspective on the large number of people involved in building democracy.

3. See that the democratic process is something alive today that they are part of because building democracy is an active process.

Discover what their understanding of this democratic tradition is like at present by asking questions:

◆ Ask: "When the Bill of Rights was drawn up, which Americans did it apply to and which Americans were not included?" Explain that white male property owners were included, and that efforts had to be made to include all Americans.

◆ Ask: "What famous people do you know who worked to include all Americans in democracy? Who do you know who worked to end slavery? Who do you know who worked for women to have the right to vote? Who do you know who worked for civil rights? Who spoke for the rights of native people? Who worked to stop hate groups in America?" Add other questions to help students search for names they already know.

GRADES: 4th–9th
FOCUS: Make a bulletin board display
MATERIALS: Drawing or brown butcher paper, green and blue paper, markers

◆ Ask: "How many people do you think there were a hundred years ago who were working to end racism? How many people today? How many people a hundred years ago were working to end sexism? How many people today? How many people in our city/town do at least one thing each year to help make the world a better place?" Help students understand (1) that famous people alone can't build democracy, and (2) each person's contribution is important.

PROJECT

THE RIVER PROJECT: DEFINITION OF TASK

◆ Introduce the project: " 'This Beautiful River' is the name we're going to use for this vast number of people who have worked to change things in America that they thought were unfair. We are going to put as many names as we can on the river as a display of people who help to make our country a place where all people have equal rights, housing, food, and jobs."

◆ "We are going to include names of any American who is alive today or a person in history."

◆ We will look for names of people who are not already known to everyone in this class.

◆ We will include local people — and they may be known to many students.

◆ At any moment there need to be as many names of females as there are of males.

◆ With each name we need to be able to write a few words to

describe what the person did or does.

◆ We're going to work in "river teams" to find at least ten names, including five women and five men.

Making The River For The Display: Ask one team of children to work on the background — to place green and blue paper, or paint brown butcher paper to indicate that it is a river.

RESOURCES

River Teams: Divide the class into groups of three or four students who work together to find names. Provide enough reference books and biographies that each team member can be looking at a book.

Librarians: Engage librarians in helping to assemble stacks of books that the teams can use.

Examples:

◆ *Book: 500 Años del Pueblo Chicano / 500 Years of Chicano History,* Elizabeth Martinez, editor, SouthWest Organizing Project, 211 Tenth Street, SW, Albuquerque, New Mexico. 1991.

◆ *Name:* Magdalena Mora, child of migrant workers and journalist, directed a victorious strike of food workers.

◆ *Book: One More River to Cross: The Stories of Twelve Black Americans* by Jim Haskins (Scholastic, 1992).

◆ *Name:* Fannie Lou Hamer, widely recognized key leader in the Civil Rights movement, especially the voter registration drive in Mississippi, whose courage and determination inspired many people.

International Peacebuilders: Look for news of groups who promote reconciliation on an international level.

◆ The Karuna Center for Peacebuilding: Using experiential learning methods to build skills, director Paula Green works in war-torn countries like Bosnia and war-threatened areas like the Middle East giving training in inter-group dialogue and conflict transformation. For a newsletter, write the Karuna Center for Peacebuilding, 49 Richardson Road, Leverett, MA 01054.

Local Peacemaker: Do you know someone who is helping a food bank, a homeless shelter, or an environmental group? Invite people who are involved in helping to create positive social change into the classroom to talk about themselves and their work. Tell them about the Beautiful River Project and ask them to bring names of people who have inspired them to add to the river.

Engaging The Help Of Parents. Create a letter for students to take home asking to interview adults in their lives for ideas of people to add to their list. The prejudice that only famous people are important is one to buck here. People may think that small local actions are not important enough, but those are just the kinds of things the Beautiful River Project can ferret out.

Examples:

◆ A neighbor who goes to the food bank and sorts food for the soup kitchen.

◆ A relative who works with families of people with AIDS.

CLOSURE

1. *Putting Ourselves in the Picture:* "Do you want to put all of our names in this river as people who are also part of it?"

2. *Celebrate the Names with Song:* Use the pattern in the song, "I Want to Know Your Name" by Sarah Pirtle (on *Linking Up;* see Resources, p. 169.)

Example:

Laura Haviland
        (echo: Laura Haviland)
Quaker woman ending slavery
        (echo: Quaker woman ending slavery)
I want to know your name.
        (echo: I want to know your name).
Chorus:
I want to know your name. I want to know your name.
We are links on the chain. I want to know your name.

The image of "being links on the chain" has been used in American history to describe working together toward social change.

3. *Presentation:* Invite another class in the school to come see the Beautiful River display. Each student reads one name and tells what that person did to help build a fair, just country for all.

✳ ACTIVITY ✳
HERITAGE QUILT SQUARES
Drawing and Research

ORIENTATION

Tell students: "Today we are going to start to make a paper quilt. Like a quilt blanket, there will be a series of squares placed together — one for each person. We will make them by drawing and writing on paper. Each square will tell information about us, our families, and our heritage."

SUMMARY

On their Heritage Squares, each student will put:

1. "Your name in fancy lettering."
2. "A symbol that relates to your family."
3. "The name or face of a famous person from history who relates to your heritage."

SCHEDULE

Students will need time for each of these phases:

1. Introduce, cut out squares, plan space, and draw name in pencil.
2. Reflect upon a symbol of family culture and draw it in pencil.
3. Research the name of a person in history who relates to your culture.
4. Draw their face or write their name on your square in pencil.
5. Complete the square by using markers to go over pencil lines.

FAMILY CULTURE

Each person has a culture and has an ethnic background. The culture of our family includes our customs and values as well as our cultural objects. Here are some questions that will help students identify what picture or word they will put on their heritage square to symbolize their family.

◆ What is important to your family?

◆ What does your family like to do on weekends?

GRADES: 4th–6th

FOCUS: Make a square for a paper quilt about family culture and about a person you admire

LENGTH OF PROJECT: One week, 30 minutes each day

Example: Go over to grandmother's house for dinner
Symbol: Dinner table

When your family relaxes together outside, what do you like to do?
Example: Fishing
Symbol: Fishing pole and fish

What games are played in your family?
Example: Bowling
Symbol: bowling ball

Does your family participate in religious or spiritual practices?
Example: We are Jewish and every Friday we celebrate the Sabbath.
Symbol: Sabbath candles and challah for Shabbat dinner

Are there special objects of clothing, jewelry, art, or furniture that remind you of your family?
Example: Rocking chair in our living room.
Symbol: A rocking chair

There is no wrong or right answer. What you are helping the child uncover is what symbol will have the most meaning for them to draw.

INSPIRATIONAL PEOPLE

Specifically suggest that students select a person from their culture and of their gender. With the help of a librarian, gather books for research. Use interlibrary loan at a public library to plan in advance for material to match the ethnicity of students to insure that every student will have books to consult. One resource is *Herstory: Women Who Changed the World,* edited by Ruth Ashby and Deborah Gore Ohrn (Viking, 1995).

Sample choices

◆ A girl of Indian heritage might select Lakshmi Bai, who resisted the British in the nineteenth century and has been called "India's Joan of Arc."

◆ An African-American girl who likes writing might select Ida Wells-Barnett, who used her outstanding journalism to fight against lynching and the intimidation of the black community in the South after the Civil War.

◆ A European-American girl of British heritage might select Emmeline Pankhurst for her inspiring fight for women's suffrage.

C L O S U R E

◆ *Ceremony:* On the day you look at the Heritage Quilt Square, and hear the students describe what they put on it and why, give a special atmosphere to the occasion. Light a candle, bring in flowers, put on music, or in some other way indicate that this is an important time. Allow individual students to explain what they have put on their squares and then receive appreciative applause.

◆ *Recommendation:* Invite parents to celebrate the completed paper quilt and attend this ceremony.

E X T E N S I O N

◆ *Social Studies:* Write reports about the heritage person you selected.

◆ *Language Arts:* Write a journal entry on how you chose your family symbol.

◆ *A Real Quilt:* Use fabric markers, pasted cloth cutouts, sewed fabric and other elements like beads, buttons, or feathers to create real squares for a real cloth quilt.

APPENDIX

The Developmental Acquisition of Skills

Even though children within the same classroom are at different developmental levels, teachers can identify specific experiences and skills that they will want to address with their whole class. Here is a rudimentary list that a faculty could use in assigning skills to grades. When teachers know that in each classroom children are incrementally developing their cooperation and conflict resolution skills, this increases the sense of teamwork within the building. It is recommended that staff meet, amplify this list with their own suggestions, and then indicate which skills they choose to focus on at their grade level. Ruth Charney, of the Northeast Foundation for Children in Greenfield, Massachusetts, uses portions of this list "as a guide to assess children's growth....[She compares] the results from before a program of class meetings with those after six months." (*Teaching Children to Care: Management in the Responsive Classroom*, pp. 78–79)

- -

SKILLS THAT CAN BE INTRODUCED ON THE K-3 LEVEL:

Cooperation
- Finding a friend to help (*example*: tying shoes).
- Participating in a cooperative game (*example:* a song game asking small groups to be eagles flying together).
- Participating in a cooperative art activity.
- Working in a pair on a task (K–2).
- Working in a trio or group of four (2nd–3rd).

Communication
- Sharing news in a group. Listening while another child shares.
- Paraphrasing what another child says.
- Maintaining eye contact.
- Waiting rather than interrupting.
- Participating in a class brainstorm.
- Setting healthy boundaries using words and body language.
- Understanding nonverbal social messages and responding receptively.
- Using "I Statements" and caring language.

Affirmation and feelings
- Saying something affirming about the work of another child.
- Sharing something positive about yourself (*example:* telling your favorites).
- Knowing what you feel, knowing when you are angry.

- Learning that people need different things when they are angry (such as comfort, being alone, physical movement, or dialoguing).
- Learning how to cool down, seeking out what you need when you are angry.
- Expressing what you feel in words once your balance of thinking and feeling is restored.
- Developing an inner voice to be able to reflect on feelings and use self-control.

Conflict resolution
- Controlling impulses (*example:* not hitting when angry).
- Making an "anger plan" for constructive behavior and carrying it out when you are upset.
- Becoming familiar with the concept, "Stop and think."
- Knowing what constructive communication looks like, sounds like, and feels like.
- Choosing to talk out a problem rather than fighting or ignoring it.
- Recognizing what makes a problem worse or better.
- Participating in a negotiation led by a teacher.
- Expanding options: coming up with more than one solution to a problem.
- Learning how to make a plan that constructively solves a problem and carrying it out.
- Using puppet plays with a teacher to explore conflicts. Participating in a role play of conflict (3rd).

Bias Awareness and Inclusion
- Talking comfortably about differences among class members.
- Understanding disabilities of classmates, thinking about how to include class members with disabilities in all classroom activities. Being a buddy on the bus or at lunch or to teach a skill with a child with a disability or special needs, to develop the classroom community.
- Noticing unfairness and responding. Interrupting bias, teasing, and exclusion.
- Learning about the variety of family cultures.
- Respecting the differences in how families of class members celebrate holidays, select food, worship, and dress.
- Recognizing bias in books and magazines.
- Gaining awareness of languages other than English.
- Learning words in any additional language spoken in the homes of other class members.

- -

4TH-6TH GRADES

Each of the skills above is important across the whole K–6 range. Teachers can work with both lists, using these additional skills and experiences for older students.

Cooperation
- Playing kickball and other familiar games with fairness and respect for all players.
- Creating pictures, murals, or dramatic improvisations in small cooperative learning groups.
- Studying material, preparing for tests, doing work sheets, or creating reports as a team.

Note: the next three items are listed in developmental order, increasing in sophistication of the group task.

♦ Working in teams using a jigsaw format where material is divided into parts, each student learns his or her part, and then combines.

♦ Dividing a task as a group to produce a single cohesive product.

♦ Investigating a problem in a group where both the task of the group and how to organize it is decided by the students (6th–8th)

Communication

♦ Paraphrasing

♦ Active listening

♦ Learning to speak neutrally about a problem, describing it without using put-downs and other "you" statements.

♦ Exploring multiple points of view.

♦ Asking open-ended questions to learn information.

♦ Affirmation and feelings.

♦ Reflecting on interpersonal skills after an experience in cooperative groups (*Example*: "I don't think we listened to each other as much as we did yesterday.")

♦ Taking the role of the "encourager" in group work.

♦ Using self-talk to know you are angry and help you stop and think.

♦ Recognizing pro-social contributions and making affirmative statements about class members. (*Example*: I like that Kyle noticed when I hadn't spoken and asked me what I thought.")

♦ Identifying aspects of self you are proud of.

Conflict resolution

♦ Participating in negotiation with peers.

♦ More sophisticated impulse control, stopping not only before hitting, but also before threats or put-downs.

♦ Developing multiple solutions to a problem.

♦ Understanding win-win situations.

♦ Looking for common ground with another person.

♦ Weighing advantages and disadvantages of a potential solution.

♦ Examining a plan for solving a conflict to see whether it can be implemented and making realistic amendments.

♦ Making an agreement and keeping it.

♦ Taking the role of a conflict manager to offer on-the-spot mediations with students (*Example*: for a recess conflict). This involves participating in specific training sessions and having ongoing support from an adult adviser.

Bias Awareness and Inclusion

♦ Understanding vocabulary words such as *targeted person* and *ally*.

♦ Learning accurate names for ethnic and racial groups and respecting the importance of calling people what they want to be called.

♦ Recognizing disrespectful put-down terms and not using them.

♦ Being able to receive feedback that a remark or behavior felt disrespectful.

♦ Intervening when bias erupts without counterattacking.

♦ Recognizing bullying and harassment and interrupting it instead of being a passive bystander.

♦ Understanding the process of stereotyping and learning how to catch one's self making unfair assumptions.

♦ Noticing gender-related bias and put-downs.

♦ Learning the names of community builders in history and today who worked for fairness and social justice.

Features of a School-Wide Conflict Resolution Program

Here is an ideal image to use as a beacon.

1. **Positive Beginning to the School Year:** The school year begins with a friendly, fun all-school meeting and school sing that sets a tone of cooperation, community, and respect for each student's participation. Peer mediators are introduced, and they perform a short skit that demonstrates what they do.

2. **All-School Problem-Solving Format:** School has one consistent format for problem solving. The words are modified for PreK–1st classes so that every classroom uses similar steps, but the concepts are expressed appropriately for all age-levels.

3. **All-School Agreements:** All school recess, lunchroom, and hallway agreements are clear. Consequences for infringement are also established. Agreements clarify that bias, bullying, and exclusion are unacceptable.

4. **All-School Terms:** A common language of terms is taught to all grades. (*Example*: "give the school listening look.")

5. **Student Mediation Program:** Trained student mediators from the 5th and 6th grades are on duty at recess and in the lunchroom to mediate student disputes. Other scheduling arrangements allow mediators to assist with conflicts that arise during other times of the day. For instance, pairs can be assigned to each classroom so that younger students build a relationship with two individuals who are peer mediators.

6. **Support for Mediation Program:** Student mediators have ongoing support from an adult adviser, have regular meetings and year-round training. A committee supporting the mediation program is set up to include representatives from students, teachers, adults on duty at recess and lunch, and parents.

7. **Classroom Rules and Agreements:** At the beginning of the school year, each classroom makes clear rules and agreements, with student imput. The topics of teasing, bias, bullying, and exclusion are addressed. Rules are reviewed and revised as needed. Conflict methods are applied consistently in daily situations.

8. **Affirmative Activities:** Each classroom participates at least weekly in activities that develop affirmation, communication, cooperation, understanding of emotions, and tolerance. These can be either embedded within the curriculum or set up as separate sessions.

9. **Classroom Structure:** Each classroom has methods for student input, discussion, feedback, expression, and group

problem solving. These could include weekly class meetings, daily meetings after recess, or student feedback groups.

10. **Focus on Cooperation:** Teaching styles use learning formats that include cooperating and linking among students.

11. **Focus on Multiculturalism:** Commitment to multicultural education in its broadest application is evident in curriculum and approach. Whatever demographic makeup the school has, all students, not just students of color, need to learn about the history, literature, and culture of all peoples. If not, the dominant message that white culture is most important, or the deeds of men in history are most important, is the message that prevails. Classrooms can focus not just on famous heroes and holidays but infuse a multicultural approach into literature, social studies and science curriculum.

12. **Focus on Interrupting Targeting:** Adults interrupt name calling, and other forms of mistreatment. They also teach students how to recognize, intervene and interrupt bias, bullying and harrassment.

13. **School Materials Promote Understanding:** School assemblies and bulletin boards reinforce the themes of affirmation, cooperation, and living in a multicultural world. Displays reflect diversity in the faces shown. Current periodicals in the library represent diverse groups. (*Example*: A school of primarily European-American children would benefit from subscribing to "Ebony Junior"). Library books are examined for bias, and new books are ordered that specifically provide a broader view of ethnicity, gender, and economic class. Films, holiday celebrations, and guest performers or speakers at assemblies bring in a celebration of "all of us" instead of "who's in the majority here." This helps children deconstruct the dominant group as "normal" and affirms everyone.

14. **Designated Bias-Awareness Concerns Staff:** A specific committee or person is designated to hear concerns about bias. The guidance counselor, or a "Diversity and Unity" committee of staff and students are empowered to help when acts of prejudice, harrassment, or oppression occur. In other words, students and parents need to know who to go to with the situation and be assured that their feedback will be re-

spected. This person or group needs to have procedure for fully acknowledging what has happened, working with the immediate situation, reading implications of what it reveals, and devising wider efforts to prevent a similar situation from occurring.

15. **Shared Responsibility:** The whole staff, not just staff who are people of color, are responsible for making sure the school is actively anti-racist. The whole staff, not just women, is responsible for making sure the school is actively non-sexist.

16. **Diversity Within Staff:** Staff hiring patterns allow several, not just one, person from a minority to be hired. The makeup of the staff evinces respect for diversity.

17. **Cultural Respect:** Set up dress codes and expectations of manners in such a way to respect cultural differences. When social expectations are set according to only the dominant group norms, this can undermine positive cultural identity formation and peer friendships.

18. **Respect for Language:** Everyone learns new language skills. Acknowledge and honor the language spoken in each child's home. Help English speakers learn the other languages of their friends. (*Example*: At a school in Springfield, Massachusetts where 70% of students speak Spanish at home, efforts are made to help English speakers learn Spanish, not just the other way around.). Instead of the melting pot approach which asks those whose language isn't standard English to fit in, schools can respect each student's "homebase" language while teaching standard English.

19. **Affirming Teaching Atmosphere:** The teaching staff works as a cooperative team. Teachers affirm each other, rather than feeling threatened by another person's success. Conflicts are addressed face to face instead of talking behind someone's back. Comfortable methods for handling conflicts are offered. Peer assistance methods encourage teachers to help each other develop skills and evaluate their work. An atmosphere is set up where it is clear there is room for each teacher to do well in her or his own way.

Index for Language Arts and Expressive Arts

ARTWORK AND DRAWING

An Encounter of Cultures, 45
Biographical Scrolls, 41
Conflict Cartoons, 114
Communicating Memories, 31–32
Cooperative Dialogue Writing, 33
Cooperative Study of Animals, 38
Drawings of Our Conscience at Work, 116
Friendly Voice Drawings, 115
Heritage Quilt Squares, 163–164
The History in Our Hands, 70–71
Making Cooperative Board Games, 66–67
Mystery Bags, 44
Opposites Meet, 122–123
Peace Flowers, 35
People Can Change, 114
Story Drawings, 63
Tribbles, 29
The Web of Human Unity, 159
What the Spirals Say, 50–53
Yes and No Drawings, 120

CREATIVE MOVEMENT

Magic Pebbles, 73
Discovery Dance, 74–75
Our Whale Hearts, 117
Movement and Writing, 75–76
Songs for Cooperation, 86
Spider Web Hands, 72
Spider Web Hand Squeeze, 160
Storytelling Dances, 77–79
Yes and No Dances, 121–122

DRAMATICS

Always Something You Can Do, 104–105
Changebringers, 119
Conflicts of Community Builders, 42–43
The Decisions of Cell Membranes, 39–40
Discovery Dance, 74–75
Heart Statements, 112–113

Picturing the Future, 46–48
School Responsibility Assembly, 15–16
Sharks, Turtles, and Kangaroos, 106–108
Storytelling Dances, 77–79
You Made Me, 110–111

MUSIC

Cooperative Songwriting, 80–85
Feelings and Conflicts, 97–98
Musical Walls and Bridges , 137–138
Naming Differences , 139–140
Singing Spanish, 153
Songs for Cooperation, 86
Talk It Out Family Night, 19 – 21
Writing Conflict Resolution Songs, 99–100

READING

Biographical Scrolls, 41
Conflict Book, 103
Conflict Resolution and Literature, 34
Cooperative History Fair, 54–55
Cooperative Study of Animals, 38
Good News Board, 25

VISUALIZATION AND LISTENING

Communicating Memories, 31–32
The History in Our Hands, 70–71
Peacemaker Council, 118–119
Listening Pairs, 64–65
Story Drawings, 63
Tribbles, 29

WRITING

Anger Poetry, 30
Choose Your Peacemaker Animal, 108
Communicating Memories, 31–32
Cooperative Dialogue Writing, 33
Cooperative Songwriting, 80–85
The Decisions of Cell Membranes, 39–40
Friendly Voices, 115–116
Peacemaker Council, 118–119
Movement and Writing, 75–76
Mystery Bags, 44
Opposites Meet, 122–123
Please Touch Table, 134–135
Picturing the Future, 48–49
Tell Me Why, 36

Resources

BIAS AWARENESS AND AFFIRMING DIVERSITY

Crawford, Susan Hoy. *Beyond Dolls and Guns: 101 Ways to Help Children Avoid Gender Bias.* (Heinemann, 1996).

Derman-Sparks, Louise and the A.B.C. Task Force. *Anti-bias Curriculum: Tools for Empowering Young Children.* (Washington D.C.: NAEYC: 1989).

Sadker, Myra and David. *Failing at Fairness: How America's Schools Cheat Girls.* (Touchstone Books, 1994).

Schniedewind, Nancy. *Open Minds to Equality: A Source Book of learning Activities to Promote Peace.* (Prentice Hall Trade, 1984, Allyn and Bacon, 1997 second edition).

Stein, Nan. *Bullyproof: A Teacher's Guide on Teasing and Bullying for Use with Fourth and Fifth Grade Students.* (National Education Association, 1996).

CONFLICT RESOLUTION AND COMMUNITY

Charney, Ruth Sidney. *Teaching Children to Care: Management in the Responsive Classroom.* (Northeast Foundation for Children, 1991).

Cohen, Richard. *Students Resolving Conflict.* (GoodYearBooks, 1995)

Johnson, Judith M. and Priscilla Prutzman. *CCRC's Friendly Classroom Mediation Manual.* (Nyack: Children's Creative Response to Conflict, 1998).

Kreidler, William.J. and Project Adventure. *Keeping the Peace in School-age Programs: Conflict Resolution and Violence Prevention.* (Educators for Social Responsibility, 1998).

Kreidler, William. *Elementary Perspectives: Teaching Concepts of Peace and Conflict.* (Educators for Social Responsibility, 1990).

Kreidler, William.J. *Creative Conflict Resolution: More than 200 Activities for Keeping Peace in the Classroom.* (Scott, Foresman & Co., 1984).

Levin, Diane. *Teaching Young Children in Violent Times: Building a Peaceable Classroom.* (Educators for Social Responsibility, 1994).

Nia-Azariah, Kinshasha et. al. *A Year of SCRC: 35 Experiential Workshops for the Classroom from Students'Creative Response to Conflict,* Center for Peace Education, Cincinatti, Ohio. (Chldren's Creative Response to Conflict,1992).

Porro, Barbara. *Talk It Out: Conflict Resolution in the Elementary Classroom.* Peaco Todd, Illustrator. (Virginia: Association for Supervision and Curriculum Development, 1996).

Prutzman, Priscilla, Lee Stern, *et al. The Friendly Classroom for a Small Planet* (Nyack: Children's Creative Response to Conflict, 1988).

Sadalla, Gail, Meg Holmberg, and Jim Halligan. *Conflict Resolution: An Elementary School Curriculum.* (Community Board Program Inc., 1990) Community Board Program, Inc., 1540 Market St., Suite 490, San Francisco, CA 94102. Telephone: 415-552-1250. Also available: videos, posters and peer mediation training materials.

Sapon-Shevin. *Because We Can Change the World: A Practical Guide for Teachers Who Care.* (Allyn & Bacon, 1999).

Schmidt, Fran and Alice Friedman. *Creative Conflict Solving for Kids.* (Peace Education Foundation, 1991).

NONVIOLENCE RESOURCES

Stand for Children–Children's Action Team (CAT), 1834 Connecticut Ave. NW, Washington, DC 20009, (800) 663-4032. Email: Tellstand@aol.com

The Fellowship of Reconciliation, P. O. Box 271, Nyack, NY, 10960, (914) 358-4601. Send for "Fellowship" Journal or information on ordering books on the practice of nonviolence.

The Highlander Research and Education Center (see p. 117) 1959 Highlander Way, New Market, Tennessee, 37820, (423) 933-3443. Send for an information packet.

The Karuna Center for Peacebuilding: 49 Ritchardson Rd., N. Leverett, MA 01054. Send for a newsletter on intercommunal dialogue and peace-building internationally. This work can be a model for children's inter-group dialogue.

EXPRESSIVE ARTS

Brody, Ed et.al. *Spinning Tales, Weaving Hope: Stories of Peace, Justice and the Environment.* (New Society Publishers, 1992).

Children's Music Network. *Pass It On! Journal.* (Children's Music Network, P.O. 1341, Evanston, IL 606204-1341).

Lyne, Sandford. *Ten-Second Rainshowers: Poems by Young People.* (NY: Simon & Schuster, 1996).

Pelham, Ruth. *Musicraft: Rhythm Instrument Building Activity Book.* (Music Mobile, P.O. Box 6024, Albany, NY 12206).

Pelham, Ruth. "Under One Sky" Recording

Pirtle, Sarah. *Linking Up: Using Music and Movement to Teach Caring, Cooperation and Communication.* (Educators for Social Responsibility, 1998). Book (350 pages) and CD or cassette recording.with 46 songs and activities.

Rogers, Sally with illustrations by Melissa Bay Mathis. *Earthsong.* (NY: Dutton, 1998).

Stone, Andrea. *Sharing Thoughts: An Anthology of Children's Songs.* (Stone Productions, 1990)

Weiss, Evelyn, Priscilla Prutzman, and Nancy Silber. *Children's Songs for a Friendly Planet.* (CCRC, 1986)

HOW TO CONTACT SARAH PIRTLE

Write: The Discovery Center for the Expressive Arts

63 Main Street, Shelburne Falls, MA 01370. (413) 625-2355

Order by mail:
- *Linking Up* book and CD or cassette recording
- Sarah's recordings produced by A Gentle Wind:
  Two Hands Hold the Earth
  The Wind is Telling Secrets
  Magical Earth.
- *Sharing Thoughts,* a collection by Andrea Stone.
- *An Outbreak of Peace,* Sarah's young adult novel.
- Find out about concerts, trainings and residencies.

For more information about these other works and links to resources referenced in this book, visit www.potteredit.com/discovery.html on the World Wide Web.

HOW TO CONTACT CCRC

The Children's Creative Response to Conflict Program

P.O. Box 271, Nyack NY 10960 (914) 353-1796

Fax: 914-358-4924 e-mail: ccrcnyack@aol.com

Find out about trainings, order books, learn about regional CCRC chapters, and receive the newsletter *Sharing Space.*